Introduction to the Law of
International Trade

Other books of interest

Contracts for the Carriage of Goods by Sea
Paul Todd

Cases and Materials on Bills of Lading
Paul Todd

Modern Bills of Lading
Second Edition
Paul Todd

Effective Retention of Title Clauses
John Parris

Making Commercial Contracts
John Parris

Introduction to the Law of International Trade

David Tiplady

BA, BLitt, PhD; Barrister; Lecturer in Law,
University of Nottingham

BSP PROFESSIONAL BOOKS

OXFORD LONDON EDINBURGH

BOSTON MELBOURNE

First Published 1989

British Library
Cataloguing in Publication Data
Tiplady, David
  Introduction to the law of international
  trade
  1. International commercial law
  I. Title
  341.7'5

ISBN 0–632–02376–7

BSP Professional Books
A division of Blackwell Scientific
  Publications Ltd
Editorial Offices:
Osney Mead, Oxford OX2 OEL
  (Orders: Tel. 0865 240201)
8 John Street, London WC1N 2ES
23 Ainslie Place, Edinburgh EH3 6AJ
3 Cambridge Center, Suite 208,
  Cambridge, MA 02142, USA
107 Barry Street, Carlton, Victoria 3053,
  Australia

Set by Selectmove Ltd, London
Printed and bound in Great Britain by
MacKays of Chatham PLC, Chatham, Kent

Contents

port of discharge – 'To arrange for an insurance upon the terms current in the trade which will be available for the benefit of the buyer' – Change of risk – Buyer's right to a policy of insurance – The duty to make out an invoice – The duty to tender conforming documents – Continuous documentary cover – Time at which documents must be tendered – Curing a defective tender of documents – The nature of an fob contract – The 'classic' fob contract – *Pyrene* v. *Scindia Navigation* – Rights and liabilities under an fob contract – Payment by documentary credit; date of opening credit – The status of the fob buyer's obligation – Duty to nominate the port of loading – The carrying ship – Delivery before loading – Summary.

– Inherent vice – Insufficiency of packing – Insufficiency of marks: latent defects – The residual defence – The carrier's obligation with regard to the bill of lading – Deviation – Reasonable deviation – Effects of wrongful deviation – Summary – The extension of the defences to third parties – The carrier's position at common law – Seaworthiness – Care of the goods – Deviation – The extension of defences to third parties – *The Eurymedon* – The carrier's right to freight

Introduction and definition – The nature of an insurable interest – A contract *uberrimae fidei* – Liability for the premium – Types of policy – Valued and unvalued – Promissory and non-promissory warranties – Proximate loss – Are the cases consistent? – The underlying principles – Exceptions: delay; inherent vice; inevitable loss – Burden of proof – Types of loss – Notice of abandonment – Partial loss followed by total loss: the doctrine of merger – The doctrine of subrogation – The suing and labouring clause – Assignment.

Introduction – Nature of a documentary credit – Types of credit – Contracts generated by a documentary credit – When does the bank become contractually bound to the seller? – Problems relating to the credit in the contract of sale – Doctrine of strict compliance – Waiver and variation – Residual liability of buyer – The contract between the buyer and the issuing bank – Restraining payment in cases of fraud – The contract between the seller and the issuing bank; the seller and the confirming bank – The contract between the issuing bank and the confirming bank – The mechanics of a documentary credit – Bills of exchange: definition and terminology – The holder in due course – Defences.

Introduction – The jurisdiction of English courts – jurisdiction over EC defendants – Jurisdiction over other defendants – Jurisdiction under RSC Order 11(1) – Exercising the discretion – Admiralty jurisdiction – The law or laws which determine international contractual disputes – Where no express choice is made – Implied intention or weighing of circumstances? – The *Bonython* approach – Contractual issues not determined by the proper law – Illegality – The doctrine of 'taint' – Lord Wright's limitations in *Vita Foods* – Each contract carries its own proper law – International torts – Interpretations of the rule in *Phillips* v. *Eyre* – Torts on board ship – Proof of foreign law.

Preface

In the mid 1960s the advent of containerisation revolutionised the mechanics of international trade regarding many types of goods. The carriage of discrete units of cargo, from inland depot to inland destination by a series of carriers under a combined transport document, replaced port to port carriage in bulk by a single carrier under a bill of lading as the typical mode of transportation in a great many instances. The practical changes which containerisation inaugurated presaged new legal problems relating, among others, to the status of the new documentation, and the liability of the several carriers.

That this book is written largely without reference to the container revolution clearly requires explanation. Two are offered. First, a great many goods – including many major commodities – continue to be sold and delivered in the traditional ways. Secondly, given the evolutionary nature of English law, it is likely that established legal principles will provide a source, or background, out of which solutions to new problems will emerge. Knowledge of those principles will continue to be essential in a changing world.

Although there are several excellent, up-to-date and detailed treatments of the law of international trade, there is no satisfactory introduction to the subject. It is hoped that this book will serve the needs of students coming new to the subject, with a background knowledge of the English law of contract, and be suitable for those taking academic or professional courses in international trade. This book is written as an introductory text to the law as it is. It does not attempt to anticipate changes which will undoubtedly occur or offer solutions to problems which are, as yet, inchoate. I hope it will be judged according to these self-imposed limitations.

I wish to thank John Dockray for help with the artwork, Ernest Wellstead of the National Westminster Bank for his insights into the practice of banking, and Suzanne Dockray for her constant inspiration.

David Tiplady

Table of Cases

Table of Statutes

References are to section numbers

Chapter 1

The Sale of Goods Under English Law

1.01 *Formation*

The theory which regulates the formation of a contract for the sale of goods is the same as that which applies to contracts in general in English law. One party is required to make a precise and sufficiently detailed communication to the other identifying the essential terms on which he is willing immediately to be bound. To these terms the other party must communicate his unqualified agreement. This is the process of offer and acceptance. The moment at which offer and acceptance fuse will, in theory, be precisely identifiable. Finally, each side must give, or promise to give, something in return for what is to be received. A contract is for the sale of goods if this exchange is of money (or the promise of money) in return for property in goods (or the promise of it): see s.2(1) Sale of Goods Act 1979.

Implementing this process can give rise to two distinct problems in international trade. First of all, where parties are dealing at a distance from each other, whether by post or by some more rapid means of communication, and finally reach agreement, there is the question of when and where their contract is made. The normal rule of English law is that a contract is made when and where the acceptance is received by the offeror. This rule is displaced when contracts are made by post. The English rule for postal contracts, which differs from that adopted in many other jurisdictions, is that the contract comes into being when and where the letter of acceptance is posted. This postal rule does not apply, however, when the parties are in instantaneous communication with each other, either by telephone, telex, or some other means: see *Brinkibon Ltd* v. *Stahag Stahl* (1983) 2 AC 34.

A preliminary question, when the parties are in places subject to different laws, is which law to apply (the offeror's, the acceptor's, or possibly the law of a third place) in order to decide whether and where a contract has been formed. Suppose, for example, that A in England sends an offer to B in Switzerland, to which B posts an acceptance which never arrives. Is there a contract, given that under Swiss law a letter of acceptance is binding only when received? This question belongs to that part of English law known as the conflict of laws, and is more fully considered in Chapter 7.

The second problem arises from the fact that in practice contracting parties do not always follow the tidy directions of the classical rubric for making contracts, outlined above. They may diverge from it in at least two respects: first, in failing to indicate all the major terms of their proposed agreement; and, secondly, in not dovetailing offer with acceptance in quite the manner demanded by theory. The approach of English law, and that adopted in, for example, the various jurisdictions of the United States which apply the Uniform Commercial Code, differ significantly. (The Uniform Commercial Code is a product of the American Law Institute, a body of jurists, legal practitioners and academic lawyers working towards the codification of American law. Although the output of the Institute has no direct legal force, several discrete pieces, including the Uniform Commercial Code, have been adopted by the legislatures of various States. Only Louisiana, with its civil law background, has failed to implement the Code in some form.) English law requires an exact congruence of offer and acceptance, and that all the terms of the proposed contract be deducible from the offer. The Uniform Commercial Code, Art. 2–204, is less stringent, and reveals a pragmatic attitude which informs the majority of the Code's provisions. It provides that 'an agreement sufficient to constitute a contract for sale may be found even though the moment of its making is undetermined', and that 'even though one or more terms are left open a contract of sale does not fail for indefiniteness if the parties have intended to make a contract and there is a reasonably certain basis for giving an appropriate remedy'.

Application of this second provision might well have produced a different result from that found by the House of Lords in *May & Butcher* v. *R* [1929] (1934) 2 KB 17n. Here parties agreed to buy and sell certain goods over a period of time, at a price to be determined from time to time. The House of Lords refused to regard this as a contract to sell at a reasonable price, and held the parties to be still in the stages of negotiation.

A more frequent problem in modern commerce is provided

not by omission but by excess. The so-called 'battle of the forms' is fought when parties do business on standard terms which do not quite mesh. The confusion which this generates is often compounded by the quite common practice of performing, or beginning to perform, agreements before their legal details have been finalised. In large organisations with separate legal and dispatch departments, it is often a case of the left hand not knowing what the right is doing.

The approach manifested in the only English case to consider the matter so far insists that the battle be fought on the classical lines (both of warfare and contract formation) laid down in the nineteenth century or earlier. In *Butler Machine Tool Co. Ltd* v. *Ex-Cell-O Corp. (England) Ltd* (1979) 1 WLR 401, following preliminary negotiations, plaintiffs sent their standard form contract containing their offer to sell a certain machine to the defendants. This offer contained two significant terms: first, a price-escalation clause, allowing the sellers to increase the offer price should manufacturing costs rise; and, secondly, a stipulation that orders were accepted only on the sellers' terms, which were therefore to prevail over any conflicting terms in the buyers' order. The defendants ordered a machine, using their own standard form, which did not include these two provisions. The sellers acknowledged receipt of this order on a tear-off slip from the bottom of the buyers' form.

After the machine had been installed, the plaintiffs claimed an additional sum to cover increased costs. The Court of Appeal held that a contract had been made on the defendant buyers' terms. The plaintiffs' offer to sell had been negated by the defendants' counter-offer, which had in turn been accepted when the tear-off slip was returned. Lord Denning MR accepted that the traditional analysis which determined this result is not always appropriate. In his opinion, a contract may be formed, as occasion demands, on the buyers' terms, on the sellers' terms, by a combination of the two, or according to the court's own version of what is fair and reasonable. The violence which these few short suggestions do to orthodox theory is severe. Lawton and Bridge LJJ, agreeing in the result with Lord Denning MR that the buyer's terms prevailed, applied the traditional analysis.

The Uniform Commercial Code provides a formula for settling the battle of the forms, in most cases, before it starts. Art. 2–207 provides that an acceptance is effective to create a contract even though it contains terms which are additional to, or differ from, those of the offer. These variations become part of the contract unless, first, the offer expressly limits acceptance to the terms of the offer; secondly, the new terms constitute a material alteration of the offer; or, thirdly, the offeror objects to them within a reasonable time. On the first two grounds the result of the *Ex-Cell-O* case in American law would have been in favour of the seller.

1.02   Is barter sale?

Somewhat surprisingly, English law, unlike American law, has failed to answer the question whether a contract of barter, or one in which goods are paid for partly in money and partly in goods or some other valuable consideration, is a contract of sale. The practical significance of this will vary from the minimal to the considerable, according to the precise matter in issue, but, fundamentally, the Sale of Goods Act 1979 will only apply if the contract is one of sale. The question has not been answered for the simple reason that it appears never to have arisen for direct consideration before an English court. Such authority as there is suggests that an exchange of goods for goods, certainly when a money makeweight is involved, may be regarded as a sale (or, strictly speaking, two sales) provided a monetary value can be assigned to the goods, but not otherwise. Hence, if a garage agrees that you may have a new car, which is available for eight thousand pounds straight cash, for five thousand plus your old car, it is fairly easy to separate this arrangement out into two contracts. It is less easy to regard the exchange of items which have no list price as a sale, or combination of sales. In *Chappell & Co. Ltd* v. *Nestle Co. Ltd* (1960) AC 87 Lord Reid expressed doubts whether, in general, part-exchange could constitute a contract for the sale of goods.

The Uniform Commercial Code, Art. 2–304, is more forthright. 'The price can be made payable in money or otherwise. If it is payable in whole or in part in goods each party is a seller of the goods which he is to transfer.' It took Roman law several hundred years to reach this conclusion, and English law has still to get there.

1.03   The classification of goods under the Sale of Goods Act 1979

English law classifies goods into various categories, in order to fulfil the different functions of the Sales of Goods Act. Though detailed consideration of these functions takes us beyond the limits of this book, three of them – the passing of property, and risk, and the availability of the remedy of specific performance – are of central importance to all contracts of international sale, and will serve to illustrate the way in which the categories are applied.

The categories are: specific, unascertained, ascertained, existing, and future goods. The first pairing and the last refer to the state of the goods at the time the contract of sale is made. Goods at that time are *either* specific *or* ascertained, *and* they are *either* existing *or* future goods. Ascertained goods are those which, at the time the contract was made, were unascertained, but which have been subsequently allocated to the performance of the particular transaction. Sometimes ascertained goods are referred to as having become specific (as, for example, by Atkin LJ in *Re Wait* (1927) 1 Ch 606), but this is sloppy and confusing terminology, and should be avoided.

Existing goods are those owned or possessed by the seller; future goods those which are to be manufactured or acquired by him after the contract has been made: s.5(1) of the Sale of Goods Act 1979. Specific goods are those which have been identified and agreed upon at the time the contract is made: s.61(1). Despite these definitions, however, the precise meaning of these terms (if, indeed, they were intended to have a precise meaning) is one of the Sale of Goods Act's great imponderables. In particular, the meaning of specific goods is difficult to determine. The concept serves a wide range of purposes. It appears in s.6 (which relates to the doctrine of mistake), s.7 (the doctrine of frustration), s.18 (the passing of property), s.19(1) (reservation of title), s.29(2) (place of delivery), and s.52(1) (specific performance). It may well be that its meaning is not constant, but varies according to the particular part of the Act under consideration.

In some instances it would seem that goods will be regarded as specific if the source from which they are to be taken is sufficiently circumscribed, even though the precise items themselves have not yet been extracted from that source. In *Howell* v. *Coupland* (1876) 1 QBD 258, Mellish LJ described a contract to sell two hundred tons of potatoes to be grown on a particular farm as an agreement to sell specific things. In *Blackburn Bobbin Co.* v. *Allen* (1918) 2 KB 467, on the other hand, the Court of Appeal was clearly of the opinion that a contract for the sale of a quantity of timber from Finland was not one for the sale of specific goods.

1.04   Specific goods and specific performance

Perhaps the most important decision in this area, however, is that of the Court of Appeal in *Re Wait*. This case concerned the availability of the remedy of specific performance to a buyer who had paid for goods but not received them. It was regarded by the judges involved as of great importance to international trade, particularly to its financing. Unfortunately, those same judges disagreed radically upon the way the case should be decided.

A Bristol firm, the plaintiffs, bought five hundred tons of Western White wheat, to be shipped from Canada, and for which they paid in full in advance. The seller, Wait, shipped one thousand tons in bulk. Having pledged the bill of lading with his bank as security for his overdraft, Wait then went bankrupt. His trustee in bankruptcy refused to deliver any wheat to the plaintiffs. They sought an order of specific performance, which the court may grant, under s.52(1) of the Sale of Goods Act, 'in any action to deliver specific or ascertained goods'. The Divisional Court held that the goods which the plaintiffs had agreed to purchase were sufficiently specific for an order to be granted. The Court of Appeal, by a majority, reversed this decision.

Atkin LJ expressed the view that to uphold the judgment of the court below would 'embarrass to a most serious degree the ordinary operations of buying and selling goods, and the banking operations which attend them'. He failed, however, to say why this would be so. He held that the goods were neither specific nor ascertained, and that the remedy of specific performance was not therefore available. Sargant LJ, dissenting, expressed his 'complete and fundamental' disagreement on both points.

The majority decision in *Re Wait* would seem to settle the question whether s.52(1) can apply to goods to be drawn from source. However, the claimants in that case would not have succeeded merely by showing that the goods were specific. Specific performance is a discretionary remedy, and normally awarded only when damages would be inadequate. Atkin LJ's judgment (and note particularly his surprise that s.52(1) should apply to ascertained goods) seems to indicate the opinion that damages will invariably be adequate to compensate for non-delivery of unascertained goods (even if subsequently ascertained) since, presumably, all the buyer requires is sufficient money to go into the market and purchase substitutes. This, however, might also be true when the goods are specific. One lot of Western White wheat is much like another, generally speaking. But for Wait's bankruptcy, (which is not taken into account in determining which remedy should be available) damages would have compensated the plaintiffs quite adequately.

Similarly, if goods are drawn from a certain source, but there is nothing special about it which reflects upon the nature and quality of the goods, then for s.52(1) purposes it seems irrelevant whether we regard the goods as specific or unascertained, since specific performance should be unavailable in any event. The crucial question throughout is whether damages is an adequate remedy. If a buyer agrees to buy one of a litter of five pups sired by this year's Crufts Supreme Champion, and the seller refuses to deliver, it is suggested that specific performance ought to be available, on the ground that the goods are sufficiently identified and damages is an inadequate remedy.

1.05   *The passing of property*

Be this as it may, it seems quite certain that, where the concept of specific goods is relevant to the passing of property from seller to buyer, it is confined to those goods which have been precisely and exactly identified before the contract is made.

With regard to the passing of property in general, one important point must be immediately clarified. The passing of property and the delivery of possession are totally distinct phenomena in English law. 'Property' is an intangible notion, and passes according to rules and principles set out in ss.16, 17, and 18 of the Sale of Goods Act, without any need for physical activity. Possession may be delivered, before, after, or at the same time as this quasi-magical 'passing of property' occurs; the two are separate and distinct events.

Nor is the passing of property dependent upon payment of the price. This, too, is a separate and distinct incident of a contract of sale and, like delivery of possession, may occur before, after, or simultaneously with the passing of property. Delivery of possession or payment of the price may, however, be evidence of when property was to pass. Indeed, according to Diplock LJ in *R.V. Ward Ltd* v. *Bignall* (1967) 2 All ER 449, 'in modern times very little is needed to give rise to the inference that the property in specific goods is to pass only on delivery or payment'. He did not expand on this statement, unfortunately.

The Uniform Commercial Code repudiates the English approach, for reasons stated in the Comment to Art. 2–101. The legal consequences of a contract of sale should follow directly from action taken under that contract, and the law should 'avoid making practical issues between practical men turn upon the location of an intangible something, the passing of which no man can prove . . .'

However, both the UCC and the Sale of Goods Act share two basic principles with regard to the shift of ownership from seller to buyer. Hence, s.16 of the Act provides that 'where there is a contract for the sale of unascertained goods no property in the goods is transferred to the buyer unless and until the goods are ascertained'. Art. 2–401 of the Code stipulates that 'title [which is used synonymously with "property" here] to goods cannot pass under a contract of sale prior to their identification to the contract'. This would indeed seem self-evident: one cannot become owner of a thing unless one can distinguish it from other things of like kind.

The second shared principle reflects the basic conceptual underpinning of the common law of contract. Thus, according to s.17 of the Act, property passes from seller to buyer when the parties intend it to pass (subject always, of course, to s.16). In like manner, Art. 2–401 of the Code lays down that 'title to goods passes from the seller to the buyer in any manner and on any conditions explicitly agreed on by the parties'.

It is when the parties have not expressed their intention regarding the transfer of property that the Act and the Code diverge fundamentally. The Sale of Goods Act, in s.18, purports to supplement the lacuna of expressed intention by deeming the parties to intend that property shall pass according to the appropriate rule from a set of five which the section lays down. The Code, however, abandons the myth of contractual intention and provides quite simply that 'unless otherwise explicitly agreed, title passes to the buyer at the time and place at which the seller completes his performance with reference to the physical delivery of the goods'.

1.06 The Section Eighteen Rules

Of the five rules for the passing of property under s.18 of the Sale of Goods Act 1979, the first three relate to contracts for the sale of specific existing goods; the fourth to contracts of sale or return; and the fifth to contracts for the sale of unascertained or future goods sold by description. Since contracts of sale or return have no place, practically speaking, in international trade, rule four will be omitted.

Under *rule one*, property passes as soon as the contract is made, provided it is unconditional and the goods are in a deliverable state. An unconditional contract is not (despite the views of the Divisional Court in *Varley* v. *Whipp* (1900) 1 QB 513) one in which there are no major terms. Such a contract is impossible, and, if this were the meaning of the phrase, rule one would have no possible application. (Although this in itself is not an insurmountable objection: other provisions of the Act have been found to have no meaning – see, for example, the interpretation of s.53(2) offered by the Privy Council in *Tai Hing Cotton Mill Ltd* v. *Kamsing Knitting Factory* (1979) AC 91.) The phrase refers to those provisions, colloquially designated 'if' clauses by Lord Diplock, which suspend the operation of a contract until satisfied: for example, I agree to sell and you to buy my goods, provided you can get an export licence.

The meaning of the phrase 'in a deliverable state' is much less clear, despite being defined in s.61(5). This stipulates that 'goods are in a deliverable state . . . when they are in such a state that the buyer would under the contract be bound to take delivery of them'. Does this mean that goods are not in a deliverable state if the buyer is not bound to take delivery because, for example, the goods are seriously defective or the parties have agreed that delivery shall take place next Thursday? This might appear to be the obvious meaning of the expression, but it would then follow that, in the absence of a contrary intention, property in defective goods could never pass. That this is not so is attested in numerous cases. Indeed, the rules regulating the buyer's right to reject defective goods are posited on the opposite assumption. Unfortunately, the cases in which the scope of the phrase has been considered have been decided upon their particular facts, without any general guidance being attempted. In *Underwood* v. *Burgh Castle Brick & Cement Syndicate* (1922) 1 KB 343, for example, a machine was sold free on rail. The Court of Appeal held that the machine was not in a deliverable state until loaded on board the railway truck. In *Philip Head & Sons* v. *Showfronts Ltd* (1970) 1 LlR 140 a carpet was to be laid by the sellers as part of the contract of sale. Mocatta J held that it was not in a deliverable state until this had been done.

From these and other cases it would seem that the phrase indicates that the seller must have fulfilled all his contractual obligations regarding the preparation of the goods for delivery.

Their state, in the sense of their quality (or even whether there is the right amount) would appear to be irrelevant.

Rule two applies to sales of specific goods in which the seller is required to put the goods into a deliverable state, and provides that property does not pass until the goods have been put into a deliverable state and the buyer has notice of this fact. Although the rule is expressed in negative terms, presumably property will then pass.

Rule three refers to sales of specific goods in a deliverable state where the seller needs to do something in order to calculate the price. The goods may need to be weighed, or tested for quality, for example. Property does not pass until the price has been ascertained and the buyer notified.

In the law of international sale *rule five* is undoubtedly the most important. It provides as follows:

(1) 'Where there is a contract for the sale of unascertained goods or future goods by description, and goods of that description and in a deliverable state are unconditionally appropriated to the contract . . . the property in the goods thereupon passes to the buyer; . . . (2) where, in pursuance of the contract, the seller delivers the goods to the buyer, or to a carrier or other bailee . . . for the purpose of transmission to the buyer, and does not reserve the right of disposal, he is taken to have unconditionally appropriated the goods to the contract.'

The common theme of the s.18 rules seems to be that, unless the parties indicate a contrary intention, property passes to the buyer as soon as possible under the contract. *Rule five* relates to goods property in which the seller cannot transfer immediately the contract is made, either because the precise goods are not yet known, or because they are yet to be manufactured or belong to someone else at the time the contract is made. Property will pass as soon as these, and any other conditions which the contract may impose, have been satisfied.

1.07   *The passing of property in cif and fob sales*

In fob transactions the seller is taken not to have unconditionally appropriated goods until they are across the ship's rail. At any time before that the seller can withdraw goods, which he may have intended at one stage to apply to the contract, and substitute others. This is well illustrated by *Carlos Federspiel & Co.*

SA v. *Charles Twigg & Co. Ltd* (1957) 1 LlR 240. Central American buyers contracted to purchase a quantity of cycles on fob terms, and paid the full price in advance. The contract quantity was packed, and the packages marked for delivery to the buyer. The sellers then became insolvent. The receiver refused to deliver any cycles, and the buyers sued him, as second defendant in this action, for conversion. They would succeed if they could show that the cycles were theirs.

Pearson J held that they were not, since there had been no unconditional appropriation. To constitute an appropriation, he said, the intention must have been to allocate particular goods to the contract once and for all, so that they and no others should become the buyers' goods. In an fob contract the decisive act is normally the last one the seller performs, which is the loading of the goods on board.

In *Biddell Bros* v. *E Clements Horst Co.* (1911) 1 KB 934 Kennedy LJ, dissenting, said that, in a cif contract, property passes upon shipment. Although his judgment, described by Lord Loreburn as 'remarkable' and 'illuminating', was adopted unanimously and without qualification by the House of Lords, on this particular point it is now universally regarded as incorrect. It is, of course, perfectly possible for the parties to a cif sale to agree that property shall pass on shipment (or, indeed, at any other time, provided the goods have been ascertained), but in a cif transaction the parties are deemed not to intend property to pass until the documents are taken up and paid for. It is specifically provided, in s.19(2), that 'where goods are shipped, and by the bill of lading the goods are deliverable to the order of the seller or his agent, the seller is *prima facie* to be taken to reserve the right of disposal', thus pre-empting the operation of Rule 5(2). In *The Parana* (1921) 1 AC 486, furthermore, it was held that the retention by the seller of a bill of lading made out to the buyer was inconsistent with an intention to pass property before the bill was surrendered. In *The Elafi* (1982) 1 All ER 208 Mustill J stated as a general rule that property in cif sales passes with documents.

It will be recalled, however, that despite the delivery of the bill of lading to the buyer, and regardless of intention, property cannot pass until the contract goods have been identified. In *The Elafi* the apparently categorical demands of s.16 seemed to clash with the requirements of common sense. Mustill J resolved the dilemma in a fashion which, if not totally convincing to purists (or perhaps only pedants) is at least in keeping with the pragmatic traditions of English commercial law. The facts of this case were complex and unusual; the judgment is nevertheless of general importance.

Cif buyers of copra sued the carriers for having negligently damaged it. The plaintiffs had bought six thousand tons from sellers who had loaded a bulk cargo of twenty-two thousand for delivery to various European buyers. The copra was damaged by seawater while the ship was at the final unloading port, but before actual discharge. At the time the damage was caused, all but the plaintiffs' copra had been offloaded at previous ports of call. The only issue was whether the plaintiffs had standing to sue.

It was accepted that the plaintiffs would have a right of action only if they were the owners of the copra at the time the damage was inflicted. Two factors threw this into doubt. First, the plaintiffs had bought the copra from the sellers, not under one contract but four, and no allocation of copra between the separate sales ever took place. Secondly, by mistake an additional quantity over and above the twenty-two thousand tons had been loaded. This amount was taken to be five hundred tons, and the sellers sold it to a broker, one Frank Fehr. Fehr in turn sold it to the plaintiffs. It remained throughout in bulk, with the rest of the copra.

Hence the dilemma. On the one hand, the plaintiffs had clearly contracted to buy all the copra on board the defendant's ship at the relevant time. On the other, no separate distribution of it among the five contracts of purchase was ever made. It would seem, therefore, that s.16 was not satisfied, and property could not as yet pass to the plaintiffs. Mustill J refused to give s.16 a literal interpretation. In his view, the purpose of the section – to identify which goods are to become the property of the buyer – is satisfied when it can be said that the whole of the bulk is designated for that particular buyer, even though no further division is made, as between the individual purchases. As the learned judge stressed, any other interpretation would lead to the absurd result that property would never pass if no allocation was made between the separate contracts, even though the buyer had taken delivery and even used the goods. By the same token, no further act of appropriation was necessary, beyond the process of exhaustion by the offloading to other buyers, which had eventually reduced the cargo to the quantity purchased by the plaintiffs.

The interposition of Frank Fehr complicates the picture. Nonetheless, Mustill J held that the purpose of s.16 was equally satisfied even though the buyer had purchased the total quantity from different sellers. Given that the goods were sufficiently ascertained for property to be able to pass, it did so according to the intention of the parties in line with the basic principle. An unconditional appropriation between the different contracts was only necessary in the absence of a contrary intention. Here, as the arbitrators had found, all three parties – the original sellers, Frank Fehr, and the plaintiffs – intended that property should pass to the plaintiffs upon ascertainment by exhaustion. The arbitrators' finding is crucial. The mere fact that, coincidentally, Fehr had sold his portion to the same buyers, as a result of which the whole bulk was to be delivered to them, is not enough to cause property to pass. If the original sellers' intention had been to pass ownership to Fehr, a further separation of the goods between the plaintiffs' four purchases on the one hand, and Fehr's single purchase on the other, would appear to be essential. Otherwise the relevant intentions could not be triggered and property could not pass. However, this apparently unavoidable result of s.17 leads inexorably to the same absurd conclusion which Mustill J so forthrightly rejected in the earlier part of his judgment. It is little wonder, when one glimpses into this conceptual chasm, that the Uniform Commercial Code has turned away from such metaphysical exercises in favour of delivery of possession as the critical event in the transference of ownership.

A particular manifestation of the reservation of the right of disposal to which s.19 refers is the so-called *Romalpa* clause. *Romalpa* clauses, the basic purpose of which is to allow a buyer the use and possession of goods while preserving some security for payment to the unpaid seller, in fact come in a variety of forms, according to the extent of protection sought, and as draftsmen attempt to accommodate or circumvent judicial restrictions on their use. One leading authority (Schmittoff, *The Export Trade*, 8th Edn, p 66) recommends that exporters always include a *Romalpa* clause in their contracts. However, their use is largely unnecessary where the seller does not allow credit, but is paid against documents. As this work is confined to these transactions, the contentious and protean topic of *Romalpa* clauses is beyond its scope. (See further, Parris, *Effective Retention of Title Clauses*, Collins, 1986.)

1.08   *The passing of risk*

Goods which are the subject matter of a contract of sale may deteriorate, or be damaged, before they pass into the buyer's ownership or his possession. Responsibility for such eventualities is allocated, between buyer and seller, by English law in a complex fashion, which has as yet not received adequate or comprehensive study by either judicial or academic commentators. In determining who shall be responsible for such loss, and to what extent, two points in time are relevant: first, the time at which the goods must match up to the contract standard in terms of quality and correspondence with description, and, secondly, the time at which property passes to the buyer.

The doctrine of *caveat emptor* – that the buyer takes the chance of the goods he purchases turning out not to be of the quality required or suitable for his purposes – is entrenched into English law by s.14(1) of the Sale of Goods Act 1979. The obligations of certain sellers in certain circumstances to supply fit or merchantable goods are specific exceptions to the doctrine. Hence qualitative deterioration, provided it does not reduce the goods below the contract standard at the time the seller must satisfy it, is always at the buyer's risk, in the sense that he must still pay the contract price for the goods. The time the contract standard must be satisfied, in the absence of contrary agreement, is when the goods are supplied to the buyer. If the goods deteriorate, so as to become unmerchantable, unfit for their purpose, or no longer to correspond to their description after that time, the buyer must still pay the full price for them. The only qualification to this is that subsequent deterioration may be evidence that the goods were not up to standard at the relevant time: see *per* Denning MR in *Crowther* v. *Shannon Motor Co.* (1975) 1 WLR 30.

Accidental damage which does not reduce the goods below the contract standard is at the risk of whichever party has property in the goods when the accident occurs, again in the absence of contrary agreement: s.20(1) Sale of Goods Act 1979. This rule produces a more complex picture. Three factors must be considered: first, whether or not the damage takes the goods below the contract standard; secondly, whether or not it occurred before that standard is applied; and, thirdly, whether or not it occurred before property passed to the buyer. Eight possible permutations arise.

Case 1: minor damage (i.e. damage not reducing the goods below the contract standard) occurs before the goods are supplied and before property passes. The buyer must pay for the goods, but the seller, being at risk for the damage, must discount the cost of the damage from the price.

Case 2: major damage occurs at the same point. The seller is in breach of his contractual obligations regarding quality or description. The buyer can reject the goods, if tendered, and claim damages.

Case 3: minor damage occurs after the goods are supplied but before property passes. The same result as in case 1 follows.

Case 4:major damage occurs at this point. The same result as in case 1 follows, since the seller has satisfied his obligations regarding quality and description, but is at risk for the accidental damage.

Case 5: minor damage occurs after property has passed but before the goods have been supplied. The buyer must pay for the goods without any discount. They are at his risk.

Case 6: major damage occurs at this point. The same result follows as in case 2. The concept of risk does not apply to damage which puts the seller in breach of his obligations of quality or description.

Case 7: any damage which occurs after the goods have been supplied and property has passed is at the risk of the buyer.

Case 8: damage occurs after the goods have been supplied and property has passed, but the buyer has a right to reject the goods for an independent reason, for example because the goods were in any event unmerchantable. This is the most difficult case. There are two possible answers. Either the buyer can reject the goods, but must discount the cost of the damage (since the goods were at his risk when the damage occurred). Or he cannot reject the goods at all (though he can still sue for damages) because he is unable to return the goods to the seller in substantially the same condition as they were in when he received them. However, making restitution of the goods in this way is a requirement of the right to *rescind* a contract (e.g. for misrepresentation.) Although it is frequently said, both by judges and academics, that a party who terminates a contract for breach is rescinding it (see, for example, *per* Devlin J in *Kwei Tek Chao* v. *British Traders & Shippers Ltd* (1954) 2 QB 459: 'a right to reject is only a particular form of a right to rescind') this is not correct. It has never been established that a buyer who exercises his right to repudiate, or cancel, a contract for breach must be able to restore the goods in their original condition, natural deterioration, the effects of inspection, and of the breach itself apart.

In an fob contract, risk passes with property when the goods cross the ship's rail (see *Pyrene Co. Ltd* v. *Scindia Navigation Co. Ltd* (1954) 2 QB 402). In a cif contract, on the other hand, risk and property normally pass at separate times. Property passes when the documents are taken up and paid for (see *Ginzberg* v. *Barrow Haematite Steel Co.* (1966) 1 LlR 333); risk when the goods are loaded. Hence the buyer remains liable to pay, though the goods have been damaged, or even totally lost, in transit: see *Groom* v. *Barber* (1915) 1 KB 316. Risk can pass even though the goods are still in bulk: see *Sterns* v. *Vickers Ltd* (1923) 1 KB 78. However, the question of how the loss is to be apportioned between the various risk-bearers when the damage is only to a proportion of the bulk has not been addressed. In *Sterns* v. *Vickers Ltd* a buyer purchased one hundred and twenty thousand gallons of spirit from a total quantity of two hundred thousand which was stored in a single tank. The goods suffered accidental damage in circumstances in which it was held that the buyer was at risk, even though his portion had not as yet been separated from the bulk and property had hence not passed to him. What the situation would have been if the spirit had been stored in more than one container, and not all of it damaged, was not considered.

1.09   The seller's responsibility for the quality, quantity and description of the goods

These matters are covered by ss.13, 14, 15, 30 and 31 of the Sale of Goods Act 1979. These vital provisions have been the subject of diverse interpretation, and their correct scope and application is not altogether clear. They will now be considered in turn.

1.10   The meaning and scope of s.13

'Where there is a contract for the sale of goods by description, there is an implied condition that the goods will correspond with the description.'

This apparently innocuous stipulation has proved to be one of the most intransigent provisions in the the whole statute, a whirlwind masquerading as a vacuum. It has refused to yield up its true meaning despite several judicial attempts at explanation and exegesis. We are left instead with a widely varying range of interpretations, of which the following is a brief account.

1.11   The literal interpretation of s.13

On one view, s.13 converts all contractual undertakings relating to description into major promises. In other words, terms which, at common law, would be classified as warranties or innominate terms, become conditions, by virtue of s.13. This, indeed, is what the section appears literally to say, although, as we have already noticed, courts are not always too concerned to abide by the strict wording of the Act, particularly where it is felt to lead to a ridiculous result. Nevertheless, the view does have some direct, and some passing support from decisions of the highest authority.

Bowes v. *Shand* (1877) 4 App Cas 455 (see further below [2.08]) lends support to this approach. The House of Lords there treated all the elements in the description of the goods – three hundred tons of Madras rice, shipped from Madras or coast, on board *The Rajah of Cochin*, bound for London, and loaded during the stated months – as of equal, and major, importance. The leading twentieth century authority is another House of Lords decision: *Arcos* v. *Ronaasen* (1933) AC 470. Here a contract for the sale of barrel staves, cif River Thames, allowed for some variation in length and breadth, but none in thickness, which was required to be exactly half an inch. On arrival, ninety-five per cent of the staves were found to exceed the required thickness, by up to one eighth of an inch (or twenty-five per cent.) The buyers rejected the goods.

The House of Lords held that they were entitled to do so. It was irrelevant in their opinion that the goods were merchantable and fit for their purpose. The buyers were entitled to demand the very goods they had contracted to buy, and need not accept others, even if these could be shown to be their commercial equivalent. (This decision can be usefully contrasted with that of the Court of Appeals of New York in *Jacob & Youngs Inc.* v. *Kent* (1921) 129 NE 889, where installers of drainage pipe were held entitled to claim the price, even though it was not the precise brand stipulated in the contract.)

The justification for this Procrustean approach, so apparently out of line with the common law criterion of intention, is that the words of description, taken together, identify the goods which the buyer has agreed to purchase. Any deviation from these precise words means that he is being tendered a commercially different commodity. This was certainly the reason which appealed to the House of Lords in *Bowes* v. *Shand*. It is further borne out by the decision of the Court of Appeal in *Re Moore & Co. and Landauer & Co.* (1921) 2 KB 519, where a buyer of canned fruit refused to take delivery, on the ground that the cans were packed in cases half of which contained twenty-four, when the contract specified that they should all contain thirty. The Court held that the buyer could reject. Scrutton LJ adopted as his own the language of McCardie J in *Manbre Saccharine Co. Ltd* v. *Corn Products Ltd* (1919) 1 KB 198. The learned judge there had expressed the same view as informed the judgments in *Bowes* v. *Shand:* that commercial men do not waste their time including immaterial provisions in their contract.

1.12   *The hybrid interpretation of s.13*

The merits of this explanation were called into question, however, in cases concerning the sale of specific goods, on the ground that such goods were, by the very fact of being specific, already identified by means other than the use of words of description. At the same time, these cases tended to confirm that, in sales of unascertained goods, all the words of description remained crucial.

A hybrid approach to s.13 was thus developed, with one criterion for unascertained goods and another for specific. The leading English case is *Harrison* v. *Knowles & Foster* (1917) 3 KB 606. Here the buyer of two sister ships sought damages against the seller for breach of the provision that each had a dead-weight carrying capacity of four hundred and sixty tons. In fact they could each carry only three hundred and sixty tons. The contract contained an exceptions clause, exempting the sellers from liability for errors of description. It was decided that, on its proper construction, this clause only applied to breaches of warranty. Hence it became vital to determine whether the term relating to carrying capacity was a condition, in which event the defendants would be liable, or a warranty, in which case they would not. Bailhache J decided that the term was a warranty. He applied the following test:

'Where the subject matter of a contract of sale is a specific existing chattel a statement as to some quality possessed by or attaching to such chattel is a warranty, and not a condition, unless the absence of such quality, or the possession of it to a smaller extent, makes the thing sold different in kind from the thing as described in the contract.'

This case might have become no more than a curious footnote

to any account of s.13 (after all, Bailhache J does not even refer to s.13, and the Court of Appeal upheld his judgment on an entirely different ground, making no reference to his carefully thought out rule) had it not formed the basis of one of the most complete, erudite, and wrong-headed examinations of the concept of description in the law of sale ever undertaken.

In *Taylor* v. *Combined Buyers* (1922) NZLR 627 Salmond J was faced with the question whether or not a particular car sold by the defendant to the plaintiff was new. Although not directly in issue, the meaning and scope of s.13 was considered at great length. The learned judge, following the *Harrison* case, concluded that, in sales of specific goods, 'the description within the meaning of the Act is the identification of the article sold by reference to the class of things to which it belongs'. In other words, s.13 here covers statements 'as to the essential or specific nature of the article sold': statements of kind, not quality or degree.

> 'In the case of unascertained goods the law is doubtless different . . . For this purpose every description and every part of the description is material, whether it relates to kind or quality, to essential or inessential attributes. The buyer is not bound to accept any goods which fail in any respect whatever to conform to the contractual description of the goods bargained for.'

Bowes v. *Shand* is cited as authority for this proposition.

The learned judge went on to illustrate his meaning from a series of decided cases. One example must serve for our present purposes. In *Cotter* v. *Luckie* (1918) NZLR 811 the buyer bought at auction a 'stud bull'. We are told that, upon delivery and trial, the animal was found to possess 'a structural defect' which prevented it from functioning as stud bulls should. It was decided that the purchaser should have his money back. This case serves well enough to illustrate the impractical, indeed the literally preposterous nature of the Bailhache formula. A difference in kind can be discerned here (and in the other cases) only because we already know what kind of thing the buyer wants. We know because, in the usual ways, he has signalled the importance of particular attributes or requirements. We cannot know that a stud bull is essentially different from any other kind of bull (or, indeed, any other animal or article of commerce) until we know whether its being a stud, or a bull, or anything else about it, is important to the purchaser. Hence, the 'kind' of thing bought is determined by reference to those ingredients of it which the particular buyer regards as definitive. Except in a world ordered in fixed and immutable Aristotelean categories, the kind or class of things in commerce is infinitely fluid. The kind of thing purchased is a function of its important characteristics, determined by reference to the individual requirements of the particular purchaser. The Bailhache test cannot be applied until we know the things it is supposed to tell us: i.e. what the conditions which go to make up the subject matter of the contract are. Nevertheless, the judgment of Salmond J remains a *tour de force*, albeit one which should serve as a warning to all future jurists of the dangers of straying from the world of practical realities into the realm of metaphysics.

1.13   Pragmatism or metaphysics?

The leading modern authority on s.13 is the decision of the House of Lords in *Ashington Piggeries Ltd* v. *Christopher Hill Ltd* (1972) AC 441. Unfortunately, no clear consensus emerges from the various speeches of their Lordships in this case, so that, although the boundaries of s.13 appear to have been pulled back from the outlying regions of *Arcos* v. *Ronaasen* and *Bowes* v. *Shand*, it is difficult to say where they now lie. In *Ashington Piggeries*, the defendant sold mink food to a breeder. The food was compounded to a formula invented by the breeder himself, and included herring meal as an ingredient. Unknown to the parties, the herring meal used by the seller had been preserved with a salt which, interacting with the meal itself, produced a chemical which was fatal to mink. The buyers claimed that the mink food did not correspond with its description.

The House of Lords, by a majority of four to one, held, somewhat surprisingly, that it did, even though it had proved deadly to the very animals it was supposed to nourish. The majority, for reasons best known to themselves, chose to ask whether the relevant ingredient in its contaminated state was still properly described as *'herring meal'*. A more obvious question would seem to be whether a compound which was fatal to mink could appropriately be said to be mink food.

Certain, by no means consistent, views on s.13 emerge from this case. One is that the section does not apply where a product has simply deteriorated, but requires that there be a substantial addition of some extraneous matter. Lord Wilberforce refused to be so categorical, preferring a broad, pragmatic approach. Would a merchant agree that the article, defective as it is, nevertheless comes within the relevant description? This is very much in keeping with the original spirit of the Sale of Goods Act, drafted against a background in which the commercial jury, composed of experts, sat to answer just such questions as this. Lord Diplock, on the other hand, treads the metaphysical edge Lord Wilberforce eschews. In his opinion, 'the "description" by which unascertained goods are sold is . . . confined to those words in the contract which were intended by the parties to identify the kind of goods which were to be supplied'. This sentiment is redeemed only by its reference to the intention of the parties. In *Gill & Duffus* v. *Berger* (1984) 2 WLR 95 Lord Diplock returned to the theme of s.13, and was able to give a more practical meaning to the idea of the kind or identity of the goods. He said that

> 'the words used in a contract of sale that refer to the goods . . . often include words that describe a characteristic as to quality or condition that they possess which distinguishes them from other goods of the same general kind. . . . [W]hile "description" itself is an ordinary English word, the Act contains no definition of what it means when it speaks in [s.13] of a contract for the sale of goods being a sale "by description". One must look to the contract as a whole to identify the kind of goods that the seller was agreeing to sell.'

Hence it would seem that, for the purposes of s.13, the 'description' of goods comprises those elements or characteristics which the parties agree are definitive. In any particular case, however, it will generally remain a question of some difficulty whether a qualitative defect does or does not bring s.13 into play.

The question can be important, despite the control on qualitative defects in s.14 and s.15, because exceptions clauses, or quasi-exceptions clauses such as conclusive inspection certificates, may cover defects which arise under one section but not another. This issue arose in *Gill & Duffus* itself, and in the earlier Court of Appeal decision in *Toepfer* v. *Continental Grain Co. Ltd* (1974) 1 LIR 11. In this case a contract for the sale of a consignment of Number Three Hard Amber Durum wheat of United States origin provided that an inspector's certificate as to quality was to be final. The inspector erroneously certified the wheat, which was in fact not of the 'hard' type. Here a term relating to quality – 'hard' – was also part of the description of the goods sold. A certificate to the effect that the goods were hard was deemed to be necessarily final as to description also. Any other result would undercut the purpose and effect of the certificate. However, as the Court of Appeal in *Toepfer's case* were careful to point out, and as the Court of Appeal in *Gill & Duffus* also emphasised, where quality and description overlap, a certificate as to quality is conclusive as to description also only in respect of the overlapping characteristics. An inspection certificate which was to be conclusive as to the quality of 'new-laid eggs' would be unchallengeable as to the fact that the eggs were fresh, but not to the fact that they were eggs at all.

1.14   *The application of s.14*

Section 14 of the Sale of Goods Act 1979 imposes two conditions upon those who sell in the course of a business. (Note that s.13 has no such limitation.) The first, contained in s.14(2), is that the goods supplied under the contract shall be of merchantable quality. The condition does not apply to defects specifically drawn to the buyer's attention before the contract is made, nor to those which any pre-contractual examination of the goods ought to have revealed. There is no obligation on the buyer to make any examination at all, however, and in an international sale he may in any event have no opportunity to do so.

1.15   *Merchantable quality*

The concept of merchantable quality has proved to be one of the most intractable in the history of the sale of goods legislation. It was, like description, left undefined by the original draftsman, and presumably for the same reason: that commercial juries would be able from their own experience and expertise to determine whether or not a particular item was merchantable, even though they might not be able to articulate the grounds for their conclusion. With the demise of the commercial jury, however, and given the ever-present need for lawyers to be able to advise commercial clients on the extent of their obligations, attempts were soon made to define merchantable quality. In 1973 the legislature introduced a statutory definition, in the Sale of Goods (Implied Terms) Act, which was subsequently incorporated into the Sale of Goods Act 1979, as s.14(6). This provides that 'goods of any kind are of merchantable quality . . . if they are as fit for the purpose or purposes for which goods of that kind are commonly bought as it is reasonable to expect having regard to any description applied to them, the price (if relevant) and all other relevant circumstances'. Courts have subsequently informed us that this represents a statutory condensation of one or more of the judicial attempts at definition, or the more felicitous aspects of them: see, for example, *per* Denning MR in *Cehave NV* v. *Bremer Handelgesellschaft* (1976) QB 44; Rougier J in *Bernstein* v. *Pamson Motors* (1987) 2 All ER 220; and the Court of Appeal in *Aswan Engineering Co.* v. *Lupdine Ltd* (1987) 1 WLR 1. On the other hand, the Court of Appeal in *Rogers* v. *Parish* enjoins us from drawing upon those earlier definitions. The statutory definition, we are told, should stand by itself, other than in exceptional cases.

In the light of these apparently conflicting tendencies by modern courts, we must content ourselves with one or two general observations. First of all, as Lord Reid commented before the statutory definition was introduced (see *Brown & Son Ltd* v. *Craiks Ltd* (1970) 1 All ER 823) and Rougier J (in the *Pamson* case) afterwards, no definition, capable of comprehending the almost infinite variety of circumstances in which the issue of merchantability may be raised, can probably be formulated. Section 14(6) is not so much a definition of merchantable quality as an open invitation to courts to treat each case on its particular facts. Perhaps, therefore, the most useful general approach is that taken by Lord Diplock in the *Ashington Piggeries* case. In his words, 'what responsibility as to the characteristics of the goods to be supplied would the buyer reasonably believe that the seller was accepting by entering into the contract?'

Another equally helpful rule-of-thumb is to ask the hypothetical question: 'can one realistically envisage an ordinary, reasonable purchaser who would wish to buy the goods, at or around the agreed price, knowing of all their defects, both patent and hidden?' This approach was taken by the House of Lords in the leading case of *Kendall & Sons* v. *Lillico & Sons Ltd* (1969) 2 AC 31. However, its actual application led to a sharp division of opinion over the crucial question of timing. At what point in time is this notional buyer's knowledge of defects to be assessed?

The issue arose in the following way. The defendants sold Brazilian groundnut extract, which they had themselves bought afloat. The plaintiff buyers in turn sold it on to a compounder of animal feed, SAPPA, who took delivery soon after the arrival of the carrying vessel. SAPPA used it to compound a feed which was purchased by the Hardwick Game Farm, who fed it to young turkeys. The turkeys died, since the groundnut extract was contaminated with a chemical which was fatal to chicks.

At some point between the death of the birds and the date of the trial, it became known that contaminated Brazilian groundnut extract could be safely used in cattle feed.

A bare majority of the House of Lords held that this later knowledge must be taken into account in assessing the merchantability of the groundnut extract sold by the defendants to the plaintiffs. Since, by the time of the trial, buyers could be found for the product in its contaminated state, it was by definition merchantable – i.e. saleable. Lord Reid observed that some knowledge acquired after delivery must be taken into account, otherwise it would be impossible to hold goods unmerchantable for latent defects. In his view, it would be artificial to include some later knowledge but exclude the rest.

This, however, does not necessarily follow. A buyer is entitled to an article which is in fact merchantable at the time of supply. Evidence of latent defects can therefore be admitted to show that superficially conforming goods were in reality defective. By the same token, if the goods cannot in fact be put to any use at the time of supply (so that no one would buy them) it seems to be irrelevant that some way of employing the goods is later discovered. This, at least was the view of the minority. In Lord Pearce's opinion, the date of delivery is crucial. This view possesses the merit of fixing attention upon a precise and significant moment of performance, rather than upon the adventitious circumstance of the date of trial. It would seem that Lord Reid was for once seduced by false logic, and that the approach taken by the minority judges is the better one.

1.16 Durability

Where a sale involves the transportation of goods from seller to buyer, then a problem may arise if the goods deteriorate while in transit. On the one hand, s.33 of the Sale of Goods Act may apply. This provides that 'where the seller of goods agrees to deliver them at his own risk at a place other than that where they are when sold, the buyer must nevertheless (unless otherwise agreed) take the risk of deterioration in the goods necessarily incident to the course of transit'. One might expect the case to be even stronger when goods are shipped at the buyer's risk, as in cif and fob sales. The application of this provision, however, presupposes that the goods are in merchantable condition when dispatched. In *Mash & Murrell Ltd* v. *Emanuel Ltd* (1961) 1 All ER 485 Diplock J stated that 'when goods are sold under a contract such as a cif contract, or fob contract, which involves transit before use, there is an implied warranty not merely that they shall be merchantable at the time they are put on the vessel, but that they shall be in such a state that they can endure the normal journey and be in a merchantable condition on arrival'. This seems to cut much of the ground from under the rule exemplified in s.33. Furthermore, it may be important to decide whether this aspect of merchantability, that the goods are reasonably durable, means that the obligation under s.14(2) is a continuing one, or one which vests only at the moment of supply, but which subsequent deterioration may prove not to have been complied with at that moment. In *Crozier, Stephens & Co.* v. *Auerbach* (1908) 2 KB 161 and in *Cordova Land Co. Ltd* v. *Victor Bros Inc.* (1964) 1 WLR 793 English buyers sought leave to issue proceedings against an overseas cif seller, on the ground that the goods on arrival in England were defective and a breach of s.14(2) had therefore been committed within the jurisdiction of the High Court. In both cases leave was denied. Both cases emphasise that the breach of s.14(2) occurs, in a cif sale, when, and where, the defective goods are loaded on board.

1.17 Fitness for purpose

The second implied condition under s.14, originally contained in s.14(1) but now to be found in s.14(3), is that goods supplied under a contract of sale shall be reasonably fit for their purpose. This condition arises whenever the buyer makes known any particular purpose for which the goods are being bought. It is displaced if the buyer either does not rely upon the seller's skill and judgment, or, though he does rely upon it, it is unreasonable in the circumstances for him to do so.

The first point to note is that 'particular purpose' does not necessarily infer a particularised one, in the sense of a purpose which is specified with any degree of particularity or detail. Still less does it signify a purpose which is in any sense unusual. A 'particular purpose' is simply a stated or specified purpose, and it may be communicated expressly or implicitly, and in wide or narrow terms. There may therefore be considerable overlap, or even exact congruence, between s.14(2) and (3) in certain cases.

Liability attaches under s.14(3) provided a buyer gives his seller sufficent information regarding the intended use to enable the seller to exercise his professional abilities in selecting the appropriate items to fulfil the contract. A seller may therefore, paradoxically, be liable even though the buyer has not told him precisely what he requires the goods for. The crucial question is whether the seller would have delivered different goods had he been given further details. If he would not, then the further details are superfluous.

The point is well illustrated in *Kendall* v. *Lillico*, where the buyer based his claim upon s.14(1) (as it then was) as well as s.14(2). Here the buyer purchased goods under the general description 'bird food' which he, in fact, fed to young poultry. It was suitable for some types of bird, but not those the buyer actually intended to give it to. However, it was not known at the time that the food was harmful to particular kinds of bird. The sellers would therefore have still delivered the same product had they known exactly the type of bird to be fed. They were held liable for breach of the implied condition of reasonable fitness.

There must be reasonable reliance, for liability to arise. In *Teheran-Europe Co.* v. *S.T. Belton* (1968) 2 QB 545 Persian buyers purchased air compressors from English sellers. The sellers were aware that the compressors were bought for resale in Persia. They turned out to be unsuitable for use in that country. The Court of Appeal held that the sellers were not liable under s.14(1). It was not enough (as some earlier authorities had suggested) that the sellers knew of the buyers' intended use. In this case it was clear that the buyers knew everything about local conditions and the sellers nothing. In such circumstances it could not be said that the buyers relied on the sellers or, if they did, that the reliance was reasonable.

1.18   The application of s.15

Section 15 implies a condition, in sales by sample, which has three parts. The first is that the bulk will correspond with the sample in quality; the second that the buyer will have a reasonable opportunity of comparing the bulk with the sample; and the third that the goods will be free from any defect, rendering them unmerchantable, which would not be apparent on reasonable examination of the sample.

The first of these calls for little comment, except to note that the provision might impose a wider liability on the seller than under s.14(2). Where the sample is of high quality, if will not be enough that the goods are merchantable if the bulk fails to match up to the sample. The second requirement adds little to the right of any buyer, under s.34, to examine the goods. The s.34 right is triggered only upon a request from the buyer, however. The s.15 right arises automatically. Further, failure to provide an opportunity to examine under s.34 may have the effect of preventing the buyer accepting the goods. Failure under s.15 puts the seller directly in breach.

The third part of the implied condition exonerates the seller from liability for defects which the sample would reveal upon reasonable examination. It should be noted that, unlike the situation under s.14(2), the buyer cannot safeguard himself by failing to make any examination, or making only a superficial one. The whole purpose of selling by sample is that the buyer should examine the sample to see what he is getting.

1.19   Delivery of the wrong quantity

The buyer is not obliged to accept goods, regardless of their quality or condition, if the wrong quantity is delivered, or the correct quantity together with goods of a different description. Section 30 of the Sale of Goods Act entitles the buyer to reject if either more or less than the contract quantity is tendered. If he accepts the tender in either case, he must pay for the goods at the contract rate.

The position is much more complicated when the seller delivers contract goods and non-contract goods together. Section 30(4) purports to cover this situation. It provides that 'where the seller delivers to the buyer the goods he contracted to sell mixed with goods of a different description not included in the contract, the buyer may accept the goods which are in accordance with the contract, and reject the rest, or he may reject the whole'.

This provision seems to cover the case when the seller delivers the whole of the contract quantity, plus other goods. After all, if he delivers more or less than that quantity, the situation would appear to fall within the earlier provisions of s.30. This is not, however, how s.30(4) has been interpreted. A leading case is *Barker* v. *Agius* (1927) 33 Com Cas 120. Here a buyer, Barker, purchased a cargo of coal briquettes, fob the Elbe river. The contract required the briquettes to be 'size two inches'. The bulk of the cargo was shipped below deck, but a proportion was shipped on deck, and this part blocked access to the holds. When the ship docked in Liverpool no berth was available, and the coal began to overheat. In order to clear a way to the holds the master bought the deck cargo from Barker. When the rest of the coal was examined it was discovered not to conform to the specification regarding size. Barker then purported to reject the whole cargo.

Superficially this might seem a case in which either the seller has delivered short, or has delivered contract goods mixed with goods of a different description, and that the buyer is therefore entitled to reject. The position is complicated, however, by s.11(4) (as it now is) of the Sale of Goods Act. This provides that 'where a contract is not severable, and the buyer has accepted the goods or a part of them, the breach of a condition to be fulfilled by the seller can only be treated as a breach of warranty, and not as a ground for rejecting the goods . . .', Barker had accepted a part of the goods by selling the deck cargo to the master.

Salter J nevertheless decided that s.30(4) overrode s.11(4) and entitled a buyer to reject goods of a different description despite having already accepted conforming goods. He decided, however, that Barker had not validly exercised this right to reject, since he purported to reject the whole cargo, and not just the non-conforming part.

An unconsidered aspect of this decision is that a buyer may be deemed to have accepted goods which are totally unrelated to those he agreed to buy, if he either signifies acceptance, keeps the goods too long, or acts towards them in a manner inconsistent with the ownership of the seller (the three instances of acceptance provided by s.35). In *Barker* v. *Agius* the non-conforming goods were still coal briquettes. Would the buyer have been deemed to have accepted them if they had been, say, sacks of potatoes instead of sacks of coal?

It should also be noted that s.30(4) only applies where goods of a different description are tendered. The buyer will not be able to accept part and reject part when his only complaint goes to quality of the part rejected. This seems anomalous. The Uniform Commercial Code allows partial acceptance where the goods accepted form a distinct commercial unit, that is 'such a unit of goods as by commercial usage is a single whole for the purposes of sale and division of which materially impairs its character or value on the market or in use'. The Law Commission has recommended a similar concept in English law.

1.20 Instalment contracts

These are regulated by s.31 of the Sale of Goods Act 1979. This provides that:

'(1) Unless otherwise agreed, the buyer of goods is not bound to accept delivery of them by instalments.
(2) Where there is a contract for the sale of goods to be delivered by stated instalments, which are to be separately paid for, and the seller makes defective deliveries in respect of one or more instalments, or the buyer neglects or refuses to take delivery of or pay for one or more instalments, it is a question in each case depending on the terms of the contract and the circumstances of the case whether the breach of contract is a repudiation of the whole contract or whether it is a severable breach giving rise to a claim for compensation but not to a right to treat the whole contract as repudiated.'

In *Gill & Duffus* v. *Berger* the master of a ship carrying goods which a buyer had purchased cif delivered them in two instalments. The contract of sale was not an instalment contract. Superficially this delivery might therefore seem to fall within s.31(1) and entitle the buyer to reject. This was not even considered. Delivery under a cif contract, for the purposes of s.31, takes place when the goods are loaded on board. At that point a full and complete consignment had been delivered. In the Court of Appeal it was, however, suggested that the buyer could reject on the grounds that the goods had been delivered short. This reasoning is incorrect for exactly the same reason, and failed before the House of Lords.

The leading case on the application of s.31(2) is *Maple Flock Co. Ltd* v. *Universal Furniture Products Ltd* (1934) 1 KB 148. This established a two-fold test for determining whether a party has repudiated an instalment contract. The first matter to establish is the proportion of the total performance represented by the instalment in which the breach occurred. It may be sufficiently substantial in itself to represent a repudiation (where, for example, there are only two, equal, instalments, and the seller defaults on the first). The second matter is the likelihood of the breach being repeated. This is a question of the facts of each particular case.

The basic question, however, is that familiar one: is the breach sufficiently serious to justify the other side in refusing further performance? Not too much importance should therefore be placed on the fact that the section refers to a repudiation of the contract. Though this term, properly employed, signifies that one party has categorically refused to recognise his contractual obligations, it does not have that connotation in s.31. In *Munro* v. *Meyer* (1930) 2 KB 312 sellers sold bone meal cif Hamburg by an instalment contract. After a substantial proportion had been delivered, it was discovered that all the meal was seriously defective. Although the sellers had no way of knowing this, and had been anxious throughout to perform the contract correctly, it was held that they had repudiated it under s.31.

1.21   *The buyer's remedies for breach of contract*

This is a subject of obvious importance, and some complexity. Unfortunately, considerations of space permit only a brief overview.

The buyer may reject the seller's tendered performance if the seller has committed a major breach of contract. A major breach may be a breach of condition, a frustrating breach of an innominate term, or a repudiation of the contract. In orthodox theory, a right to reject is synonymous with a right to terminate further performance of the contract. However, the better view may be that the seller should, in certain circumstances, be allowed to cure his defective tender by retendering conforming goods, provided sufficient time remains to enable him to do so.

1.22   *Rejection of shipping documents*

In a cif contract the situation is more complicated. It is generally said (following the judgment of Devlin J in *Kwei Tek Chao* v. *British Traders & Shippers Ltd* (1954) 2 QB 459, but note the criticism of Winn LJ in *Panchaud Freres SA* v. *Et. General Grain Co.* (1970) 1 LlR 53) that a cif buyer has two separate rights of rejection. One relates to the documents, and the other to the goods themselves. The documents may be rejected if they are defective on their face, for instance by being wrongly dated or by indicating that the goods were not loaded in good order and condition. The goods may be rejected, even though the documents are in order and have been taken up and paid for, if the goods themselves are seriously defective, for instance by being unmerchantable. The buyer cannot, however, reject conforming documents because he suspects, with whatever justification, that the goods are defective.

In *Gill & Duffus* v. *Berger* Lord Diplock categorically asserted that 'a refusal by the buyer to accept the tender of shipping documents which on the face of them conform to the requirements of a cif contract . . . amounts to a breach of condition', entitling the seller to cancel the contract. Recognition of this principle, in his opinion, underpins the system of financing through bankers' commercial credits, on which so much of international trade is based. To refute it would accordingly do great damage to that system.

This statement must be seen in context. Other cases demonstrate that, in certain circumstances, a cif buyer is entitled to reject an apparently correct bill of lading. In *Gill & Duffus*, the buyers sought to reject the bill because, as they rightly suspected, the goods did not correspond to the contract quality. This was something about which the bill had nothing to say. All the details of the bill were not only superficially, but actually, correct, and the buyer ought to have accepted it, reserving his right to reject the goods on arrival. If, however, the bill (or any other document for which the contract calls) inaccurately records information which it is the function of the bill to contain and transmit, then the buyer can reject it. As Scrutton LJ said, in *James Finlay Ltd* v. *Kwik Hoo Tong* (1929) 1 KB 400: 'it is an essential part of the [cif] contract that genuine documents relating to the goods complying with the contract should be tendered to the buyer'. A cif buyer is therefore entitled to reject a bill of lading which is not an accurate record of the shipment of contract goods.

In *J. Aron & Co. Inc.* v. *Comptoir Wegimont* (1921) 1 KB 435 cif buyers rejected documents dated within the shipment period on the ground that the goods had in fact been shipped out of time. McCardie J held that the date on the bill was only *prima facie* evidence of the date of shipment, and that the rejection was justified. Similarly, the buyer can justify rejection of documents by showing that the goods were not in fact shipped aboard the contract vessel, even though the bill of lading indicates that they were. In *Bergerco USA* v. *Vegoil Ltd* (1984) LlR 440, a c & f contract for the sale of peas called for shipment direct from port to port.

In fact the goods were loaded on board a vessel which was scheduled to call, and did call, at intermediate ports. There was no indication of this routing on the bill of lading, which simply named the ship. Hobhouse J seems to accept without demur that the buyers might have rejected the documents, had they acted in time. In the event, they were still able to reject the goods.

The situation is somewhat more straightforward when the documents are inconsistent on their face with the requirements of the contract of sale. As *Bowes* v. *Shand* illustrates, a buyer can reject documents, if they show that the goods were shipped out of time. Similarly, if the bill of lading indicates that the wrong amount was loaded, or does not represent the exact amount purchased, it can be rejected. In *Re Keighley, Maxted & Co. and Bryan, Durant & Co.* (1894) LT 155, sellers tendered bills of lading for an amount in excess of that which the buyers had agreed to buy. The sellers contended that this was a good tender, since the contract contained a provision allowing them to ship excess amounts, which were to be for their own account. The Court of Appeal had little difficulty in rejecting this contention. It was admitted that, if the contract had simply provided for a fixed quantity, only a bill relating to that quantity would constitute a good tender. When variation in quantity is permitted, the bill of lading must still equate to the amount delivered, otherwise it could not serve its purpose as a document of title.

If the cif buyer fails to take up the documents, no question of rejecting the goods can arise, since the goods cannot be delivered to him for the purpose of examination and acceptance other than against the bill of lading (or delivery order) without altering the nature of the contract. On the other hand, if the buyer does take up the documents, he may find himself in an invidious position with regard to the goods. If the documents reveal a defect in the goods on their face, the buyer may be deemed to have waived the defect (if he was actually aware of it: *Shipton Anderson & Co.* v. *Weston* (1922) 10 LlLR 762) or be estopped from pleading it (even though not actually aware) if he accepted the documents in circumstances which would lead a reasonable man to believe that the defect was being condoned. Thus, in the *Panchaud Freres* case, a cif buyer took up documents which revealed that the goods had been shipped out of time without bothering to read them. He was not allowed to reject the goods afterwards, on the ground of late shipment. If the goods were defective in a way not discoverable from the documents, however, then the right to reject them on that ground would, generally speaking, remain unimpaired.

1.23   Damages, following acceptance of latently defective documents

On the other hand, the documents may conceal a defect in the goods, or the circumstances of their shipment, which ought to have been shown. As a result the buyer may feel himself obliged to accept both documents, and eventually the goods themselves, if the defect is not apparent from the state of the goods. For example, documents are occasionally misdated, to create the impression that the goods were loaded within the shipment period, when in fact they were not. If the buyer is ignorant of the deception, he will perforce accept both the documents and, later, the goods themselves. Even if he becomes aware of the defect before the goods arrive, he will often feel constrained to accept them, since to reject will give the seller both the price, paid against the documents, and the goods, and leave the buyer no security at all. In *Taylor & Sons Ltd* v. *Bank of Athens* (1922) Com Cas 142 buyers claimed damages for late shipment, having accepted a misdated bill of lading and the goods themselves, in the belief that they were shipped in time. McCardie J awarded them only nominal damages, on the ground that the breach must be treated as a breach of warranty, and no difference was shown between the value of the goods as actually shipped and the value of goods shipped during the contract period.

Learning the lessons of this decision, buyers in *James Finlay & Co. Ltd* v. *Kwik Hoo Tong* sued in similar circumstances, not for the defect in the goods which the late shipment constituted, but for the defect in the documents represented by the incorrect date. The Court of Appeal held that this breach had deprived the buyers of their right of rejection, which, on a falling market, they would undoubtedly have exercised. They were therefore entitled, in damages, to the difference between the market price of the goods and the contract price, an award which effectively placed them in the same position as if they had been able to exercise their right to reject. In the *Kwei Tek Chao* case, Devlin J reached the same result where the buyer had accepted the goods knowing by then that the bill of lading had been misdated.

In *Proctor & Gamble Ltd* v. *Becher GmbH* (1988) 2 LlR 21, however, the Court of Appeal refused to extend the Finlay rationale to a situation in which the goods had in fact been shipped within the shipment period but the bill of lading nevertheless bore the wrong date of shipment. The Court accepted that it is a condition of a cif contract that the bill of lading carry the correct date, and that the buyers would certainly have rejected the documents had they known of the misdating. They distinguished the preceding cases, however, on the ground that there the misdating had concealed the fact of another, earlier, breach: that the goods had been shipped out of time. Had the bill been correctly dated in *Finlay* or *Kwei Tek Chao* the buyer would have had, and been aware of, a right to reject. In this case, accurate dating would have revealed the opposite: that the goods had in fact been shipped in time. Similar reasoning appears in *Benjamin on Sale*, 3rd Edn, para 1770, where it is suggested that the Finlay principle be confined to cases in which the concealment in the documents deprives the buyer of a right to reject *the goods*. This passage was approved by Kerr LJ in the *Becher* case.

It is difficult to perceive the theoretical justification for this limitation. In both *Finlay* and *Kwei Tek Chao,* on the one hand, and *Becher* on the other, the seller has committed the same breach: that of misdating the documents. His motivation for this – whether to cover up an earlier breach or whatever else – would seem to be irrelevant. The buyer would have rejected the documents had he known of the breach, and of this right the breach deprived him. He cannot be said to have been deprived of his right to reject the goods since, as we have already seen, he would have had no such right had he taken up documents which were patently defective.

Nor is principle mollified by reference to the basic function of contract damages which, as both Kerr and Nicholl LJJ remind us, is to put the innocent party in the position he would have occupied had the contract been properly performed. The unusual feature of the *Finlay* approach is that restitutionary damages are in effect awarded where the contract has nevertheless been carried out. The real reason why the Court of Appeal has chosen to retrench appears in the judgment of Nicholls LJ. In his view, the right to reject for purely technical (i.e. financially immaterial) breaches is an anomaly, and not to be extended. This, though the learned Lord Justice does not acknowledge it, is the creed of *Hongkong Fir* v. *Kawasaki Kisen Kaisha*, masquerading as orthodoxy (see further below [2.09]).

1.24   Rejection of goods

A buyer is not taken to have accepted goods until he has had a reasonable opportunity to examine them, after they have been delivered to him. For this purpose a cif buyer will be allowed a reasonable time after discharge of the goods, even though delivery is deemed to take place when the goods are loaded. It was argued in *JW Schofield & Sons* v. *Rownson Drew & Clydesdale Ltd* (1922) 10 LlLR 480 that, under an fob sale, the goods must be examined at the place of loading. The Court of Appeal held that each case must be decided on its particular facts. In *Napiers* v. *Dexters Ltd* (1926) 26 LlLR 184 the court held that, on the facts, an fob buyer could not reject for short delivery, having taken the goods on board and carried them to their destination.

A buyer who keeps goods beyond a reasonable time cannot later reject them. In *Manifatture Tessile Laviera Wooltex* v. *Ashley* (1979) 2 LlR 28, a buyer delayed rejecting until he had ascertained what the attitude of his own sub-buyer would be. It was held that, in the circumstances, such behaviour was reasonable and the right to reject had not been lost. A buyer is not required to reject at the earliest possible opportunity.

A buyer who rejects defective goods cannot retain possession of them as security for repayment of the price: see *J.J. Lyons & Co.* v. *May & Baker Ltd* (1923) 1 KB 685.

1.25   Anticipatory repudiation

A contracting party may reject the other's performance not only at the time it is tendered, but beforehand. This is known as anticipatory repudiation and, if unjustified, anticipatory breach. One of the most intractable and contentious decisions in this area of law, and indeed in the whole law of contract, is that of the Court of Appeal in *Braithwaite* v. *Foreign Hardwood Co.* (1905) 2 KB 543. Twenty years after the case was decided, opposing counsel (by this time the country's leading commercial judges) were involved in acrimonious debate regarding its meaning and correctness (see the judgment of Lord Sumner (previously Hamilton J) in *British & Bennington Ltd* v. *North Western Cachar Tea Co.* (1923) AC 48) and that of Scrutton LJ in *Continental Contractors Ltd* v. *Medway Oil & Storage Co.* (1925) 23 LlLR 124). Even the facts are in dispute, with different reports of the case suggesting different sequences of events.

This much can be said. The plaintiffs were cif sellers of a quantity of wood. They intended to allocate a certain consignment to the fulfilment of this contract. This consignment was defective. Around the time documents relating to this consignment were to be tendered to the defendant buyers, the defendants repudiated the contract, on a ground which later turned out to be without foundation. The sellers, having resold the consignment at a loss, sued for damages. Substantial damages were awarded to them, but the buyers were credited with a sum reflecting the defective quality of the wood.

Controversy has been generated largely by the fact that the decision appears to be at odds with a principle enunciated by Lord Sumner in the *British & Bennington* case itself. There he said that a party who repudiates a contract for a reason which is unjustified is not precluded from relying upon another, valid, ground, even though he was originally unaware of it. Why, therefore, should the buyers in *Braithwaite* be liable at all if, at the time of their repudiation, it was the fact that the sellers would be unable to perform their part?

An explanation can be found in the arcane and artificial law of anticipatory breach, coupled with the peculiar incidents of a cif sale. According to the generally accepted theory, a wrongful anticipatory repudiation of contractual obligations is not in itself a breach. The innocent party is given the option of treating it as a breach by terminating the contract in response to it. It is as if the repudiator has made an offer to cancel the contract and pay damages, which the other side is free to accept or refuse. If the innocent party chooses to continue with performance, the wrongful repudiation becomes legally irrelevant.

With this in mind, we can return to *Braithwaite's case.* If, at the time the sellers accepted the buyers' anticipatory breach, they had themselves already wrongfully repudiated, then clearly that repudiation had not been accepted by the buyers. Hence, according to orthodox theory, it was irrelevant. There was no actual breach in existence at the time of the buyer's repudiation on which they could subsequently rely in accordance with the *Bennington* principle. There was merely a situation out of which, had they known, they could have created a justification.

This seems to be the explanation offered by Greer LJ in *Taylor* v. *Oakes Roncoroni* (1922) 38 TLR 349. It assumes, crucially, that the sellers were not already in anticipatory breach by having shipped defective goods: in other words, that they would have had an opportunity to cure by appropriating other goods to the contract.

Whatever the correct rationale of *Braithwaite's* case, it now seems generally accepted that the buyer is entitled to offset against any damages a sum representing the diminished value of the defective goods. However, as Collins MR pointed out in *Braithwaite* itself, and Scrutton LJ reiterated in *Continental Contractors* v. *Medway*, this follows more as a matter of common sense than strict law.

1.26   *The buyer's right to damages*

The buyer, in addition to or instead of rejecting and cancelling may seek damages. When he claims damages for non-delivery, he will ordinarily recover the difference between the contract price of the goods and the market price at the time they should have been delivered: see s.51(3) of the Sale of Goods Act 1979. In a cif sale in which the seller fails to tender documents (or tenders defective documents which are rejected) the market price of the goods at the date correct documents should have been tendered provides the appropriate measure: see *Sharpe* v. *Nosawa* (1917) 2 KB 814. Where the goods themselves are not delivered, or rejected, the market price at the date when delivery should have occurred, or when rejection takes place, is taken. For the purposes of s.51, the destination of the carrying ship, and not the port of loading, is regarded as the place of delivery: see *Lester's Leather & Skin Co. Ltd* v. *Home & Overseas Brokers Ltd* (1948) 82 LlLR 202. Similarly, damages for breach of an fob sale are calculated against the market price at the place where the buyer is able to examine the goods: see *Van Den Hurk* v. *Martens & Co. Ltd* (1920) 1 KB 850.

When the buyer accepts defective goods, he may recover in damages the difference between the actual value and the value of conforming goods. In *Obaseki Bros* v. *Reif & Son Ltd* (1952) 2 LlR 362 it is suggested that the calculation is made according to the value of the goods at their ultimate destination. In *Aryeh* v. *Lawrence Kostoris & Son Ltd* (1967) 1 LlR 63 Diplock LJ expressed the view that 'where, to the knowledge of both buyer and seller, goods are bought cif or fob for shipment to a particular market, the relevant values to be taken into consideration are the values of the goods upon the market on arrival there.'

Where the buyer, to the seller's knowledge, has bought these particular goods in order to fulfil a contract for their resale, the resale contract price may be utilised instead of the market value. Otherwise the fact of resale is irrelevant, since, with sufficient damages to bring the defective goods up to market value, the buyer can go into the market and acquire other, conforming goods to satisfy his resale obligation (see *Re Hall Ltd & Pim* (1928) 33 Com Cas 324 and *Williams Bros* v. *Agius Ltd* (1914) AC 510).

1.27   The seller's right to sue for the price

This is regulated by s.49 of the Sale of Goods Act 1979. The seller may recover the price in two instances. First, if it is due on 'a day certain', and the buyer fails to pay on that day, the seller may sue for it. In *Stein Forbes* v. *County Tailoring* (1916) 115 LT 215, a cif seller sued for the price upon the buyer's refusal to take up the shipping documents. Atkin J held that the price was not payable on a day certain and the action failed. The second instance in which the price is recoverable is where property has passed to the buyer and the terms of the contract regarding payment have been satisfied. In the absence of any specific provision this means that the seller must have delivered, or been ready and willing to deliver, conforming goods, in accordance with s.27. In *Colley* v. *Overseas Exporters Ltd* (1921) 3 KB 302 an fob buyer wrongfully failed to nominate a vessel onto which the seller could load the goods. The seller, having delivered them to the dockside, claimed the price. McCardie J held that the claim must fail. Property in an ordinary fob sale passes only after the goods are over the ship's rail. The fact that the buyer's breach had prevented this requirement from being satisfied did not affect the outcome.

Chapter 2

CIF and FOB Contracts

2.01 Introduction

There is a variety of types of sale contract which parties to an international transaction might utilise. Of these the most important are the cif (cost, insurance, freight) and fob (free on board) types. In practice, parties may not always (or even usually) conform to the strict requirements of each type, and are just as likely (whether by accident or design) to produce a hybrid contract which has characteristics taken from different varieties. Nevertheless, a considerable body of case law has grown up around the two principal types. This forms the basis of any understanding of modern practice, and is the likely source of any future developments stimulated by such relative innovations as containerisation. It is to this body of law which we now turn.

2.02 The nature of a cif contract

The essential characteristic of a cif contract of sale is that, while the seller undertakes to be responsible for transportation and insurance cover to a named destination, the buyer nevertheless agrees to pay, not against delivery of the goods at that destination, but against tender of a set of documents comprising invoice, bill of lading, and insurance policy.

Until as late as 1911 it seems to have been arguable that, unless there was an express stipulation to the contrary, the buyer's obligation to pay arose only upon delivery of the goods at the port of discharge. In *Biddell Bros* v. *E. Clements Horst Co.* (1911) 1 KB 214 cif buyers of brewing hops informed their sellers that they were not prepared to pay for the goods before arrival. The sellers in consequence declined to ship the goods. The buyers' action for non-delivery was founded upon sections 28 and 34 of the Sale of Goods Act 1893. Section 28 provides that, 'unless otherwise agreed, delivery of the goods and payment of the price

are concurrent conditions . . .'. Section 34(2) stipulates that,
'unless otherwise agreed, when the seller tenders delivery of the
goods to the buyer, he is bound on request to afford the buyer
a reasonable opportunity of examining them for the purpose of
ascertaining whether they are in conformity with the contract'.

Until the buyer has examined the goods, he is deemed not
to have accepted them. The plaintiffs argued, with sufficient
plausibility to convince a majority of the Court of Appeal, that the
combined effect of these provisions was, either, that they were
not obliged to pay until delivery of the goods at their destination;
or, if delivery were deemed to have taken place at an earlier point,
to postpone their obligation to pay until a reasonable opportunity
for examination had been afforded.   Hamilton J, at first instance,
Kennedy LJ, dissenting in the Court of Appeal, and the whole of
the House of Lords, rejected the plaintiffs' contentions. In the
view of Hamilton J (based upon considerable personal knowledge
of commercial practice – upon which the majority of the Court
of Appeal said he was wrong to draw!) a cif contract is either
an exceptional case (encompassed within the prefatory phrase
'unless otherwise agreed') or possession must be deemed to have
been given when the goods were loaded and the documents
tendered to the buyers. He did not address the argument based
upon s.34(2).

Kennedy LJ, whose 'remarkable judgment', according to Earl
Loreburn LC, 'illuminates the whole field of controversy', took
the view that s.28 is satisfied by the readiness and willingness
of the seller to give possession of the bill of lading, which constitutes symbolic delivery of the goods themselves. With regard
to examination, cif contracts are, in his opinion, an exception to
the rule in s.34. He then proceeded to examine the second part
of the cif dichotomy. A buyer who has paid against conforming
documents can nevertheless reject the goods if, on arrival, they
are found not to be of contractual standard. In this way the
buyer obtains 'the essential and peculiar advantage' of being
able to deal with the goods while still in transit (through his possession of the documents) while at the same time maintaining his
statutory rights regarding the quality and condition of the goods
themselves. However, the point at which compliance with those
rights is determined is the loading or shipment of the goods, and
not their disembarkation or final delivery. From loading onwards,
the goods are at the buyer's risk for any accidental loss, damage,
or deterioration. The seller's obligations are satisfied once he has
loaded conforming goods on board.

It was therefore established in the *Biddell Bros* case, in conformity with commercial practice if at the expense of strict statutory interpretation, that delivery of the goods themselves into the hands of the buyer is not of primary importance in a cif sale. Nor is the deficient condition of the goods on arrival, or any malfunctioning in the final delivery process from ship to buyer, in itself a matter of legitimate complaint by the buyer against the seller. Its only relevance is as evidence that the goods did not in fact conform when loaded. In cif transactions the embarkation of the goods and the subsequent tender of the relevant documentation replace physical delivery and the transference of property as the two salient incidents in the contract of sale.

2.03   Sale of documents or sale of goods?

Because of this, that most experienced and astute of commercial judges, Scrutton J, felt it appropriate to refer to a cif contract as a sale, not of goods, but of 'documents relating to goods' (see *Arnold Karberg & Co.* v. *Blythe* (1915) 2 KB 388). Although this description attracted stringent criticism from the Court of Appeal in the same case (they appear to have taken it literally), Scrutton J's dictum nonetheless captures the essential functional characteristic of cif sales. The learned judge was in fact pointing out that many of the particular problems associated with this form of sale can be resolved by recalling the central place which the documents occupy. (He himself, when elevated to the Court of Appeal, noted that the criticism levelled against his observation was basically semantic (see *Finlay* v. *Kwik Hoo Tong*) as did McCardie J in *Manbre Saccharine Co. Ltd* v. *Corn Products Co. Ltd* (1919) 1 KB 198). Although a cif seller retains his statutory responsibilities for the condition and quality of the goods, and for his right to pass title to them, nevertheless these considerations literally take second place to the documents themselves.

This fundamental point is further illustrated by the parallel cases of *Arnold Karberg & Co.* v. *Blythe* and *Theodor Schneider & Co.* v. *Burgett & Newsam* (1915) 2 KB 388 which arose upon virtually identical facts and were heard together. Cif contracts made in the spring of 1914 between English parties called for shipment of goods from China to Europe. In each case the sellers arranged for shipment aboard a German registered vessel. In *Burgett & Newsam* the policy of insurance was also German: in *Blythe* an English policy was taken out.

The documents were tendered during October 1914, and re-jected by both buyers. By this time, following the outbreak of the Great War, the German carriers had taken refuge in neutral har-bours. The question whether the sellers were entitled to be paid, even though the goods were tied up indefinitely, many thousands of miles away, was decided in favour of the buyers. (meaning?)

The reasons for this must be clearly understood. The fact that the goods might never arrive, certainly not in the predictable future, was considered irrelevant. The tender of documents might have been impeccable, and discharged the sellers' duty, even if, to the sellers' knowledge, the carrying ships were already at the bottom of the sea when the tender was made. In such a case, the insurance policy would simply come into its own, taking over the role of the invoice and bill of lading. These documents enable the buyer to take delivery if the goods arrive. The insurance policy (provided it covers the risk which has materialised) enables him to claim their insured value if they do not arrive. Thus the invoice and bill, on the one hand, and the insurance policy on the other, fulfil complementary functions in the cif package. Goods lost through an uninsured peril are at the buyer's risk, provided the seller has supplied the usual insurance cover.

A change in status between contracting parties, from business associates to enemy aliens, is not at the buyer's risk. In the instant cases the outbreak of war resulted in such changes coming about. In both cases the buyers would be unable to enjoy the benefits of the contract of carriage, and in one the contract of insurance, since to do so would be illegal. The fact of illegality frustrated the relevant contracts, rendering them totally void for the future.

These cases emphasise that the documents must be good – i.e. capable of being enforced or their benefits otherwise enjoyed – at the moment of tender. It is not enough that they were good at the time they were issued. Once again, the paramount importance of the tender of effective documents is demonstrated.

The extent of this hegemony of documents is further shown by the fact (attested to in the *Manbre Saccharine* case) that a cif seller can allocate to the contract documents relating to a cargo which has already been lost at sea, even though the contract is for the sale of unascertained goods, and even though the policy (provided it is in the usual form) does not cover the risk which has caused the cargo to be lost. It is therefore irrelevant to a cif sale that the seller is unable to fulfil the definitive obligation of an ordinary seller, which is to make the buyer owner of the goods. As McCardie J observes in the *Manbre Saccharine* case, certain provisions of the Sale of Goods Act require transposition before they can be applied satisfactorily to cif transactions.

Nor can the cif seller choose to tender goods rather than documents, or the cif buyer demand the goods before, or instead of, the documents. The point is well summarised by McCardie J during the course of his judgment in *Manbre Saccharine*. He said:

> 'the essential feature of an ordinary cif contract as compared with an ordinary contract for the sale of goods rests in the fact that performance of the bargain is to be fulfilled by delivery of documents and not by the actual physical delivery of the goods by the vendor. All that the buyer can call for is delivery of the customary documents. This represents the measure of the buyer's right and the extent of the vendor's duty. The buyer cannot refuse the documents and ask for the actual goods, nor can the vendor withhold the documents and tender the goods they represent.'

2.04   Gill & Duffus v. Berger

Hence the cif contract, although undoubtedly one of sale, seems to be so more by adoption than progeniture. Sometimes a court will lose sight of this distinctive feature of the cif type, especially when the parties have deviated from the pure form and introduced additional provisions into their contract which lean towards either the fob or ex-ship types (or sometimes, schizophrenically, both.)

In *Gill & Duffus* v. *Berger* (1983) 1 LIR 622 the Court of Appeal fell into just such error, and as a result attached unwarranted significance to events which developed at the time and place of arrival. Fortunately, the House of Lords, lending unanimous support to one of Lord Diplock's most incisive judgments, were able to set the matter right.

The case concerned the cif sale of five hundred tons of Argentinian beans. The contract provided that the beans were to be inspected upon arrival by a named company. If satisfied, the company was to issue a certificate of quality, which was to be conclusive. The buyers rejected the documents on the ground that they did not include the certificate. This, it was decided, was not a valid ground of rejection. As Lord Diplock pointed out, it would have been impossible for the documents to have included the certificate, since it could not be issued until after the arrival of the goods. Nevertheless, this 'ex-ship' feature of an otherwise straightforward cif sale was an immediate source of dispute and confusion.

The carrying vessel arrived at its destination, Le Havre, discharged four hundred and fifty tons of beans, then left for another port. The sellers obtained a certificate for the amount landed and again tendered the documents. They were again rejected, and this time the sellers accepted the rejection as putting an end to the contract.

The following day the carrying vessel arrived back at Le Havre and discharged the balance of the cargo. It was then discovered (as the buyers had suspected all along) that the goods did not meet up to their contractual specification. The question of the buyers' right to reject was referred to arbitration.

The matter eventually came before Lloyd J. In a judgment of Solomon, he split the loss between the two parties, deciding in favour of the sellers with regard to the amount covered by the conclusive certificate of quality, and the buyers with regard to the remainder. The Court of Appeal, by a majority, allowed the buyers' appeal. In the words of Sir John Donaldson MR, 'even if a buyer is not justified in rejecting the documents, and these buyers were not [because they were impeccable] the seller cannot complain if the buyer can show that, upon examination the goods were found to be disconform [*sic*] with the contract'. The only question, therefore, was whether the buyers, in the face of the conclusive evidence provision relating to the inspection certificate, could indeed show this to be so.

The Master of the Rolls and Slade LJ took the view that the defective fifty-five tons, to which the certificate did not relate, must either be discounted in the notional delivery of the goods – in which case the seller had delivered short – or they constituted goods of a different kind, mixed with contract goods, and so the whole consignment could be rejected under s.30(4). Goff LJ, dissenting, was of the opinion that it was for the buyer to show that no certificate of quality would have been issued for the fifty-five tons by any reasonable firm of inspectors. Since they could not do so, it must be assumed that all five hundred tons conformed to the contract. However, he, too, agreed that a cif buyer can justify an otherwise wrongful rejection of conforming documents by proof that the goods themselves could have been rejected.

In the House of Lords Lord Diplock revealed the fundamental misunderstanding of cif contracts (and of trade practice) which such views entail. As we have already seen (above [1.25]) a repudiating party can bring forward a valid reason for his repudiation, even though at the time he was unaware of it and hence gave an invalid reason or none at all. This, however, does not allow a cif buyer to reject conforming documents because it transpires that the seller would have been unable to deliver conforming goods. Once again, the standard rules are displaced in the special regime of cif transactions. The seller's obligation to load conforming goods, and the buyer's obligation to accept conforming documents, are independent of each other, so that a failure to observe the one does not, in itself, justify a refusal to perform the other.

The practical justification for this is not far to seek. Financial institutions, which commonly fund such transactions, deal only in documents. They have neither the time, resources, nor expertise to inquire into the quality or condition of the goods themselves, still less to delve into the legal and transactional niceties of the sale contract – even supposing they have access to its terms. A bank to which apparently correct documents have been tendered, but which is nevertheless instructed by its client, the buyer, to reject those documents on the client's view that the goods they represent are somehow suspect will find itself in an invidious, and often impossible, position.

So far as rejection for short, or mixed, delivery at the port of discharge is concerned, this can never be relevant. The reason given by Lord Diplock is that no delivery can take place unless the buyer accepts the documents, since it is by means of the documents that delivery is effected. An equally cogent reason is that s.30 applies in any event to delivery at the point of loading, not unloading, and the fact that the carrier chooses for his own reasons to deliver short, or piecemeal, is, as far as the seller's obligations are concerned, neither here nor there.

2.05 *The significance of the cif designation*

In *Biddell Bros* v. *E. Clements Horst*, the plaintiff buyers contended that the designation of a contract as cif, unless accompanied by such words as 'payment against documents', was simply an accounting device. It signified that the price to be paid by the buyer included carriage and insurance, but no more.

In particular it did not specify when payment became due. The eventual decision of the House of Lords established that the cif designation indicated a particular type of contract, with its own peculiar incidents and implications.

Nevertheless, it is trite law that a mere label does not automatically classify the type of contract to which it may be attached. Just as a jar labelled 'raspberry jam' may be found to contain pickled onions, so a contract, said to be cif, might turn out to be a quite different creature, when all its terms are examined together.

Such a situation arose in the case of *Comptoir D'Achat* v. *Luis de Ridder Ltd (The Julia)* (1949) AC 293. Here Argentinian sellers sold Belgian buyers five hundred tons of rye, cif Antwerp. The contract, on a London Corn Association standard form, contained additional provisions. By these the sellers were to pay for any deficiency in weight, guaranteed condition on arrival, and made themselves responsible for all averages (i.e. accidental losses). Furthermore, although the contract called for tender of a bill of lading or delivery order at the sellers' option, and a policy or certificate of insurance, the practice of the parties (who had done business with each other over a number of years) was such that no document of title, and no insurance cover specific to the buyers' consignment, ever reached the buyers' hands.

While the carrying vessel, *The Julia,* was at sea, Belgium was invaded, and Antwerp occupied by hostile forces. The sellers, who had *The Julia* under charter, arranged for her to make for Lisbon, a neutral port. On arrival there the cargo was sold, for a price below that which the buyer had paid. The buyers claimed repayment of the purchase price on the ground that the contract of sale was frustrated and they had in consequence suffered a total failure of consideration (see *Fibrosa* v. *Fairbairn* (1943) AC 32).

If this were truly a cif contract, the buyers' contention would fail. They had been provided with such documentation as the parties' business practice required, and therefore the sellers' obligations would have been discharged. On the other hand, if the contract called for actual delivery – an 'arrival' or 'ex-ship' contract – it was equally clear that no such delivery could now take place at the designated port, and the contract would in the circumstances be frustrated by intervening impossibility, before any benefit at all had been conferred on the buyers.

The House of Lords decided that the contract was in truth of the arrival type. All the circumstances were examined, in order to determine the parties' contractual intention regarding their particular relationship. It was acknowledged that the strict form of cif contract can admit some modification and still remain within the parameters of the type. Hence, for example, the seller might be empowered to tender a delivery order, or a certificate of insurance, instead of a bill of lading or policy. Nevertheless, 'the object', in Lord Porter's words, 'and the result of a cif contract is to enable sellers and buyers to deal with cargoes or parcels afloat and to transfer them freely from hand to hand by giving constructive possession of the goods which are being dealt with.' The practice adopted by the parties here made such dealings effectively impossible. The additional responsibilities taken on by the sellers emphasised the importance of the actual arrival of the goods, and supported the conclusion that this was not a cif contract, despite the use of that designation.

The cif clause in this particular sale served the purpose which the buyers in *Biddell Bros* had unsuccessfully argued it should generally serve: as an indication merely of the items covered by the price paid. Whether the inclusion of a cif clause has any presumptive significance, or deserves any particular weight when ascertaining the parties' intention, was a matter left unresolved by the House of Lords in *The Julia*. Lord Porter was of the opinion that it should be taken into account; Lord Simonds took the view that it should not.

2.06 The obligations of the seller under a cif contract

These were outlined by Hamilton J in the course of his judgment in *Biddell Bros* v. *E. Clement Horst*, in a passage which has been referred to or quoted with approval on a number of subsequent occasions. The learned judge said:

[T]he meaning of a contract of sale upon cost, freight and insurance terms is so well settled that it is unnecessary to refer to authorities upon the subject. [This form of words is, incidentally, a familiar judicial conceit, often indicating that, although the opposite is in fact the case, this particular judge has settled the matter in his own mind.] A seller under a contract of sale containing such terms has firstly to ship at the port of shipment goods of the description contained in the contract; secondly, to procure a contract of affreightment, under which the goods will be delivered at the destination contemplated by the contract; thirdly to arrange for an insurance upon the terms current in the trade which will be available for the benefit of the buyer; fourthly to make out an invoice . . .; and finally to tender these documents to the buyer . . .'.

This is a useful adumbration of the seller's duties. However, each of its five elements (not six: Lord Atkinson, in *Johnson* v. *Taylor* (1920) AC 144 miscounts) needs to be fleshed out before its implications can be fully understood. It must also be borne in mind that the parties remain free to make their own particular arrangements. The general law of contract allows parties to stipulate for whatever allocation of responsibilities and risks best suits them. As we have just seen, even within the cif form, it is possible to adjust and vary to some extent the fine tuning of the basic obligations.

2.07 'To ship at the port of shipment goods of the description contained in the contract'

This is a composite obligation. Three distinct elements to it can be discerned. The first suggests that the seller must actually ship the goods. This is not, however, strictly correct. The seller is responsible for contract goods being loaded on board, but he can discharge this obligation by himself acquiring goods that have already been shipped by someone else. In other words, he can buy goods afloat. It is not, however, sufficient that the goods have been made ready for shipment, for instance by delivering them to the carrier ready for loading, unless the contract so provides. In *Hindley & Co.* v. *East Indian Produce* (1973) 2 LIR 515 defendant sellers sold fifty tons of Siamese jute to plaintiff buyers, c & f Bremen. The sellers had bought the jute afloat, or so they believed. In fact, although the documents were superficially in order, no jute had ever been loaded on board the designated vessel. Nevertheless, the defendants claimed to have performed their duties as c & f sellers by tendering apparently conforming documents. They founded this contention upon the admitted fact that they had not been parties to the original shipment, but merely an intermediate party in a string of sales.

Kerr J had little hesitation in rejecting this remarkable plea. Despite the emphasis in cif (and c & f) sales upon the tender of correct documentation, such transactions remain sales of goods, and the duty of the seller either to ship contract goods, or, if he is selling goods which he has himself bought afloat, the undertaking that such goods have actually been shipped, is fundamental. By the same token, the presentation of an apparently satisfactory bill of lading is insufficient, if there is no actual shipment behind it. Such a document can never be a document of title, nor can it be 'valid and effective' as required by *Arnold Karberg* v. *Blythe*.

The goods must be put on board the correct vessel, that is to say either the ship, or type of ship, specified in the contract, bound for the nominated destination by the designated route.

2.08   Time of shipment

Implicit within Hamilton J's statement of the seller's duty to ship is that shipment will take place within a certain time. A cif contract will in fact usually specify the loading date or period. If it is silent, a reasonable time will be allowed: see s.29(3) of the Sales of Goods Act 1979.

The obligation to load in time is generally regarded as a major term, or condition, of the contract. Its breach therefore entitles the buyer to cancel the contract without proof of loss. However, this interpretation is not apparent from the relevant section of the Sale of Goods Act itself. Section 10(2) provides that 'whether any other stipulation as to time [i.e. other than one relating to payment] is or is not of the essence of the contract depends on the terms of the contract'.

The leading English authority is the House of Lords decision in *Bowes* v. *Shand* (1877) AC 455. Though this predates the first Sale of Goods Act, it nevertheless remains a cornerstone of modern commercial law. However, it does suggest a slightly eccentric interpretation of the apparently candid language of s.10(2).

In *Bowes* v. *Shand*, sellers of rice sought damages for non-acceptance of the goods. Two contracts, in identical terms, each called for the shipment of three hundred tons of Madras rice, to be shipped from Madras of Madras Coast, for London, on board a named ship. The sellers were allowed the months of March and April in which to load. In the event, approximately seven-eights of the total quantity was put on board during three days of late February. Bills of lading were issued for the amounts loaded on each of these days. The balance was finally loaded by 3 March, and a bill of lading for that amount then issued. The buyers pleaded that the rice had not been loaded during the period specified in the contract, and that they were consequently not bound to accept it.

The Court of Appeal refused to give a literal meaning to the stipulation for shipment, on the ground, as expressed by Mellish LJ, that to do so would place an additional burden on the seller without any corresponding benefit to the buyer. It would in fact simply hand the buyer a windfall opportunity to escape from his bargain should the market have turned against him, or other factors extraneous to the contract have made his bargain a bad one.

The House of Lords, in a classic expression of nineteenth century economic liberalism, held that such matters as the balance of benefits and burdens, and the supposedly inequitable exploitation by one party of purely technical breaches by the other, were irrelevant considerations in law. It was for the parties to make their own bargain, assigning benefits and burdens between themselves as they saw fit. Merchants, Lord Cairns LC opined, were not in the habit of including in their contracts terms which were not important. This, although he himself thought it 'a sufficient answer' to the question in issue, seems to ignore the obvious fact that not all terms are regarded as of equal importance, even by merchants. In Lord Cairns' view, however, it was not for the courts to speculate upon reasons why particular terms were included, but simply to give effect to their plain meaning. The stipulation as to shipment was, furthermore, a part of the description of the goods. Rice shipped out of time – whether prematurely or belatedly – was a different commercial entity from rice shipped within the designated period. Today, not only s.10, but s.13, would therefore be in issue.

Despite the neutral language of s.10(2), as a result of *Bowes* v. *Shand* it is established that a stipulation as to time of shipment has the presumptive status of a condition. Indeed, it would seem that all time of performance clauses, other than those relating to payment, are now regarded *prima facie* as conditions (see, for example, *The Post Chaser* (1981) 2 LlR 695: time for declaring ship; and *Bunge* v. *Tradax* (1981) 1 WLR 711: time by which ship expected ready to load). In the words of Megaw LJ in *Bunge* v. *Tradax*: 'this rule of law . . . has not been regarded by the mercantile community as failing to conform with what is commercially desirable and appropriate'. This is presumably for the reason given by Lord Roskill in the same case: 'parties to commercial contracts should be entitled to know their rights at once and should not . . . be required to wait on events before those rights can be determined'.

The need for certainty and predictability in commerce was also emphasised by Megaw LJ in *The Mihalis Angelos* (1971) 1 QB 164.

2.09 What determines the right to reject?

Nevertheless, it seemed for a season that the revolutionary judgment of Diplock LJ in *Hongkong Fir Shipping Co.* v. *Kawasaki Kisen Kaisha* (1962) 2 QB 26 might require the rationale of principles such as that enunciated in *Bowes* v. *Shand* to be re-evaluated. Diplock LJ took the view that, in the absence of special circumstances, an innocent party's right to cancel a contract for breach was dependent upon the seriousness of the consequences emanating from the particular breach in issue, and not upon the prior classification of the term broken. This approach was felt to be more consonant with the demands of justice, and consistent with the development of the common law in modern times.

The two competing approaches had in fact already been set against each other, in *Bowes* v. *Chaleyer* (1923) 32 CLR 159, a case concerning a time of performance provision. By the narrowest majority the High Court of Australia preferred the view taken in *Bowes* v. *Shand*. Here a contract for the sale of a quantity of silk called for delivery in two parts; 'half as soon as possible; half two months later'. The seller failed strictly to comply with this provision, but the buyer suffered no loss as a result. The buyer repudiated the contract because the market had turned against him, and the seller sought damages. It was not until the defendant had taken legal advice that he became aware of the possible significance of the plaintiff's failure to ship strictly in accordance with the time provisions of the contract. He then used it to justify his own refusal to perform.

The High Court of Australia held that he could do so. The most notable feature of this case, however, is a ringing dissent, delivered jointly by Isaacs and Rich JJ. In terms which anticipate uncannily the judgment of Diplock LJ in *Hongkong Fir*, (and echo that of Cardozo J in *Jacob & Youngs Inc.* v. *Kent*, although the later cases show no awareness of their predecessors) the two judges decry the injustice and insensitivity of the *Bowes* v. *Shand* approach. 'No honest reasonable merchant' in their view would have dreamt of basing his defence upon such an arid technicality. Any other approach than that which they now espoused – based upon the seriousness of the breach – 'establishes the tyranny of mere words over substance'.

Be this as it may, the view that a buyer's right to cancel should be a function of the seriousness of the particular breach, in time of performance cases, is no longer tenable, in the light of the authoritative observations in *Bunge* v. *Tradax*. Good business practice is one thing; the strict rights given under law are another.

2.10   Named ship: ports of shipment and discharge

Whether, as part of the cif seller's first duty, the goods must be shipped aboard a particular vessel is a matter of construction of the contract of sale. In *Bowes* v. *Shand*, for example, the House of Lords included shipment on the named vessel, *The Rajah of Cochin*, as part of the description of the contract goods. In *Thomas Borthwick Ltd* v. *Bunge Ltd* (1969) 1 LIR 17, on the other hand, a contract for the sale of soya bean meal cif Avonmouth, provided that shipment was to be aboard *The Bristol City* (expected ready to load between the third and fifth of January) or substitute vessel. It proved impossible to load onto *The Bristol City*, and the sellers eventually shipped on *The Montreal City*, which issued bills of lading of the twenty-seventh of January. The buyers refused to accept the tender of these bills. Browne J held, as a matter of construction, that the contract did not fix a time of performance. Therefore, following s.29(2) of the Sale of Goods Act 1893 (s.29(3) of the 1979 Act) shipment must take place within a reasonable time. He further held, on construction, that the sellers were not restricted to loading an alternative ship which was also expected ready to load within the given dates, or one which the shipowners had put into service in place of *The Bristol City*. It was sufficient that *The Bristol City* was in fact unable to take the goods, and that the substitute was available within a reasonable time of making the contract. As has long been established, a clause 'expected ready to load' does not commit the seller to loading within the stipulated period, but is simply an undertaking that this is his honest belief and expectation. The undertaking is, however, a condition of the contract: see *The Mihalis Angelos*.

Whether it is a term of the contract that the goods be shipped from a particular port may also be a matter of construction. Once again, in *Bowes* v. *Shand*, the House of Lords indicated that the place of embarkation was a part of the description of the contract goods and therefore a provision of major importance. Many cif contracts omit to specify the loading port, however, or do so in general terms, giving the seller an option to ship from a range of localities (e.g. 'Brazilian port/s not north of Santos': *Panchaud Freres SA* v. *Etablissements General Grain Co. Ltd* (1970) 1 LlR 53).

In *Toepfer* v. *Cremer* (1975) 2 LlR 118 the question of the nomination of loading port arose in a slightly unusual fashion. Sellers here sold USA soyabean meal under a standard form contract which did not stipulate a loading port. There were provisions for an extension of loading time in the event of delay caused by *force majeure*. Should an extension be claimed, however, the sellers were required to give the buyers notice stating which port or ports they had intended to ship from. Any shipment thereafter (when the *force majeure* had abated) was required to be from among these nominated ports. The sellers gave notice, stating their intention to ship from 'Mississippi River port(s)'.

The Court of Appeal held that this nomination was good, and that it was unnecessary for the particular port or ports to be named. It would seem to follow that the seller in such a case must ship as soon as any one of the ports within the geographical range becomes open or available, even though it is not the one he had originally intended to use.

Counsel for the buyers contended that it was open to the seller to name a range of ports as wide as he wished: for example, 'All United States ports'. Orr LJ felt that such a specification would be too wide. Tantalisingly, he gave no indication of why this would be so, or what factors would set the parameters of choice. The Mississippi River region is a major growing area for soya beans, and for the production of meal, but these facts cannot be decisive. Why should the seller not be free to carry the goods overland, say to a Gulf or North Atlantic port, and ship from there?

The port of discharge is obviously crucial in a cif contract. It may be named specifically, or chosen from a set of named ports, or from a geographical range. Whichever party has the choice of port must exercise it within a reasonable time. Unless the contract states otherwise, the choice, it is suggested, is that of the seller.

In *SIAT* v. *Tradax* (1978) 2 LlR 485, (1980) 1 LlR 53 sellers sold buyers approximately five thousand tons of Brazilian soya bean meal, cif Venice, and chartered a ship to carry the goods. Four separate groups of documents, including eight bills of lading, were tendered to the buyers. They accepted the first group, but rejected the other three. No point was taken that the contract was not severable, and the parties agreed to treat each bill separately. The goods were eventually landed at Venice, and sold for an amount considerably below the contract price.

The bills in the second and third groups indicated that the port of discharge was 'as per Charterparty'. Those in the fourth group gave it as 'Ancona/Ravenna'. The buyers were not supplied with a copy of the charterparty. Both Donaldson J, at first instance, and the Court of Appeal, held that the bills in the second and third groups were defective. No copy of the charterparty had been delivered, and the buyers could not tell from the face of the bills, or from the other documents, whether the carrying vessel was in fact bound for Venice. Megaw LJ, delivering the judgment of the Court of Appeal, was prepared to assume, but not decide, that the provision of a copy of the charterparty, showing unequivocally that Venice was the port of discharge, would render these bills of lading valid.

The bills in group four were defective on their face. Although counsel for the sellers made a bold attempt to argue that they nevertheless should have been accepted, Megaw LJ found such an argument 'inconceivable' and impossible to take seriously.

2.11 Conclusive evidence of shipment

Sellers occasionally attempt to anticipate the rejection of a defective bill by incorporating into the contract of sale some form of provision which purports to make the bill rejection-proof. For example, in *James Finlay & Co.* v. *Kwik Hoo Tong*, buyers who sold on to sub-buyers provided in the contract of resale that 'the bill or bills of lading shall be conclusive evidence of the date of shipment'. Goods were shipped under wrongly dated bills, but it was assumed by the Court of Appeal that the conclusive evidence clause would have prevented the sub-buyers from raising the matter. The Court of Appeal also held, however, that the buyers would have been justified in rejecting the bills themselves, even though they could have required their own sub-buyers to accept them. To stand on one's strict legal rights in such a situation was recognised as potentially disastrous business practice.

In *SIAT* v. *Tradax* the parties contracted using GAFTA form 100, clause 11 of which provides, *inter alia*, that no clerical error shall entitle the buyers to reject. The sellers, however, also incorporated into the contract their own, wide-reaching provision, known as the Tradax Documents Clause. This required the buyer to take up the documents, regardless of whether they contained errors or omissions, or were in apparent conflict with the terms of the contract of sale. In return, the sellers guaranteed performance in accordance with the contract of sale. As Donaldson J pointed out, this clause is Draconian, and changes the whole documentary basis of the contract. Whether in his view the contract was as a result of this clause an arrival contract and not cif is not made clear. The learned judge did emphasise, however, that in view of the stringency of this particular provision, it was to be strictly construed. He held, and the Court of Appeal affirmed, that the sellers had not in the event given the proper form of guarantee for which the clause called, and the sellers could not therefore invoke its protection.

2.12   Description of goods shipped

The third aspect of the cif seller's initial duty is to ship goods 'of the description contained in the contract'. The word 'description' here must be taken, not simply in its s.13 sense (whatever that is) but to include also the quality and quantity of the goods, and the seller's right to sell them.

2.13   'To procure a contract of affreightment under which the goods will be delivered at the destination contemplated by the contract'

This is the second of the cif seller's duties, according to Hamilton J in the *Biddell Bros* case. However, Hamilton J's was an unreserved judgment, and his words must not be taken at face value. As we have already seen, a cif seller is not liable should the goods fail to arrive at their destination, provided conforming goods were shipped. In fact, this second obligation is better expressed by Atkin KC (later Lord Atkin) as counsel for the defendants in the *Biddell Bros* case. The seller must effect a contract for the carriage of the goods to their destination, but he is under no obligation (as Hamilton J's words imply) to ensure their ultimate arrival.

The precise extent of this second obligation will depend, in the words of Lord Radcliffe in *Tsakiroglou* v. *Noblee Thorl* (1962) AC 93, upon 'the commercial nature or purpose of the adventure that is the subject of the contract'. Once more, it may be helpful to examine this provision in its three constituent parts.

2.14   *Making the contract of carriage*

The duty to 'procure a contract' does not require that the seller actually make the contract with the carrier. His duty is to obtain a contract of carriage, and this he can fulfil either by engaging the services of a carrier directly, or by taking over a contract already made by an earlier party in a chain of sales. Section 1 of the Bills of Lading Act 1855 provides that 'every consignee of goods named in a Bill of Lading, and every endorsee of a Bill of Lading, to whom the property in the goods therein mentioned shall pass upon or by reason of such consignment on endorsement, shall have transferred to and vested in him all rights of suit, and be subject to the same liabilities in respect of such goods as if the contract contained in the Bill of Lading had been made with himself'. The cif seller, having become a party to the contract of carriage in this way, can in his turn and by the same means pass it on to his buyer. If, on the other hand, the seller has himself made the contract of carriage with the carrier, he can transfer it to his buyer as consignee or first endorsee.

2.15   *The terms of the contract of carriage*

The second aspect of this duty is to obtain a contract on terms which are current or usual at the time the contract of carriage (not the contract of sale) is made. The point is well illustrated by the case of *Tsakiroglou* v. *Noblee Thorl*. Here cif sellers sold a quantity of Sudanese groundnuts, to be shipped from a West African port to Hamburg during the months of November or December 1956. At the time the contract was made, the usual route from West Africa to Europe lay through the Suez Canal. During the two shipping months, however, the canal was, unexpectedly, closed. An alternative route, via the Cape of Good Hope, involved a journey of over eleven thousand miles, as against one of less than four thousand five hundred through Suez. Freight rates at the beginning of the shipment period were twenty-five per cent higher than they had been at the time the contract of sale was made; by its close they had doubled. The sellers refused to ship the goods, arguing that these unanticipated changes had frustrated the contract of sale. In other words, the new state of things was not within the ambit of their contractual risk, and did not represent the sort of circumstances in which they had agreed to deliver.

The House of Lords rejected this superficially plausible contention. The cif seller, they held, must ship by the route which is customary or usual at the date of shipment, not the date of the cif contract itself.

How does one determine whether an available route is 'customary and usual'? The House of Lords turned this question on its head by asking whether the route is expressly or impliedly prohibited. An express prohibition should be fairly obvious. An implicit prohibition will be inferred if the goods cannot be carried to their destination, to arrive in the agreed condition and in the agreed time. In *Tsakiroglou* there was no stipulated time for delivery and the goods were not required for any seasonal market. The contract allowed for wide variations in the speed of the carrying vessel. Hence it could not be said that the delay in delivering the goods at Hamburg made necessary by the much longer journey around the Cape was of any particular importance. Nor was the condition of the goods threatened: they would arrive in substantially the same state as if they had come by the shorter way.

Lord Radcliffe also noted that the new route did not require the goods to be specially packed or stowed. It would seem, however, that if the new route is one which the cif seller can be properly required to employ, it is a customary and usual route, and he should therefore bear the costs inherent in its use. It is, generally speaking, part of the seller's duty to ship the goods in a condition whereby they can withstand the rigours of the journey. If, for example, the goods require refrigeration on the new route, or particularly sturdy packing, this should be for the seller's account. It is a truism of the doctrine of frustration that increased expense alone – even if increased beyond the point at which the contract ceases to be commercially worthwhile for one party – does not frustrate the adventure.

2.16 Cif seller's obligation regarding arrival at the port of discharge

Finally, it should be re-emphasised that the cif seller is under no obligation to ensure the arrival of the goods at their destination. His delivery obligations are satisfied upon shipment. Nevertheless, the seller must not do anything to prevent or impede the eventual delivery of the goods into the hands of the buyer. This is merely an extension of the almost universal implied term that neither party shall prevent the due performance of the contract by anyone involved in it. One of the reasons why the House of Lords in *The Julia* decided that the contract there was not cif was because the sellers had *The Julia* under charter and were, in the event, able to order it to discharge at a different port. As it happened, *The Julia* was originally chartered to Hamburg (the sale contract port) and it was therefore necessary for the sellers to renegotiate with her owners for rerouting to Lisbon. The case would have been all the stronger had the original charter given the sellers the power to alter the route.

This aspect of the cif seller's second duty is well illustrated by the decision of the Court of Appeal in *Colins & Shields* v. *Weddel & Co.* (1952) 2 ALL ER 337. Here sellers under a modified cif contract sold ox-hides for delivery at Liverpool. The contract contained a clause permitting transshipment, and gave the sellers liberty to supply a so-called ship's delivery order in place of a bill of lading.

The sellers in fact shipped the goods on board a vessel bound for Manchester, and a bill of lading was issued for that destination. The sellers, having acknowledged this error to the buyers, managed to have the owners of the carrying vessel clause the bill 'in transit to Liverpool'. The buyers nevertheless rejected it, and arbitrators held that they were entitled to do so. Meanwhile the ship arrived, and discharged the hides at Manchester. The sellers arranged for them to be carried by barge to Liverpool, and tendered the buyers a document addressed to the Master Porter of the Hide Berth at Liverpool Docks, ordering him to deliver the hides to the buyers. This, the sellers said, constituted a 'ship's delivery order'. The buyers again refused to accept.

Before Sellers J the buyers contended that a valid delivery order can only emanate from a valid bill of lading, and a valid bill of lading was one which evidenced shipment to the correct destination. Since no such bill was ever issued, the validity of the so-called delivery order became a secondary matter. For good measure, the buyers also contended that a document addressed to a master porter rather than to the ship itself, could not be a ship's delivery order, properly described. Sellers J accepted both contentions.

It follows that, generally speaking, a cif seller must ensure that a bill of lading, made out to the contract destination, is tendered to his buyer. It is perfectly possible, where the contract allows for transshipment, for the journey to proceed in stages and with different vessels. But the bills of lading issued by them must form a chain linking the port of embarkation with the port of discharge. A delivery order, even if in all other respects valid, cannot take the place of a bill of lading. Its function, as explained by Denning LJ in the *Weddel* case, is to enable a buyer to take delivery out of bulk, where only one bill of lading has been issued for the whole consignment, but it has been sold to several buyers. A delivery order is, therefore, a subordinate document.

2.17   'To arrange for an insurance upon the terms current in the trade which will be available for the benefit of the buyer'

No contrast was presumably intended by Hamilton J between 'procuring' a contract of carriage, and 'arranging' for insurance. Just as the cif seller can transfer to his buyer a contract of carriage made by a previous party, so he can assign a contract of insurance either made by himself, or between the insurer and a previous party. Section 50(3) of the Marine Insurance Act 1906 provides for the assignment of policies of marine insurance 'by endorsement thereon or in other customary manner'.

A similar question arises as in connection with the terms of the contract of carriage: at what time do we determine whether or not the terms of the insurance are those current in the trade? *Tsakiroglou's* case shows that, for the contract of carriage, the relevant time is when the contract of carriage is made. A comparable issue with regard to insurance arose in *Groom* v. *Barber* (1915) 1 KB 316. Cif sellers sought damages against their buyers for non-acceptance of documents. The goods to which the documents related had been lost by the sinking of the carrying ship during the Great War. This occurred after the contract was made but prior to the tender of documents. The buyers contended that the insurance cover which the sellers had effected was not on the usual terms since it did not cover war risk.

The contract of sale was made before war broke out. At that time the terms current in the trade did not include war risk. Such cover had, however, become standard by the time the contract was performed. Atkin J decided that what is usual is to be judged at the time the contract of sale is made. The learned judge offered no explanation why this should be so, although he seemed to regard it as a general rule, rather than a finding appropriate to the particular facts before him, where the seller had himself bought the goods afloat.

It is difficult to find the justification for this approach. It would seem to follow from it that, if circumstances change in the interval between making the contract of sale and taking out the insurance, the seller is nevertheless entitled to effect cover which is no longer normal. Such a rule might as easily lead to his having to effect excessive cover as to his effecting cover which is inadequate. Either way, the rule seems a strange one, and it is difficult to isolate any circumstances which dictate that the usual terms of the contract of insurance should be determined in a different manner from the usual terms of the contract of affreightment. In practice, however, the contract of sale will often specify the amount of cover to be provided.

The rule postulated by Atkin J seems to be supported inferentially by the judgment of Rowlatt J in *Law & Bonar* v. *British American Tobacco Co. Ltd* (1916) 2 KB 605. There is no further authority on this point.

2.18   Change of risk

If circumstances change in the interval between the making of the contract of sale and its implementation, and risks increase, is the seller under any duty to notify the buyer, so that the buyer himself can take out extra insurance cover? Section 32(3) of the Sale of Goods Act 1979 suggests that he is. It provides that 'unless otherwise agreed, where goods are sent by the seller to the buyer by a route involving sea transit, under circumstances in which it is usual to insure, the seller must give such notice to the buyer as may enable him to insure them during their sea transit; and if the seller fails to do so, the goods are at his risk during such sea transit'.

Rowlatt J considered the question in the *Law & Bonar* case, however, and gave a negative answer. The seller's only duty is to take out the usual insurance. The learned judge did, however, leave to one side the question whether s.32(3) might apply where the seller effects unusual cover. Presumably Rowlatt J had in mind the case in which the contract itself entitles the seller to underinsure. Here, s.32(3) might apply. On the other hand, if the contract makes this provision, it is arguable that the contract also constitutes the required notice (cf the judgment of Hamilton LJ in *Wimble* v. *Rosenberg* (1913) 3 KB 743. It seems to be assumed in *Wimble's case* that s.32(3) can have no application whatever to cif contracts, but the point was not fully argued or developed.)

2.19 Buyer's right to a policy of insurance

In the absence of contrary agreement, the buyer is entitled to be given a policy of insurance, and may therefore reject anything less, such as a certificate or broker's cover note. The inadequacies of such lesser documents were emphasised by McCardie J in *Diamond Alkali Export Corp. v. Bourgeois* (1921) 3 KB 443. He noted in particular that the full terms of the policy of insurance would not be included (other than referentially) and that the buyer would have no way of knowing them unless he had access to the policy itself. He also noted two difficulties that might arise under the Marine Insurance Act 1906. Firstly, s.50(3) of that Act provides for assignment by endorsement of policies only. A certificate or other document would require to be assigned under what is now s.136 of the Law of Property Act 1925. Secondly, s.22 stipulates that 'a contract of marine insurance is inadmissible in evidence unless it is embodied in a marine policy'.

McCardie J was undaunted by the fact that his judgment was out of line with the current business practice of tendering documents other than policies. As he indicated, the difficulties 'can be easily, promptly, and effectively met by the insertion of appropriate clauses in cif contracts'. This is in practice now done, and standard form contracts typically provide that the cif seller may tender a policy or certificate of insurance at his option.

Whatever type of document is used, however, it must represent specific and discrete insurance cover for the buyer's goods, and be held exclusively by him or on his behalf. In *The Julia*, defendant sellers shipped a cargo of seven hundred thousand tons of rye, of which they sold five hundred thousand to the plaintiff buyers. The delivery order sent to the buyers indicated that the bearer had a proportionate share in the insurance effected on the total consignment. The House of Lords decided that this failed entirely to achieve one of the basic purposes of the cif contract, and was an important factor in their Lordships' conclusion that the contract in question was not cif at all.

2.20 The duty to make out an invoice

The invoice itemises the goods and services for which the buyer is to pay. Often in practice freight will be discounted, the buyer himself paying it to the carrier on arrival. The effect of an error in the invoice was considered by Rowlatt J in *Berg & Sons* v. *Landauer*

(1925) 23 LILR 249. Here a contract for the sale of peas provided that the seller should tender a provisional invoice giving the name of the carrying ship and the date on which the bill of lading was made out. By a clerical mistake the invoice gave the date of the bill as 1 February, when the correct date was in fact 2 February. Both dates, however, fell within the shipping period. The buyer refused to accept the peas, on the ground that correct dating of the invoice was a condition of the contract.

Rowlatt J held that the purpose of provisions such as this was to enable the buyer to know as accurately as possible exactly where he stood with regard to the goods. All such terms were therefore *prima facie* to be regarded as conditions. The buyer's repudiation was justified, even though it was not shown that he suffered any loss. However, the learned judge drew no distinction between the right to reject the documents and the right to reject the goods, and it is not clear from the facts whether or not the documents were ever accepted. If they were, then it would seem that this decision cannot stand with that of the Court of Appeal in *Proctor & Gamble* v. *Becher* (above [1.23]).

2.21   The duty to tender conforming documents

The seller's final duty is to tender documents representing the contracts of sale, carriage, and insurance to the buyer, plus any other documents for which the contract may call, such as pre-shipment certificates of inspection, certificates of origin, export licences, and so forth.

Even if the documents are intrinsically sound when issued, the buyer may be entitled to reject them because of the circumstances existing at the time of tender. As we have already seen, a bill of lading or insurance policy must be valid and effective at the time of presentation. In other words, it must give the buyer full rights against the carrier or insurer which the original contracting party initially enjoyed. In *Arnold Karberg* v. *Blythe* the carrier (and in an associated case, the insurer) had become an enemy alien by the time the bill and policy was tendered to the buyer. The Court of Appeal held that the buyer was, in consequence, entitled to reject.

2.22   Continuous documentary cover

The bill of lading must also give the buyer continuous documentary cover. That is to say, the protection which the bill ensures must operate from the beginning of the contract voyage to the end, without break or interruption, and confer direct rights of suit against a responsible carrier. This requirement is best illustrated by the decision of the House of Lords in the leading case of *Hansson* v. *Hamel & Horley Ltd* (1922) 2 AC 36. Here goods were sold cif Kobe or Yokohama, for carriage from Norway. In the event the goods were shipped from a Norwegian port for Hamburg, where they were transshipped onto another vessel for carriage on to their destination. The bill of lading issued on behalf of the second carrier did not cover the earlier portion of the transit from Norway to Hamburg. Even though the goods had been safely delivered to Hamburg it was held that the buyer could rightly reject the bill of lading. He was entitled to a document which would have given him a direct right of action had the goods been lost or damaged during the earlier voyage. The fact that no such loss or damage had occurred was irrelevant.

Where – as happens often in practice – the contract allows for transshipment, the cif seller must either ensure that the initial bill, issued by the first carrier, covers the whole journey, in the sense that the first carrier accepts responsibility for due delivery at the destination, or the subsequent bill imposes retrospective liability for the earlier part of the transit. Although Lord Sumner, giving the leading judgment of the House of Lords in the *Hansson* case, was prepared to admit the validity of subsequent bills, he did so subject to the overriding requirement that they be issued within a reasonable time of the commencing of the initial voyage. A transshipment bill issued some time after initial shipment can never be valid. Nor, it follows, will it be enough for the seller to issue a bill covering the journey from port of loading to port of transshipment, with an undertaking to procure a bill covering the remainder of the voyage. Unless the contract provides otherwise, complete shipping documents must be tendered to the buyer within a reasonable time, or as soon as possible, after the initial shipment.

The cif buyer is entitled to reject a bill whereby the carrier who issued it purports to limit his liability to that part of the carriage actually performed by him. This occurred in *Holland Columbo Trading Society Ltd* v. *Segu Mohamed Khaja Alawdeen* (1954) 2 LIR 45. The Privy Council, speaking through Lord Asquith, advised that 'a bill of lading with a transshipment clause is not necessarily a bad tender under a cif contract, but . . . a bill of lading issued by a shipowner who by the transshipment terms in it disclaims all liability in respect of the goods in the event and as from the time of transshipment' fails to give the continuous documentary cover from the outset to which the cif buyer is entitled.

2.23   *Time at which documents must be tendered*

Somewhat surprisingly, the cif buyer is not entitled to receive the bill of lading in time for him to take delivery of the goods when the ship arrives at its destination. This, at least, was established in the old case of *Sanders* v. *Maclean* (1883) 11 QBD 327, and appears not to have been challenged since. Here cif buyers contended that it was an implied condition of their contract that the bills of lading should be forwarded to them in such time either as to be available at the port of delivery when the carrier arrived, or at least in such time as to arrive before the master incurred charges such as storage or demurrage (i.e. for taking longer to unload than the contract of carriage allowed). The Court of Appeal felt it unnecessary actually to decide the issue, but Brett MR was categorically opposed to any such implication, and he had the qualified approval of his brother judges. In the Master of the Rolls' view, the seller's only obligation was to 'make every reasonable exertion to send forward the bill of lading as soon as possible after he had destined the cargo' for that buyer.

In Brett MR's opinion, an express term in a cif contract requiring the seller to make the bill available at a particular time would not be a condition of the contract. Interestingly enough, he took this somewhat heterodoxical approach – the judgment of the House of Lords in *Bowes* v. *Shand* being still quite recent – because of the inherent unreasonableness of allowing a buyer to reject even though he may have suffered little or no loss. Nevertheless, more recent decisions express a clear preference for the relative certainty that follows a categorical classification of time of performance provisions to the supposed fairness or commercial expediency of judging each matter according to the seriousness of the particular outcome.

Toepfer v. *Lenersan-Poortman NV* (1980) 1 LlR 143 is a leading modern authority. Here the contract called for payment not later than twenty days after the date on the bill of lading. Bills were issued on 11 December. Nine days later the carrying ship ran aground. Eventually the cargo was transshipped and arrived some time in April. In the meantime delivery orders had been tendered to the buyers in February. These the buyers rejected, as being out of time. The Court of Appeal decided that the provision relating to payment fixed the date on which payment was due, and that it was the duty of the sellers to tender documents in time for the buyers to effect payment on the due date. Furthermore, this obligation, in keeping with time of performance obligations generally, was a condition of the contract.

This approach was followed by Lloyd J in *Cerealmangi v. Toepfer; The Eurometal* (1981) 1 LlR 337. The contract there provided that, if the shipping documents were not to hand by the time the vessel arrived, sellers should provide buyers with alternative documentation, against which payment should be made. The learned judge ruled that the alternatives must be provided at the time of the ship's arrival, and not within a reasonable time of it, in order that the buyer should be able to take immediate delivery of the goods. As a matter of the interpretation of a particular clause, this seems unexceptional. For the moment, however, Brett MR's view that a cif buyer is not entitled to be put in a position to take immediate delivery from the ship is still valid. Nevertheless, the view belongs to a world in which the time taken to carry goods was far less predictable than today, and documents were delivered by methods as tardy and hazardous as those employed to carry the goods themselves. In an age of air transport, not to mention the electronic transmission of facsimile documents (which may well become an acceptable method of tendering documents) it is increasingly difficult to see any justification for the late-Victorian rule.

2.24 Curing a defective tender of documents

The question whether a cif seller can withdraw the tender of defective documents, and retender conforming ones (assuming that sufficient time remains to do this) has not, as yet, received the categorical and reasoned response which one might like. A related, and also unsatisfactorily answered, query is whether the cif seller can alter or amend the defective documents themselves, so as to bring them into line, and retender those.

These questions have, however, been touched on in a number of cases. Thus, in *SIAT v. Tradax*, following the rejection of three groups of documents, the master purported to correct the defects by inserting the correct destination into each bill of lading. Donaldson J described the master's behaviour as 'a wholly extraordinary proceeding', and ruled that the buyers were entirely justified in rejecting the altered bills. The buyers, he said, were entitled to documents which would pass freely in the trade, and an altered bill was not such a document. He excepted from this pronouncement the correction of minor clerical errors, provided the correction was made before the bill was issued and was duly signed or initialled.

In the Court of Appeal Megaw LJ endorsed Donaldson J's opinion, but pointed out that the requirement that the error be amended before issuance, and the correction signed or initialled, might be unduly restrictive. He made the further important observation that amendments attempted after the bill of lading had been endorsed to a third party constituted a purported unilateral variation of the contract of carriage, since the bill of lading as between carrier and endorsee *was* that contract, rather than merely evidence of it.

In *Proctor & Gamble* v. *Becher* (1988) 1 LIR 88 an incorrectly dated bill of lading was tendered. Leggatt J observed that the buyers could have rejected the bill, 'but the [sellers] would still have been able to represent it . . .'. He did not develop the point, but seems to have been saying that the very bill might have been represented (presumably after amendment) rather than a substitute bill obtained. In the Court of Appeal Kerr LJ said that, undoubtedly, it was open to cif sellers to make a second tender if they could, but that in practice this will not often be possible. Again, tantalisingly, the point was developed no further. With regard to the tender of amended documents, it is submitted that the view of Donaldson J in the *SIAT* case established the basic guideline, and that amended documents may be validly tendered only when, and to the extent that, the amendments in question pass muster in the trade. The circumstances in which this will be the case are likely to be very limited.

In *SIAT*, Megaw LJ acknowledged that a cif seller has the right to present correct documents, if an earlier tender of defective documents has been rejected. In an ordinary sale of goods, the breach of a condition is regarded as a repudiation of the contract, which in orthodox theory justifies immediate cancellation by the innocent party. This analysis stands in the way of recognising a general right of cure in the law of sale. If Megaw LJ's opinion regarding cif sales is correct, it provides yet another example in which the provisions of the Sale of Goods Act require to be stretched, in order to accommodate the cif form within it.

Not all authorities seem to acknowledge that such a right exists, however. In *Kwei Tek Chao* v. *British Traders & Shippers Ltd*, Devlin J equated the right to reject (whether goods or documents) with the right to cancel the contract. In his opinion, 'wherever there is a breach of condition there is a right to rescind the contract'.

A decision sometimes cited in favour of a right to cure a defective tender of documents is that of the Court of Appeal in *Borrowman, Phillips & Co* v. *Free & Hollis* (1878) 4 QBD 500. It is not a particularly strong authority. Cif sellers of maize offered the cargo of a particular ship, which the buyers rejected on the ground that the documents were not available at the time of the offer. The sellers then offered the cargo of an alternative vessel, which the buyers also rejected, on the ground that there was no right of substitution. The Court of Appeal held that the second tender ought to have been accepted.

On close examination of this decision it will be seen that the sellers had not actually made a defective tender (be it of documents or goods) but merely notified their present, but equivocal, intention to do so, to which the buyers immediately objected. The sellers thereupon changed their intention, the buyers persisted in their repudiation, and neither goods nor documents were in the event ever tendered. The Court of Appeal, in fact, signified that if the sellers had given the buyers an unequivocal notice of their intention to appropriate a particular cargo to this contract, the notice could not be withdrawn.

However, collateral support for a right to retender can be found in the judgment of Goff J in *Societe Italo-Belge* v. *Palm Oils; The Post Chaser* (1981) 2 LIR 695. Here cif sellers were required to inform their buyers of which ship would be carrying the goods, as soon as possible after sailing. The learned judge said, *obiter*, that 'even if an invalid, i.e. non-contractual declaration were to be made, and were to be rejected, I can see no reason in principle why the sellers should not subsequently, if within the time scale contemplated by the contract, cure the defect by making a fresh, valid declaration'. This, of course, assumes that no estoppel arises from the buyer having acted to his detriment on the declaration.

2.25   The nature of an fob contract

'An fob contract is one under which the seller is to put the goods on board at his own expense on account of the buyer', according to Buckley LJ in *Wimble, Sons & Co. Ltd* v. *Rosenberg & Sons* (1913) 3 KB 743. This dictum identifies two of the basic features of an fob contract. It is submitted that they are the only two which are definitive, and that the further obligations of buyer and seller under this form of contract derive either from the general law of sale or from the specific characteristics of the contract in question. The two features are: first, the seller must see that the goods are loaded, the cost of which is chargeable to him; and secondly, that further expenses, such as cost of shipment, insurance, and unloading, are chargeable to the buyer.

2.26 The 'classic' fob contract

It has become the practice, however, both in cases and textbooks, to talk in terms of the 'classic' fob contract, and variants of it. Just as the cif contract has a model form, which the parties are free to vary or depart from to an extent, so, too, does the fob contract. In the absence of indications to the contrary, one is entitled to assume that the incidents and characteristics which attach to these model forms apply, unless (*pace* the House of Lords in *The Julia*) the cif and fob designations are to be totally disregarded. Beyond this assumption, however, it is submitted that it serves no purpose to talk in terms of a *'pure'* or *'classic'* contract of either type.

In *the Parchim* (1918) AC 157, for example, a so-called c & f contract for the sale of Chilean saltpetre called for loading at Taltal, a Chilean port, and delivery at one of a range of European ports. The contract required the buyers to take over the charter of the carrying ship from the sellers, to nominate the port of discharge, to be responsible for variations in freight and, in certain circumstances, to provide a substitute carrier. As Lord Parker of Waddington, delivering the advice of the Privy Council, observed, 'the contract has far more of the characteristics of a contract fob Taltal than it has of a contract cif European port'. The provisions of the contract were examined in detail in order to determine whether property had passed from German sellers to Dutch buyers before the cargo was seized as prize of war. The Privy Council held that property passed upon shipment, and not upon payment in exchange for documents. This is consistent with the contract being fob rather than c & f. In truth, however, the contract was a hybrid, or mongrel, as in practice so many international trade contracts are.

2.27 Pyrene v. Scindia Navigation

With this in mind, we turn to the judgment of Devlin J in *Pyrene* v. *Scindia Navigation* (1954) 2 QB 402. This detailed exegesis upon the nature of fob contracts has given rise to considerable difficulties. The plaintiffs sold certain machines fob London, with the buyers making all arrangements for carriage to Bombay aboard the defendant's vessel. One of the machines was dropped and damaged, through the defendant's negligence, while being loaded. The contract of carriage was intended to be covered by a bill of lading issued under the Hague Rules. The sole question before Devlin J was whether the defendants were entitled to take advantage of a limitation of liability contained in those Rules, even though, in the event, no bill was actually issued. Devlin J found in favour of the defendants, by a process of reasoning which must be regarded as suspect.

The learned judge, having decided certain preliminary matters relating to the scope of the Hague Rules, addressed the crucial question of whether the sellers were privy to the contract of carriage, to which the Rules applied. In reaching his conclusion that they were, he examined the nature of fob contracts, and identified three types. Under the first, so-called 'classic' type, 'the buyer's duty is to nominate the ship, and the seller's to put the goods on board for the account of the buyer and procure a bill of lading in terms usual in the trade'. Here, according to the learned judge, the seller is a party to the contract of carriage, 'at least until he takes out the bill of lading in the buyer's name'. This assumes that, in a classic fob contract, the seller makes the contract of carriage with the nominated carrier. (In what capacity is not stated.) The learned Editor of *Benjamin on Sale* (3rd Edn., p 1141) endorses this view, adding that the position is even stronger when the seller takes the bill of lading in his own name.

Neither authority explains why the issuance of a bill of lading in the buyer's name **is** of any relevance to the privity question. If the seller does in fact engage the carrier, either as principal or as agent for the buyer, this will be demonstrable through the application of the ordinary principles of the law of contract, which will operate before the bill is issued. Devlin J does not explain why the issuing of the bill should effect a change. If, however, it is assumed that the buyer will acquire contractual rights and liabilities under s.1 of the Bills of Lading Act 1855 such an assumption would, in the typical case, be incorrect. That section operates only where the buyer acquires property in goods 'under or by reason of' the bill. In an fob contract the buyer typically acquires property when the goods pass over the ship's rail, which will usually occur before the bill is issued. Furthermore, s.1 has the effect of adding the buyer to the contract of carriage, not of substituting the buyer for the seller. Devlin J's dictum seems to assume that the seller will drop out of the contract once the bill is issued in the buyer's name.

It is, in fact, far from clear just what Devlin J is trying to tell us in these few, critically vague, observations. Although he invokes *Wimble* v. *Rosenberg* as a decision in which a 'classic' fob contract was supposedly described, there is no indication that the Court of Appeal there regarded the involvement of the seller in making the contract of carriage as a feature of the paradigm fob arrangement. The second example given by Devlin J is where 'the seller is asked to make all the necessary arrangements . . .'. This, sometimes called an fob contract with additional services, clearly involves the seller in making the contract of carriage, and may differ from a cif contract only in the arrangements for payment and passing of property, and in the fact that changes in freight and insurance rates will be for the buyer's and not the seller's account. The only point of direct contrast between these first two types of fob arrangement which Devlin J makes explicit is that, in the second type, the fob seller may take the bill of lading in his own name.

The third example involves the buyer engaging the ship and procuring the bill of lading, often through the services of a booking agent at the port of loading. This was the type in issue in the *Pyrene* case itself and, according to Devlin J, the only one to raise a privity problem with regard ot the seller. In his view, however, the practical requirements of the transaction demand that the seller be treated as a party to the contract of affreightment. At no point in his judgment does the learned judge suggest what consideration the seller provides to the carrier in this third case.

It is respectfully submitted that there are few sound conclusions to be drawn from this highly questionable judgment. Especially it must be doubted whether the normative fob contract – i.e. that which provides the benchmark from which the parties must show their intention to depart, if they wish to avoid its implications – is the 'classic' type as described by Devlin J. The bare fob contract requires the buyer to engage the carrying vessel. In the absence of provision to the contrary, the fob seller can presume that this will be done and, furthermore, that he is not a party to the contract of carriage. Diplock J's definition of a 'classic' fob contract, which appears in *Ian Stach Ltd* v. *Baker*

Bosley Ltd (1958) 2 QB 130 is to be preferred. There he said that it is the duty of the buyer to find shipping space and to determine the date and place of shipment. Though, as he noted, there are as many exceptions to this rule as there are examples of it, it should nevertheless apply unless the parties intended otherwise.

2.28   Rights and liabilities under an fob contract

We must now consider what the respective rights and liabilities of buyer and seller will be under a standard fob contract. The position of the carrier will be exactly that which he occupies under a cif agreement. In other words, he will be expressly bound to the original contracting party; enjoy or attract the rights and liabilities which s.1 of the Bills of Lading Act 1855 confers, where applicable; and be party to an implied contract, should *Brandt* v. *Liverpool Steam Navigation Co.* (1924) 1 KB 575, or any other principle of implication, apply. The carrier fulfils exactly the same function regardless of the type of sale arrangement involved, and very often he will neither know nor care how the contract between buyer and seller is designated.

It is generally accepted that risk passes to the fob buyer when the goods have passed the ship's rail, in the standard fob contract. It is also generally assumed that property passes at the same time, in accordance with the basic presumption of the law of sale that risk and property pass together: see s.20 of the Sale of Goods Act 1979, *Federspiel* v. *Twigg* (1957) 1 LIR 240 and *Colley* v. *Overseas Exporters* (1921) 3 KB 302. Is the fob seller, however, obliged to pass property at this point, so that he will be in breach of contract unless protected by a specific provision?   This question was addressed by Hobhouse J, at first instance, and by the Court of Appeal, in *Mitsui & Co. Ltd* v. *Flota Mercante Grancolumbia SA* (1988) 1 WLR 1145. A Columbian company, Vikingos, sold prawns to a Japanese firm, Columbia Fisheries, on fob terms. The prawns were shipped on board the defendant's vessel, which was engaged by the sellers for carriage to Japan. The sellers took a bill of lading in their own name. The plaintiffs paid eighty per cent of the price in advance. Upon discharge the prawns were found to be damaged. The plaintiffs' right to recover in tort against the carriers turned on the question whether they were the owners of the goods during the whole of the period of carriage.

Hobhouse J held that they were, despite s.19(2) of the Sale of Goods Act 1979. This provides that 'where goods are shipped, and by the bill of lading the goods are deliverable to the order of the seller or his agent, the seller is *prima facie* taken to reserve the right of disposal'. Following s.19(1), property does not pass to the buyer where a right of disposal is reserved.

Hobhouse J held that the reservation of a right of disposal was inconsistent with the fob seller's duty to pass property on shipment. Since he had no grounds for concluding that the sellers intended to break their contract, he took the view that the presumption raised by s.19(2) could not apply to an fob sale.

This approach was based upon a fundamental misunderstanding of the nature of fob contracts, which the Court of Appeal proceeded to expose. The fob seller, no less than any other, requires some security that the full price will be paid. He is therefore entitled to retain his property in the goods until that security is furnished. Somewhat surprisingly, the Court of Appeal went on to decide that the payment of eighty per cent of the price, and the provision of a letter of credit for the balance, was not sufficient. In the words of Staughton LJ, 'even the most copper-bottomed letter of credit sometimes fails to produce payment'. The seller is therefore entitled to retain property until he has in fact been fully paid. Staughton LJ summarised the basic obligations which arise under an fob contract as follows: 'The expression "fob" determines how the goods shall be delivered, how much of the expense shall be borne by the sellers, and when the risk of loss or damage shall pass to the buyers. It does not necessarily decide when the property is to pass'.

It should perhaps be added that, in the unlikely event of the contract making no provision for the time and manner of payment, s.28 of the Sale of Goods Act 1979 will apply, and it will be 'cash on delivery'. In other words, the buyer will be liable to pay when the goods are on board. In this event he will be entitled to a bill of lading in his own name and the seller who takes a bill in his name will, as Hobhouse J said, be in breach. In *Stach* v. *Baker Bosley*, Diplock J noted that 'the classic fob contract provide[s] for cash . . . against documents'.

2.29   *Payment by documentary credit; date of opening credit*

In a large number of modern transactions, however, the contract will provide for payment through the medium of a banker's documentary (or 'commercial') credit. (In other words, the buyer will arrange for credit to be made available to the seller locally, through the international banking system: see further below, Chapter 6). The question of when this credit must be opened was considered by Diplock J in the *Baker Bosley* case. An fob contract for the sale of steel was made between two brokers which (being a 'classic' fob contract properly so-called) allowed the buyer to select the date of shipment within a given period. Payment was to be by confirmed letter of credit. The sellers contended that this must be opened, at the latest, by the beginning of the shipment period. The buyers argued that it need only be made available a reasonable time before they themselves called for the goods to be shipped.

Diplock J upheld the seller's contention. In a cif contract, it was already clearly established that a credit must be opened at the beginning of the shipment period (see *Pavia & Co. SPA* v. *Thurmann-Nielson* (1952) 2 QB 84). Diplock J ruled that the same should be true in fob transactions.

The reasons for this require careful scrutiny. A cif seller is entitled to choose the actual date of shipment, when the contract calls for shipment within a designated period. As soon as he performs his part, he is entitled to be paid. Hence it follows that the means of payment must be in place from the outset, since the seller may choose to ship at the earliest time. The alternative would require the seller to notify the buyer of the intended shipment date, which would introduce an additional stage into the cif process, with all its attendant problems.

This reasoning does not apply to fob sales. Here the buyer chooses the shipment date. Since he is obviously required to inform the seller of this in any event, no further complication seems to be added, by tying the date of opening the credit to within a reasonable time of the date of shipment. However, in Diplock J's opinion, it does introduce a fatal element of uncertainty into commercial transactions. As the learned judge pointed out, the parties were middlemen, links in a chain of sales of uncertain length joining producer and user. The buyer, it was said, could not possibly know just how long a reasonable time for opening the credit would be, since it would depend upon circumstances which were beyond his knowledge. Diplock J mentioned three: the length of the chain between himself and the ultimate seller; the time it would take to bring the goods to port; and whether the goods were in stock or required manufacture.

Diplock J over-emphasises the importance or relevance of these circumstances. As to the length of the chain of sales: the implication appears to be that the longer it is, the more time will be needed to transmit the shipping information from one end to the other, and so the longer will be the 'reasonable time' required. In days of instantaneous world-wide communications this reason seems to possess little more than superficial plausibility. Furthermore, though a chain may be long in theory, it may be short in practice. It is not uncommon for the same goods to pass through the hands of a trading house several times in the course of its journey from producer to user. Even in a chain in which each party is aware only of those immediately linked to him, it would seem that the necessary information can pass down the chain with sufficient rapidity to cause little interference with the calculation of the notice which the particular seller need be given.

Diplock J's two other circumstances would appear to be totally irrelevant. The first seller in an fob chain will have taken both into account in agreeing to his own delivery period. Each subsequent seller, if he has any sense, will also have contracted for a delivery term during which he can be sure of being able to perform. In practice, performance of a chain of fob sales will be effected by the first fob seller putting the goods on board a vessel nominated by the last fob buyer, and not in a jerky series of transshipments, as each buyer in the chain nominates his own ship, and each seller fulfils his obligations by putting the goods on board it. In short, the matters referred to by Diplock J are not factors which should affect the fob seller's ability to perform within a given scale of time. There seems no particular commercial advantage, and no greater certainty, in fixing the buyer's obligation to open the credit to the first possible date of shipment than to the actual date of shipment. If, on the other hand, it is to be performed within a reasonable time before either, then again there seems no compelling reason, other than a superficial symmetry with cif contracts, for preferring the one date rather than the other. The cost to the buyer will be the same in either case. It can, however, be argued that, since the seller must be ready to perform throughout the shipping period, he should have the assurance that the credit is in place throughout the whole of that period.

2.30   The status of the fob buyer's obligations

Diplock J also decided in *Stach* v. *Baker Bosley* that the duty to open the credit in time is a condition of the contract, since it was 'obviously a term which went to the root of the contract'. Other of the fob buyer's obligations which require to be performed within a certain time have also been designated as conditions, in line with the approach taken to time of performance clauses in cif contracts. In *Bunge* v. *Tradax* (1981) 1 WLR 711, for example, an fob buyer was required to give 'at least fifteen consecutive days notice' of the probable readiness of their vessel to load the goods. This the House of Lords held to be a condition of the contract, despite the fact it could not be predicated that every breach of it would inevitably deprive the seller of the whole of his consideration. (This, it will be recalled, was Diplock LJ's criterion of a condition in *Hongkong Fir Shipping Co.* v. *Kawasaki Kisen Kaisha*). In *Gill & Duffus* v. *Societé Pour L'exportation des Sucres SA* (1985) 1 LlR 621 Leggatt J similarly ruled that the obligation to nominate the port of loading was a major term, so that fob sellers were entitled to cancel the contract when the nomination was made a day late. In each case the importance of certainty in commercial contracts was emphasised.

2.31   Duty to nominate the port of loading

In the former of these cases the sellers had the choice of loading port. In the latter the choice was the buyer's. When the contract is silent, three separate situations might arise. First, the port of loading will be named in the contract, and there will be no problem of nomination. Secondly, and exceptionally, the contract may say nothing at all about the matter. In such an unlikely eventually, the agreement might either be void for incompleteness, or it may be possible to imply a term that one or other party is to nominate a loading port. Thirdly, the contract may name a range of ports, or a geographical area, such as 'Hull, Grimsby or Immingham' (*Modern Transport Co.* v. *Ternstrom & Roos* (1924) 19 LlLR 345) or 'Benelux port' (*Stach* v. *Baker Bosley*).

In *Boyd & Co.* v. *Louca* (1973) 1 LlR 209 the contract was for the sale of a quantity of herring meal 'fob stowed good Danish port'. The buyers failed to name a port, and the sellers sought damages for breach. Kerr J held that the obligation fell upon the buyers, who were accordingly liable. He did so for reasons analogous to those advanced by Diplock J in *Stach* v. *Baker Bosley* regarding the time for opening a credit. First, to place the obligation on the seller would introduce another stage into the transaction; secondly, the nomination would need to be made a reasonable time before the opening of the shipping period, which would introduce the problems of uncertainty which so deterred Diplock J in the earlier case.

2.32   *The carrying ship*

In fob contracts, it is the buyer's right and obligation to name the carrying ship. That vessel must be a suitable one: in other words, capable of loading the contract cargo. Suitability relates not merely to the vessel's physical capabilities – for example, its ability to enter or load at the contract port – but to its legal condition. The nomination of a vessel belonging to an enemy alien would be obviously inadequate. Difficulties have arisen where a licence is required before particular goods can be shipped. Is it part of the seller's obligation to deliver conforming goods, or the buyer's, to provide a suitable ship, to obtain the licence? The question was considered by the House of Lords in *A.V. Pound & Co. Ltd* v. *Hardy & Co. Inc.* (1956) AC 588. It was decided that there was no general rule, but that the question must be answered on a case by case basis.

What is the position when the vessel chosen turns out to be unable to take delivery? Is the buyer free (or, indeed, obliged) to nominate a substitute ship, assuming that there remains time enough for him to do so? The matter was considered by Widgery J in *Agricultores Federatos Argentinos* v. *Ampro SA* (1965) 2 LlR 157. Here, fob buyers of maize nominated a vessel which, owing to unforeseen circumstances, could not arrive at the loading port in time. The sellers gave notice to the buyers of their intention to cancel the contract. The buyers found a substitute vessel which, by working overtime, could have completed loading within the contract period. The buyers were, however, unable to persuade the sellers to accept the substitute nomination, and the vessel was unable to load. The buyers sought damages.

According to Widgery J, the general law applicable to an fob contract 'merely is that the buyers shall provide a vessel which is capable of loading within the stipulated time'. He regarded it as a matter of courtesy that the buyers actually inform the sellers of the name of the ship, and held that they were free to change their minds and send forward a different vessel, provided that the substitute was a suitable alternative, in that it could load the cargo in time.

The contract in this case allowed for a loading period of ten days. It was originally expected that the first named ship would arrive on the seventh day. In the event the substitute would only have been ready on the final day. The question did not arise, and Widgery J did not consider the position regarding expenses incurred by the sellers in storing the goods for the additional three days, nor the more serious question of liability in the event that the goods had deteriorated or been damaged in that intervening period.

The question of storage charges might be solved by an implied term laying the cost on the buyer. The issue of risk (on the assumption that deterioration was not proof of unmerchantability) might be determined by s.20(2) of the Sale of Goods Act 1979. This provides that, 'where delivery has been delayed through the fault of either buyer or seller the goods are at the risk of the party at fault as regards any loss which might not have occurred but for such fault'. This solution assumes that the buyer is somehow at fault by failing to provide the original ship, which will not necessarily be the case. Again, it may be possible to imply a term that the buyer shall pay.

A problem of a rather different kind arose in *J. & J. Cunningham Ltd* v. *Munro Ltd* (1922) 28 Com Cas 42. A contract for the sale of bran called for October shipment, fob Rotterdam. The sellers had the goods at the port by mid-month, but the buyers were only able to find shipping space some two weeks later. In the interval the bran deteriorated, and the buyers refused to accept it when the time came to load. The sellers contended that the bran was at the buyer's risk from the date it arrived at Rotterdam.

Hewart LCJ rejected this contention, thus firmly establishing the principle that the buyer has the choice of loading date in an fob contract. The Lord Chief Justice did, however, consider hypothetically the problem we have raised above, in which the buyer gives one loading date, the seller brings his goods forward, the buyer then substitutes a later date, and the goods go bad. In a rather long-winded and confused passage (in the course of which the learned Lord Chief Justice appears to adumbrate a rather extreme version of the doctrine of promissory estoppel) Hewart LCJ eventually decided that the goods would be at the buyer's risk and the seller would be able to recover the price (or the equivalent as damages) notwithstanding the deterioration. He appeared not to notice that, on the facts before him, the buyer had accepted part of the goods, and allowed him to reject the defective balance, which is contrary to the principle set out in s.11 of the Sale of Goods Act.

2.33   *Delivery before loading*

In the course of his judgment, Hewart LCJ commented that an fob buyer might be disentitled from rejecting goods after loading, if he has already previously accepted them. While it may be theoretically possible for an fob buyer to accept goods prior to delivery, one must be careful to distinguish acceptance of the goods from taking delivery of them. The decision of Bailhache J in *Maine Spinning Co.* v. *Sutcliffe & Co.* (1918) 87 LJKB 382 establishes that an fob buyer cannot demand that the goods be delivered to him other than over the ship's side. Here fob sellers were unable to obtain the necessary export licences. The buyers claimed to be entitled to take delivery on land. Bailhache J held that the fob term enured to the mutual benefit of both parties, and could therefore be dispensed with only by mutual consent. Presumably a contract in which the parties waive performance of the fob term ceases to be an fob contract, and it would be no defence for a seller failing to deliver on land that the buyer would, for example, have been unable to procure a suitable vessel within the designated time.

2.34   *Summary*

Businessmen rarely pattern their affairs according to the law's formal categories (being often ahead of them). Although the theoretical divisions between cif and fob contracts are, in many instances, easy to state, we have now studied enough examples to know that, in practice, they are often blurred through adaptation, alteration, or ignorance. As a result the courts, normally sensitive to the needs of the business world, have refused to force contracts into one of the standard types. They have instead tended to take each case as it comes, and construed the contract according to its terms, without especial regard to its supposed classification.

In the light of this, it may seem that the fob and cif designations are little more than a shorthand method of incorporating certain terms into contracts, and that those terms may be displaced by the presence of other, incompatible provisions in the same agreement.

Commercial reasons for choosing one form of contract rather than another are unlikely to involve detailed consideration of their different legal implications. Economic and political factors, such as government incentives to utilise domestic shipping or insurance services, and the relative stability or volatility of the freight and insurance markets, as well as supply and demand of the particular goods themselves, will be much more influential. There follows, however, a list of the principal legal distinctions (and similarities) between cif and fob contracts.

1. CIF: the seller can ship at any time within the shipment period.
   FOB: the buyer can call for shipment at any time within the shipment period.
   In either case the goods must be loaded on board within the designated time, and the fob buyer must therefore allow the seller sufficient time to accomplish this.
   In each case failure to comply with the loading obligation constitutes a breach of condition.
2. CIF: the seller determines the carrying vessel and the loading port, if the contract is silent.
   FOB: the buyer does so.
3. CIF: the seller's delivery obligation is fulfilled on loading, to the extent that the buyer's obligation to pay then arises.
   FOB: the same is true.
4. CIF: the buyer nevertheless has a right to inspect the goods on discharge, and may reject them if their condition indicates that they were defective when loaded.
   FOB: the time and place at which the buyer should examine the goods depends upon the particular circumstances.
5. CIF: property passes to the buyer when documents are exchanged for payment, on the assumption that the goods are identified.
   FOB: property passes when the goods are put over the ship's rail, on the same assumption.
   These rules are based upon the parties' supposed intentions, and can be displaced.
   In both cases risk of accidental damage or loss passes to the buyer on loading.
6. CIF: the seller must tender conforming documents within a reasonable time.
   FOB: the seller may not be concerned with this: it will depend upon the particular type of fob contract.
7. CIF: the buyer, if he is paying by banker's credit, must open it at the latest by the beginning of the shipment period.
   FOB: the same appears to be the case.

8. CIF: the seller is entitled to be paid on tender of conforming documents. To this extent a cif sale is a sale of documents.

FOB: the seller is entitled to be paid on loading. In practice, however, the date of payment is likely to be deferred, in which case the passing of property will also often be deferred.

9. CIF: the seller must obtain any necessary export licences and clearances.

FOB: there is no fixed rule.

10. CIF: if the seller is prevented from shipping, he must use his best endeavours to buy goods afloat.

FOB: there is no such obligation. Goods are never in practice bought fob afloat.

11. CIF: the buyer's contractual rights against the carrier arise under s.1 of the Bills of Lading Act 1855, or under the rule in *Brandt's* case.

FOB: if the buyer has engaged the carrier, his rights against him arise under the common law of contract. If he has not, they will depend upon whether property has passed 'upon or by reason of' the bill of lading being made out to him. Where property passes on loading this will not be the case. Since, however, the buyer is liable to pay the freight, the *Brandt* principle will frequently be applicable.

12. CIF: the buyer's rights in tort will depend upon his having property in the goods at the relevant time, or a right to possession of them.

FOB: the same is true.

13. CIF: the contract of sale may be frustrated by delay in transit or by re-routing.

FOB: this question has not been considered judicially, but frustration may be more difficult to establish.

14. Application of the principles for the assessment of damages may vary, according to whether the contract is cif or fob, in relation to the time and place of assessment.

Chapter 3

The Bill of Lading

3.01 Introduction

A bill of lading is a document issued by or on behalf of a carrier acknowledging the shipment of goods on board a particular vessel, or that goods have been received for shipment. The former is known as a 'shipped' bill and the latter as a 'received for shipment' bill. It is also a direction to deliver the goods to a named person (a 'straight consigned' bill) to the order or assigns of a named person (an 'order' bill) or to bearer (a 'bearer' bill.) Whether, in the absence of specific provision, the cif buyer is entitled to a shipped bill will, generally speaking, depend upon the custom of the particular trade to which the sale relates, or the practice of the particular port at which the bill is issued. Although shipped bills are regarded as superior to received bills, it may, as we shall see, be to the buyer's advantage to be given a received bill, as this will enable him to deal with the goods at the earliest time.

3.02 The validity of received bills

The validity and effectiveness of received bills has been a matter of some dispute, however. In *Diamond Alkali Export Corporation* v. *Bourgeois* (1921) 3 KB 443, McCardie J denied that a received bill was a bill of lading, properly so-called, at all. As he pointed out, the seminal case of *Lickbarrow* v. *Mason* (1787) 2 TR 83, which first gave judicial recognition to the mercantile practice of regarding bills of lading as documents of title, was confined to shipped bills. Section 3 of the Bills of Lading Act 1855 (see further below [3.11]) is similarly limited. On the other hand, the Privy Council in *The Marlborough Hill* (1921) 1 AC 444 apparently decided that a received bill and a shipped bill were in principle no different. That decision was subjected to radical criticism in the *Diamond Alkali* case, but nevertheless followed by Lloyd

J in *Ishag* v. *Allied Bank International* (1981) 1 LlR 92. The learned judge felt that the Privy Council in *The Marlborough Hill* had acknowledged a general trade practice of recognising received bills as documents of title. Under the latest revision of the Uniform Customs and Practice for Documentary Credits (see further below, Chapter 6) banks will now accept received bills, unless the credit specifically calls for a shipped bill, or a received bill is inconsistent with some other provision of the credit itself. On the other hand, the expression 'bill of lading' when it occurs in Incoterms (sets of standard terms for the various types of international sale contract, promulgated by the International Chamber of Commerce and in worldwide use) refers to a shipped bill.

With the gradual displacement of traditional methods of shipment by such innovations as containerisation, for certain types of goods, and the consequent shifting of the focal point of delivery to the carrier from the dockside to the inland container depot, there is little doubt that the classic shipped bill of lading is being displaced by new forms of documentation, such as the combined transport document. In those areas where the bill of lading remains paramount, a received bill is usually a much less effective document than a shipped bill. The reasons for this are several. First, a received bill is no guarantee of shipment. Secondly, it may cause a gap in the continuous documentary cover to which the cif buyer is entitled. (see *Yelo* v. *Machado* (1952) 1 LlR 183). It is no evidence of the date of shipment, which can be of critical importance. It does not identify the carrying ship. It may present difficulties to a bank in deciding whether it is a proper document under a commercial credit. A received bill can, however, be converted into a shipped bill by the simple expedient of noting the fact of shipment on it, when shipment eventually takes place.

3.03   Contents of a bill of lading

The bill will be signed by the carrier, or on his behalf, and will describe so far as possible the nature, condition and quantity of the goods to which it relates. In practice considerably more information than this will be contained in the bill, including a full statement of the terms of the contract of carriage.

3.04   The functions of a bill of lading

A bill of lading is commonly said to have three functions. It is a document of title of the goods; a receipt for the goods; and it either is, or is evidence of, a contract for their transportation. (It is evidence in the hands of the party shipping the goods. It is the contract itself in the hands of a subsequent transferee.)

3.05   The bill of lading as a document of title

Just what is a document of title? In layman's terms, it is a document evidencing ownership of goods described in it, or the right to their possession. A statutory definition can be found in s.1(4) of the Factors Act 1889. This comprehends any document, including a bill of lading, 'used in the ordinary course of business as proof of the possession or control of goods, or authorising or purporting to authorise . . . the possessor of the documents to transfer or receive goods thereby represented'. There is no common law definition of a document of title, but its essence would seem to be that, by mercantile custom, dealings in the documents – for instance, their sale or pledge – are regarded as dealings in the goods which those documents symbolically represent. It will be seen that the statutory definition is rather wider, and comprehends documents which simply constitute proof of possession or control.

In the absence of provision in the contract, a cif buyer is entitled to a bill of lading which enables him to deal freely with the goods; in other words, one which possesses the common law quality of transferability. In *Soproma* v. *Marine & Animal By-Products Corporation* (1966) 1 LlR 367, therefore, the rejection of a 'straight consigned' bill (i.e. one specifying delivery to a named party, with no provision for transferability) was held to be justified. Echoing the sentiments of Lord Porter in *The Julia*, McNair J said that 'the essential characteristic of [cif and c & f] contracts is that by the shipping documents the buyer to whom property passes under the bill of lading is given contractual rights against the shipowner, which rights he can by endorsement transfer to a subsequent purchaser'. Transferability cannot be implied, as was decided by the Privy Council in *Henderson & Co.* v. *The Comptoir D'Escompte De Paris* (1873) LR 5 PC 253. 'In order to make bills of lading negotiable [transferable?] some such words as 'or order or assigns' ought to be in them', according to Sir Robert Collier.

An additional justification for rejecting the bill in the *Soproma* case was the fact that it was endorsed 'freight collect'. The cif form, by definition, places responsibility for freight on the seller. It often happens in practice that the buyer will actually pay the freight, upon the arrival of the carrying vessel. In such cases, however, freight will be discounted from the invoice. No such arrangement was made in *Soproma*. Hence the bill as tendered failed to fulfil one of its basic functions, which is to allow the holder to obtain possession of the goods as of right from the carrier. No accompanying document demonstrated that freight had in fact been paid, and the bill was therefore bad on its face.

The other side of the coin is that the carrier must deliver to the party entitled under the bill of lading, and to that party alone. As Lord Denning emphasised in *Sze Hai Tong Bank* v. *Rambler Cycle Co. Ltd* (1959) AC 576: 'a shipowner who delivers without production of the bill of lading does so at his peril'. Here carriers delivered goods to consignees, who did not hold the bill of lading, against an indemnity from the consignee's bank. A widely drawn exceptions clause in the contract of carriage purported to exonerate the carriers for misdelivery. The Privy Council held that the literal scope of this clause must be cut down so that the main object of the contract of carriage might be achieved. That object is the delivery of the goods against the bill of lading. The bill of lading holder was therefore entitled to damages for misdelivery.

In *Brown Jenkinson & Co. Ltd* v. *Percy Dalton Ltd* (1957) 2 QB 621 a majority of the Court of Appeal held the contract of indemnity to be illegal, and deprecated its widespread use.

The significance of the bill of lading as a document of title is well described by Bowen LJ in *Sanders* v. *Maclean*, in a passage which deserves full quotation.

'A cargo at sea while in the hands of the carrier is necessarily incapable of physical delivery. During this period of transit and voyage, the bill of lading by the law merchant is universally recognised as its symbol, and the indorsement and delivery of the bill of lading operates as a symbolic delivery of the cargo. Property in the goods passes by such indorsement and delivery of the bill of lading, whenever it is the intention of the parties that the property should pass, . . . And for the purpose of passing such property in the goods and completing the title of the indorsee to full possession thereof, the bill of lading, until complete delivery of the cargo has been made on shore to someone rightfully claiming under it, remains in force as a symbol, and carries with it not only the full ownership of the goods, but also all rights created by the contract of carriage between the shipper and the shipowner. It is a key which in the hands of a rightful owner is intended to unlock the door of the warehouse, floating or fixed, in which the goods may happen to be.'

3.06 When issued in sets

In *Sanders* v. *Maclean*, cif buyers refused to accept the bills of lading on the ground that they had been issued in a set of three, of which only two had been tendered. The Court of Appeal commented upon the practice (still current) of issuing bills in multiple copies, noting that this was generally done in order that the seller, and possibly the carrier, should have a copy for their own records and in case the original should be lost. They also noted that the practice left open the possibility of fraud: the copies of the bill could be used to dispose of the cargo away from the buyer either before or after he had accepted and paid against the original. It had recently been decided, by the House of Lords in *Glynn Mills & Co* v. *East & West India Dock Co.* (1882) 7 App Cas 591 that a carrier who delivered the goods to someone in possession of a copy bill could not be sued by the buyer who held the original and whose goods they were. The Court of Appeal in *Sanders* v. *Maclean* took the view that such fraudulent dealings were an inherent risk in the practice of issuing multiple bills, but that the buyer was nevertheless only entitled to one copy. In their opinion, the indorsement and delivery of any copy of the bill had the effect of neutralising the others, which thereupon ceased to be effective documents of title.

It follows that the tender of one copy of a bill of lading after another has already been made available to a third party would not be an effective tender. There would, of course, be no way of knowing this from the face of the bill itself.

The potency of the bill of lading as a document of title is well illustrated by the decision of the Court of Appeal in *Cahn & Meyer* v. *Pockett's Bristol Channel Steam Packet Co* (1899) 1 QB 643. This involved an action by a buyer of goods against a carrier, for wrongful refusal to deliver them. The goods had in fact been stopped in transit, on the instructions of the shippers and original owners. They had contracted to sell the goods to a buyer, and had delivered a bill of lading to him together with a bill of exchange for acceptance and return. Section 19(3) of the Sale of Goods Act provides that, in such circumstances, the transfer of property in the goods is conditional upon acceptance of the bill of exchange. The buyer did not accept the bill of exchange. Indeed, he was already insolvent when the documents were sent to him. Nevertheless, he purported to sell the goods to the plaintiff, and delivered the bill of lading to him. Applying s.25(2) of the 1893 Act (s25(1) of the 1979 Act) the Court held that the plaintiff had bought the goods from someone who had himself agreed to buy them, and who was in possession of a document of title with the consent of the seller. As a result, property passed to the plaintiff. The fact that the original seller's consent to possession was conditional was deemed to be irrelevant.

3.07   The passing of property

If the bill of lading is properly to fulfil its function as a document of title, the rules regulating the passing of property in the Sale of Goods Act must not be allowed to draw attention away from the tendering of the bill as the critical event in transferring ownership rights. Hence it may be necessary, once more, to give certain provisions of the Sale of Goods Act a special interpretation, in order to harmonise them with the cif form.

This was in fact done, by the House of Lords, in *Smyth* v. *Bailey* (1940) 3 All ER 60. The Court of Appeal in this case had held that property in a cif sale passed upon the seller giving the buyer notice that particular goods had been appropriated to the contract. Lord Wright, with whose speech the rest of their Lordships agreed, said that such a view would 'have serious consequences in unsettling the course of business generally in cif contracts', and should be 'explicitly and fully controverted'. Lord Wright noted that property passes when the parties intend it should pass, provided the goods are specific or ascertained. He also pointed out, however, that parties seldom make their intention known, or even give thought to the matter at all. In such circumstances, their 'intention' is to be sought in sound commercial practice. It is common for merchants to raise bridging finance, to cover the period between shipment and payment, by pledging the shipping documents with a bank. This requires that the seller have the general property in the goods. As Lord Wright stressed, 'these credit facilities, which are of the first importance, would be completely unsettled if the incidence of property were made a matter of doubt'.

3.08   *The bill of lading as evidence of the facts stated in it*

A typical bill of lading will contain a considerable amount of factual information relating to the goods and their shipment. It will, for example, specify the ports of loading and discharge, the carrying vessel, and the date the goods were loaded. The quantity, or weight, and apparent condition of the goods will also be noted. In contracts which are subject to the Hague–Visby Rules (see further below [4.12]) the shipper is entitled to demand that the bill of lading contain the following information:

(a) the leading marks necessary for identification of the goods, as the same are furnished in writing by the shipper before the loading of the goods starts, provided such marks are stamped or otherwise shown clearly upon the goods if uncovered, or on the cases or coverings in which the goods are contained, in such a manner as should ordinarily remain legible until the end of the voyage;
(b) either the number of packages or pieces, or the quantity or weight, as the case may be, as furnished in writing by the shipper; and
(c) the apparent order and condition of the goods. The carrier is not obliged to give the information in (a) or (b) if either he reasonably suspects it to be inaccurate, or has no reasonable means of checking its accuracy.

Article III rule 4 of the Rules provides that a bill of lading containing the above information shall be *prima facie* evidence of the receipt by the carrier of the goods as described. Furthermore, proof to the contrary cannot be admitted once the bill has been transferred to a *bona fide* third party.

It will be noticed that the Rules entitle the shipper to a received bill. Although, as we have seen, the pedigree of received bills has been cast in doubt, they do give the shipper the benefit of a document of title which he can immediately use to deal with the goods: see *per* Brown J in *Hugh Mack & Co. Ltd* v. *Burns & Laird Lines Ltd* (1944) 77 LlLR 377.

3.09   *Where the Hague–Visby Rules do not apply*

The position is somewhat different where the Rules do not apply. In a number of cases, decided by and large before the Rules were first introduced (as the Hague Rules, in 1924) various aspects of, or statements within, the bill of lading were examined, and their contractual or evidential significance considered. The only general conclusion to be drawn from these decisions is that it seems impossible to attribute an overall status to the different elements of a bill. Some may be contractual terms; some may be mere representations; some may give rise to evidential presumptions; and some may have no legal significance whatsoever.

As a starting point, we should consider the crucial, and controversial, rule in *Grant* v. *Norway* (1851) 10 CB 665. Here a ship's master signed bills of lading for goods which had never in fact been put on board. The question arose whether the shipowner was bound by his employee's statement in the bill that they had, and therefore liable for non-delivery. Did the master's authority, as agent for the shipowner, go so far? The Court of Common Pleas held that it did not. The master's authority was to do whatever was usual in the management of the ship. To sign for goods never actually loaded was not usual, and all parties likely to be affected by the bill (the plaintiffs happened to be pledgees of it) were deemed to know that it was not.

This rule, though it has been criticised, still stands. It may, indeed, extend beyond the case in which no goods are loaded and apply, by analogy, to situations in which goods of a different quality or kind from those signed for are put on board. In *Cox* v. *Bruce* (1886) 18 QBD 147 plaintiff endorsees of a bill of lading sued the carrier, when it transpired that the goods delivered were of a lower quality than that indicated in the bill. The master had in fact made out the bill using the quality-denoting marks given to him by the shipper. It was impossible to determine upon superficial inspection that the goods were not of that quality.

The Court of Appeal held that the rule in *Grant* v. *Norway* is not limited to the case of goods which were never loaded. The master's authority is confined to the making of statements relating to the outward condition of the goods. He is not employed as a judge of quality, and businessmen are therefore deemed to know that his powers as agent to bind his principal are accordingly circumscribed.

Statements regarding *apparent* condition are within the master's remit, however. In *Compania Naviera Vasconzada* v. *Churchill & Sim*

(1906) 1 KB 237 buyers of timber claimed damages against the carrier when the wood was delivered badly stained by petrol. The bill of lading stated that the goods had been shipped in good order and condition. It was proved that the timber was already visibly damaged when loaded on board. Channel J said that 'a captain is expected to notice the apparent condition of the goods, though not the quality'. By this we may assume that the shipowner is bound by the master's statements regarding the former, but not the latter.

In what way is he bound? Channel J held in the case above that the words in a bill of lading 'shipped in good order and condition' do not form a term of the contract of carriage. The carrier is, however, liable to deliver the goods in the same condition in which he received them. The phrase in the bill can be used to raise an estoppel against the carrier. That is to say, he will be prevented from disproving its truth, provided it constitutes a statement of fact upon which someone to whom it was addressed has acted on it, to his potential detriment, in the belief that the statement was true. Channel J held that the buyers had acted in this fashion, because they had accepted the bill as a good tender from the sellers, and duly paid the price of the goods. He came to this conclusion despite the fact that the buyers could (and did) obtain an award for the return of the price, on the ground that the sellers had not shipped goods of the contract quality. The plaintiff's prejudice presumably lay in the trouble, uncertainty, and expense of recovering from the sellers (even though it has been held, in *Cook* v. *Wright* (1861) 1 B & S 559 that an award of the remedy sought is, in law, complete compensation for such matters). In the event, the plaintiffs did not seek to enforce their award against the sellers, who were a foreign company.

3.10 *Grant* v. *Norway and s.3 of the Bills of Lading Act 1855*

It has been suggested that s.3 of the Bills of Lading Act 1855 was passed in order to mitigate the rigours of, and indeed to entirely displace, the rule in *Grant* v. *Norway*. If this were so, it has failed signally to achieve its objective. The section provides that 'every bill of lading in the hands of a consignee or endorsee for valuable consideration, representing goods to have been shipped on board a vessel, shall be conclusive evidence of such shipment as against the master or other person signing the same, notwithstanding that such goods or part thereof may not have been so shipped . . .'.

Two things should be noted at once. First, the section does not create a cause of action, but merely raises a statutory estoppel (of which detrimental reliance is not a part). Secondly, the estoppel is raised against the signer of the bill, not his employer. Since this is its compass, it is difficult to see how the *Grant* v. *Norway* hiatus is bridged.

Nevertheless, in *Parsons* v. *New Zealand Shipping Co.* (1901) 1 QB 548 the Court of Appeal seemed prepared to assume that this was, indeed, the effect of s.3. This important, and difficult, decision on the extent to which statements in a bill of lading bind the carrier deserves careful attention. Plaintiff buyers of frozen New Zealand lamb sued the carriers for short delivery. The bills of lading included identification marks which had been inserted by the sellers. These indicated that the lamb carcases were marked 'Sun Brand 622X' or 'Sun Brand 488X'. In fact some were actually marked 'Sun Brand 522X' and 'Sun Brand 388X', although the total quantity was correct. On a falling market the buyers refused to accept the carcases, and sought damages against the carriers. (The interesting question of how these would be calculated was never considered.)

The Court of Appeal decided, unanimously, that the plaintiff's claim failed. They did so, however, for significantly different reasons. The Master of The Rolls, A.L. Smith, decided that the carriers would have been liable on the statement in the bill, but for the presence of an exceptions clause in the contract of carriage covering misdelivery. In his view, all the details of the marks were important: they enabled the buyer to distinguish his goods from others of the same kind which might be on board; they described the subject matter of his insurance (and they might, although the Master of the Rolls did not take the point, to be the marks by which the buyer had sold the goods on). It was of no relevance, in his opinion, to show that the goods tendered were of exactly the same quality and commercial value as those he had contracted to take.

The majority judges, Collins and Romer LJJ, held that the precise number on the markings was unimportant, and could be totally discounted. The last figure, which was constant, described the quality of the lamb. The first, which varied, was relevant only to the seller's internal bookkeeping, and was completely immaterial to the buyers or anyone else.

Paradoxically, both approaches are correct, and simply represent different interpretations of the facts. The principle to be deduced from this case would seem to be as follows. If the condition in which goods were shipped is described in the bill of lading in terms which correspond to the description of the goods in the contract of sale, the buyer cannot reject the goods, even though the bill contains additional words of description, going beyond, but not varying, those used in the contract of sale. If a buyer buys five thousand tons of Canadian wheat, and the bill notes the shipment of five thousand tons of Canadian Western White wheat, the buyer cannot complain. He has what he agreed to pay for. Hence Collins LJ is able to say that 'a contract for the sale of Sun Brand lambs, second quality, of the Christchurch company's freezing, might have been satisfied equally well out of either mark or out of both indiscriminately'. This is correct, once it is established that the mark was not part of the description. This, however, is not done by establishing that the article described in the bill of lading had the same commercial value as that described in the contract of sale (see *Arcos* v. *Ronaassen* and *Manbre Saccharine* v. *Corn Products*, above [1.11]). The seller is allowed to ship, and the carrier sign bills for, goods of a more precise description than that used in the contract of sale, provided the additional description does not take the goods outside the parameters of the sale requirements. In A.L. Smith MR's opinion, just this had happened. As he puts it, if one buys ABC champagne, ABC champagne must be tendered, and it is to no purpose to say that XYZ champagne is just as good (or even better).

So we are returned to the old, endlessly difficult, question of separating words of description from the rest. Since these goods were bought afloat, and insured under a policy which used the same numerical designation of the goods, and since in all three judges' view the buyer would have had difficulty in actually getting his goods out of the ship if the bill and carcase numbers did not correspond, there is a lot to be said for the approach of the Master of the Rolls.

But if this be correct, ought the carrier not to have escaped liability in any event, albeit by a different route? There are three possible views of the significance of the carcase markings. Either they were irrelevant, in which case no liability for their accuracy attaches. Or they related to the quality of the animals, in which case the carrier is not liable, following *Cox* v. *Bruce*; or, as A.L. Smith MR thought, they related to the *kind* of goods being carried, in which case, since goods of that kind had not been loaded, the shipowner would escape liability under the rule in *Grant* v. *Norway*.

Grant v. *Norway* is, however, only mentioned in the judgment of Collins LJ. He seems to accept that the owner could be liable for statements relating to kind. A.L. Smith MR is clearly of the opinion that s.3 of the Bills of Lading Act 1855 establishes liability. However, on the view of *Grant* v. *Norway* taken in *Cox* v. *Bruce*, Collins LJ's judgment is inconsistent, and that of A.L. Smith MR simply wrong.

3.11   The scope of s.3

What, therefore, is the true scope of s.3? The question was considered by Mocatta J in *V/O Rasnoimport* v. *Guthrie & Co. Ltd* (1966) 1 LlR 1. The plaintiffs here were indorsees of a bill of lading issued by the defendants, who were port agents of shipowners onto whose vessel a cargo of rubber had been loaded. The bill indicated that two hundred and twenty five bales had been shipped, when in fact only ninety were actually put on board. Mocatta J held that the defendants were liable for breach of a warranty that they had the owner's authority to sign the bill. This form of liability is a well-recognised, albeit somewhat anomalous aspect of the law of agency, whereby an agent may be liable to third parties if he claims an authority which he does not possess. Liability cannot arise, however, if the third party is aware that the agent is unauthorised. Counsel for the defendants would therefore seem to have been on strong ground when he argued, following *Grant* v. *Norway* and *Cox* v. *Bruce*, that the limits of a master's powers to bind his principal are well known. (No point was taken that the party signing the bill was not the master.) Mocatta J, however, took the view that the authority of masters, and agents generally, is not well known. This observation directly contradicts what was said by Lord Esher MR in *Cox* v. *Bruce*, as well as *Grant* v. *Norway* itself. The learned judge went on to hold, however, that s.3 could not raise any estoppel against the owners, since the section was, on its face, directed only against the actual signer of the bill. While the learned judge accepted that this could include the person authorising signature, or on whose behalf the bill was signed, in his view it was not right 'to stretch the words "other person signing the same" to cover the owners . . .'.

Mocatta J did accept as correct a submission by counsel for the defendants which appears not to have been considered directly before. It was taken to be undoubtedly correct that the signature of the master on a bill of lading stating that goods had been shipped raised a *prima facie* presumption against the shipowner. The owner would, as a result, be put to proof that shipment had not taken place. If he could not rebut the presumption he would be liable for non-delivery, despite the rule in *Grant* v. *Norway*.

3.12 The bill of lading as evidence of the contract of carriage; the bill of lading as the contract of carriage itself

A bill of lading in its barest form is a receipt for goods shipped, or to be shipped, whether or not on a particular vessel, signed on behalf of the carrier. It need contain no further detail than this. In practice, however, bills of lading will state some or all of the terms on which the carrier has agreed to carry the goods. The contract of carriage will have been made before the bill of lading was issued. Indeed, the carrier (or his agent) will have taken possession of the goods, and issued the bill, in part performance of his obligations under that contract.

The idea that, as between buyer and carrier, the bill of lading contains the terms of the contract, whereas, between the original parties, it is only evidence of them, was expressed by Lord Esher MR in *Leduc* v. *Ward* (1888) 20 QBD 475. However, he proceeded to obviate the point of the distinction by declaring that, when the terms of the contract of carriage are reduced to writing, in the form of the bill of lading, the parol evidence rule applies to prevent the introduction of extraneous terms. The full force of the distinction was restored by the judgment of Lord Goddard CJ in *SS Ardennes (Cargo Owners)* v. *SS Ardennes (Owners)* (1951) 1 KB 55. Here plaintiff goods owners shipped goods aboard the defendant's vessel, following an oral undertaking by the defendants to carry the goods direct to London. The bill which was eventually issued contained a provision permitting the carrier to deviate. The ship in fact discharged goods at an intermediate port before going on to London, as a result of which the plaintiffs incurred additional import duties and lost the market advantage of an earlier arrival. Lord Goddard CJ held that the oral promise was part of the contract of carriage. *Leduc* v. *Ward* was an action between carrier and endorsee, between whom the bill of lading was the contract. The contract in the *Ardennes* case had been made between carrier and shipper before the bill was issued, and there was therefore scope for it to include the oral term. Lord Esher's idea that the issuing of the bill reduced the terms of the contract to those contained in the bill seems to have been rejected by implication, if not in so many words.

3.13   Delivery orders

As we have already noticed, cif contracts often provide that the seller may at his option tender a delivery order in place of a bill of lading. A delivery order may, by the custom of the particular trade, be a document of title. Certainly delivery orders fall within the statutory definition of documents of title in s.1(4) of the Factors Act 1889. However, unlike the bill of lading, there is no fixed form or content which a so-called delivery order must possess or follow. In particular, there is no requirement that the document be issued between particular parties. In *The Julia*, for example, a delivery order was drawn by one agent of the seller upon another, who was to take delivery of the goods from the carrier and deliver them to the buyer. In *Colins & Shields* v. *Weddel* a delivery order was addressed by the carriers to the master porter of a Liverpool dock. However, if the contract is truly cif, rather than simply described as such, then the delivery order must be capable, as nearly as possible, of fulfilling the functions of a bill of lading. As such, it must give the buyer direct rights against the carrier. In both the above cases, the delivery order was deemed inappropriate to the cif form of contract.

The nature and requirements of a delivery order in a cif contract were considered by Kerr J in *Krohn & Co* v. *Thegra NV* (1975) 1 LlR 146. A contract for the sale of manioc chips cif Rotterdam was made on GAFTA 100, a standard form of contract much used in the grain and feedstuffs trade. This provides that the seller may tender either a shipped bill of lading, or a ship's delivery order, or 'other delivery orders in negotiable and transferable form'. The sellers tendered delivery orders which had been issued by charterers and addressed to their local agents in Rotterdam. The buyers rejected them on the ground that they were not ship's delivery orders. Kerr J noted that there is no clear definition of a delivery order. The expression is imprecise, and takes its meaning from the particular context in which it is used. The fact that the term occurs in a cif contract is, however, important. The documents tendered to the cif buyer must be such as give him, as far as possible, control over the goods: in other words, ownership of them and direct contractual rights against the carrier. While a delivery order cannot achieve these objectives to the same extent as a bill of lading, a delivery order tendered under a cif contract should approximate as closely as possible to a bill of lading.

These objectives can be achieved, by the person in possession of the goods being ordered to deliver to the buyer, and by his acknowledging this obligation to the buyer himself (i.e. by so-called attornment). Alternatively, the person in possession might undertake directly with the buyer to deliver to him. A delivery order addressed to, or issued by a person not in possession fails to achieve the basic objectives of the cif form. In the opinion of Kerr J, tender of any other kind of delivery order than a ship's delivery order as described by him would be insufficient under a cif contract. As *The Julia* shows, however, the fact that the contract allows a different kind of delivery order to be tendered may indicate that the contract is not cif at all.

Chapter 4

The Carriage of Goods by Sea

Introduction: the incorporation of charterparty terms into contracts for the carriage of goods by sea

In the previous chapters we have examined the arrangements for transporting the goods as an aspect of the contract of sale cif or fob. In this chapter the contract of carriage itself assumes centre stage, and we will look in detail at its provisions and implications. First of all, however, we need to consider a preliminary matter.

The owner of a cargo-carrying vessel may, in general, employ his ship for profit in one of two ways. Either he may himself seek for parties who wish goods transported from place to place, selling space on his vessel until its whole capacity is filled or, the shipowner may hire out the ship and crew to someone who then takes over the burden – and benefit – of finding cargoes (if he does not wish to use the vessel solely to carry his own goods). This latter arrangement is called a *charterparty*. It may last for a predetermined period of time, or cover a specific voyage. In a voyage charterparty, the charterer agrees to pay the owner freight: that is, a sum calculated according to the amount of cargo shipped. This will usually be accompanied by an undertaking to load a specified minimum quantity. Insofar as the charterer falls short of this target, he will be required to pay so-called 'dead freight'. A time charterer engages to pay a hire charge.

We are not concerned here with the relationship between the owner and charterer, except insofar as it affects or has implications for the contract of sale. We should note first of all, therefore, that when a chartered vessel is engaged to carry goods, the contract of carriage is usually made between the goods owner and the shipowner, not the goods owner and charterer. This is the case even though the contract of carriage may have been negotiated by the charterer and the profits from it go to him. Unless a charterer hires a ship to carry his own goods, a charterparty is essentially a speculative venture in which the shipowner transfers to the charterer the risk of fluctuations in market rates and demand, in return for a guaranteed fixed income from his vessel. In either instance, all aspects of the vessel's employment and management remain, generally speaking, within the owner's control. Hence the actual contracts of carriage are, as a rule, made by the shipowner; and the master, when he issues the bill of lading, usually does so on the owner's behalf.

In *Manchester Trust* v. *Furness* (1895) 2 QB 539 shipowners wished to show that they were not parties to the contract of carriage. They had chartered their vessel on terms which provided that the captain and crew were to be the agents of the charterers for all purposes. Bills of lading issued by the master purported to include 'other conditions as per charterparty'. The goods were misdelivered. The plaintiff, as indorsee of the bill of lading, sought damages from the shipowners. They denied liability on the ground that they were not parties to the contract of carriage contained in the bill.

The Court of Appeal held that the words in the bill of lading which referred to the charterparty only had the effect of incorporating into the contract of carriage those provisions of the charterparty which related to the payment of freight, and whatever else was to be performed when the cargo was delivered. To include anything beyond this would, in the opinion of Lopes LJ, 'require very clear and explicit words'. The plaintiff's action succeeded.

Since particular terms in the charterparty may be more favourable to shipowners than the provisions of the contract of carriage, attempts have frequently been made to incorporate the relevant parts of the one contract into the other, by means of a reference in the bill of lading of the kind discussed in the *Furness* case. Occasionally it has been the bill of lading holder who has wished to take advantage of a charterparty term. This has generated a series of cases in which the effectiveness of the various attempts has been assessed, and a set of principles enunciated. Unfortunately, these are not altogether clear, or free from contention.

4.02 *Thomas* v. *Portsea SS Co. Ltd*

A leading authority is the decision of the House of Lords in *Thomas* v. *Portsea SS Co. Ltd* (1912) AC 1. The subsequent history of the law on this subject can be summarised as an attempt to determine just what was decided in this case, and whether or not it should be followed. The facts, at least, are fairly clear. The respondent's ship was under charter; the charterparty contained an arbitration clause. A cargo was shipped by a third party, to whom a bill of lading was issued. The bill stipulated that deck cargo was to be a shipper's risk, 'and all other terms and conditions and exceptions of charter [sic] to be as per charterparty'. The bill was endorsed to the appellants, who wished a dispute between themselves and the carriers to be referred to arbitration, as the charterparty provided. The House of Lords determined that the arbitration clause was not a part of the contract of carriage.

There appear to have been two grounds for this decision. First of all, the general phrase 'terms and conditions' was to be construed by reference to the type of contract in which it occurred. A bill of lading is concerned with the carriage and delivery of goods, and with payment for that service. The phrase in question should be so construed as to bring into the contract of carriage from the contract of charter only those provisions in the charter which relate directly to the objects of the contract of carriage. The second ground for decision lay in the scope of the arbitration clause itself. It applied in terms to disputes arising out of the charterparty. The dispute in issue arose out of the contract of carriage. Hence it is difficult to see that the clause could have had any application in any event, unless there were indications elsewhere that the parties intended bill of lading disputes to be included within its scope. Several of their Lordships indicated that the parties must use 'distinct and specific' (Lord Atkinson), or 'explicit and precise' (Lord Robson) terminology if they wished to include charterparty terms in the contract of carriage. Several of their Lordships also made reference to the fact that the bill of lading was a negotiable instrument. Although this was obviously felt to be significant, the point was unfortunately left undeveloped.

4.03 Subsequent developments

Virtually every aspect of this decision has been the subject of later comment. As a result, the law in this area is somewhat murky, despite recent pronouncements by both the House of Lords and the Court of Appeal. In *The Merak* (1965) P 223 the plaintiffs chartered a vessel by a contract which contained an arbitration clause, and which further provided that all bills of lading issued under it should include specific reference to the arbitration clause. Third parties shipped a cargo of timber, for which bills of lading were issued. These purported to incorporate 'all the terms conditions and clauses of the charterparty', but failed, by a clerical oversight, to refer specifically to the arbitration provision. The bills were endorsed to the plaintiffs. The timber was damaged during the voyage, and the shipowners sought arbitration of the plaintiff's claim.

The first striking fact is that the plaintiffs were parties both to the contract of charter and the contract of carriage. One would therefore assume that they were familiar with the terms of both agreements. However, at first instance, Scarman J held this fact to be irrelevant in deciding whether the charterparty terms were a part of the contract of carriage. The reason for this initially surprising conclusion exposes the significance of the unexplained references in *Thomas* v. *Portsea* to the fact that a bill of lading is negotiable. The contract which the bill represents must receive a consistent interpretation, no matter in whose hands it happens at present to be. Coincidentally, the plaintiffs were both charterers and holders of the bill. Although, as charterers, they were deemed to be cognisant with the terms of the charter, a different holder of the bill of lading would not necessarily possess such knowledge. Particular terms in the bill could not mean one thing in the hands of one holder and something else in the hands of another. As the learned judge concluded: 'if such instruments may be construed by reference to extraneous circumstances, their mercantile purpose will be frustrated and commercial confidence in them undermined'.

Nevertheless, he proceeded to hold that the words of the bill were sufficient in themselves to incorporate the arbitration clause from the charterparty. In doing so, he seems to have given a wider meaning to the judgments in the *Thomas* case than appears justified. In Scarman J's view, that case is authority for the proposition that a general reference in the bill to the terms of the charterparty will be sufficient to incorporate all charterparty provisions which are *not inconsistent* with the subject matter of the bill of lading. In other words, not only are those terms included which are clearly and directly connected with the carriage of goods, but also those which are capable of being applied to or are not manifestly incompatible with it.

The Court of Appeal affirmed the decision. Both Sellers and Davies LJJ seemed to feel, however, that the fact of the plaintiff being privy to the charterparty was a circumstance which should be taken into account. In Davies LJ's opinion, the correct explanation of the *Thomas* case lies in the fact that the arbitration clause there applied only to disputes arising under the charter. Both he and Russell LJ held that general words can be sufficient to bring a charterparty term into the contract of carriage, even if the term in question is not directly connected to the objectives of the carriage, provided the term refers to the bill of lading.

This liberal approach may, at least in part, be the result of a less jaundiced judicial attitude towards arbitration clauses, or exclusive jurisdiction clauses, which have the effect of denying the parties immediate access to the English courts. Certainly the judgment of Lord Gorell in *Thomas* v. *Portsea* was heavily influenced by this particular prejudice.

The approach taken in *The Merak* was reviewed by a differently constituted Court of Appeal in the *The Annefield* (1971) 1 All ER 406, a case which involved substantially similar facts. The later court held that a clause in a charterparty which is not directly germane to the bill of lading may nevertheless be incorporated into the contract of carriage either by explicit words in the bill of lading or in the charterparty.

The relatively brief, and unreserved judgments in this case must be understood against the background of the specific facts. In both *The Merak* and the *The Annefield* the bill of lading holder was also a party to the contract of charter. It was perfectly possible for him to agree with the shipowner, in the charterparty, that particular provisions of the charter should be a part of any subsequent contract they might make together in the future. Such an agreement cannot, however, be binding on third parties who might be drawn into the later contractual nexus through the transfer to them of a bill of lading. In order to commit these parties to the terms of the charter, specific words of incorporation must be employed in the bill itself (see *per* Collins MR in *Temperley* v. *Smyth* (1905) 2 KB at 800).

The high ground of liberalisation was achieved, and surrendered, within a period of two years. In *Astro Valiente Compania Naviera SA* v. *Pakistan Ministry of Food & Agriculture; The Emmanuel Colocotronis* (1982) 1 All ER 823, sellers of wheat chartered the plaintiffs' vessel. Defendant buyers were consignees under the bill of lading, which purported to include all the conditions of the charterparty. The shipowners claimed the right to arbitration. Staughton J held that the effect of recent authority was that it was incumbent upon the holder of the bill of lading to familiarise himself with the terms of the charterparty, once the wording of the bill had alerted him to the charterparty's existence. General words suffice to incorporate all charterparty terms which are not inconsistent with the provisions of the bill of lading.

The approach of Staughton J was criticised by the Court of Appeal in *Skips A/S Nordheim* v. *Syrian Petroleum Co; The Varenna* (1983) 3 All ER 645. *Thomas* v. *Portsea* had established that general words of incorporation were to be taken to refer only to those provisions of the charterparty which governed the shipment carriage or delivery of the goods. This interpretation had been adopted and relied upon by businessmen ever since. In Donaldson MR's words: 'this is a corner of the law where the commercial customers, shipowners, shippers and receivers attach supreme importance to certainty, and where particular phrases have established meanings and effects it is not the policy of the law to seek to change them even if, in the absence of precedent, there would be a case for so doing'. Oliver LJ criticised the notion that the scope of an incorporating provision can be determined by reference to an entirely different contract.

4.04 Liberal construction of incorporated charterparty terms

In cases from *The Merak* onwards, it seems to have been accepted that, where the parties to the contract of carriage clearly express their intention to bring in a particular provision from the charterparty, it may be necessary for the court to alter the express language of that provision so that it harmonises with the contract of carriage. In Denning MR's words in *The Annefield*, the process of construction 'may involve a degree of manipulation of the words in order to fit exactly the bill of lading'. The extent to which this is permissible was considered by the House of Lords in *Miramar Maritime Corporation* v. *Holborn Oil Trading Ltd* (1984) 3 WLR 1. Owners of a chartered vessel claimed demurrage, calculated according to the terms of the charterparty, from consignees. The bill of lading gave notice of the charter and provided that all its terms applied to and governed the rights of the parties to the bill.

The demurrage clause in the charterparty imposed liability on the 'charterer'. The shipowners contended that this should be 'manipulated' so as to cover consignees and holders of the bill of lading. The House of Lords rejected this contention. Lord Diplock, with whose speech the rest of their Lordships agreed, noted that the interpretation for which the shipowners contended would impose upon holders 'a potential liability to pay an unknown and wholly unpredictable sum'. This was the sort of risk no sane businessman would undergo. In this case there happened to be only one consignee of the whole cargo. Had there been several consignees, a 'whole host' of questions would have arisen regarding the apportionment of liability amongst them, were the shipowners' argument to be accepted. Furthermore, other clauses in the charter did refer to the consignee expressly. It therefore followed, as a matter of semantics, that the parties must have intended to omit the consignee from liability under the demurrage clause.

Having indicated at the beginning of his speech that the appeal was being heard in order to give the House an occasion to establish the limits of the power of 'verbal manipulation', Lord Diplock ended with a negative statement of principle. There is no rule, he said, that allows a court to substitute 'bill of lading holder' for 'charterer' in charterparty provisions which are directly relevant to the bill of lading. Presumably a court may do so only when, having construed the charterparty as a whole, it is decided that to do so will achieve the business objectives of the contract of carriage.

4.05   Summary

The foregoing may be summarised as follows:

1. Apparently wide words of incorporation which are coupled with a specific provision in the contract of carriage may be narrowed down so as to encompass only those clauses in the charterparty which are cognate to the specific provision. Thus, in *Thomas* v. *Portsea*, the bill of lading also provided that the consignee should pay freight, 'with other conditions as per charter'. The House of Lords said that the general words must be construed by reference to the specific, and thus limited to charterparty provisions relating to freight. This is the so-called '*eiusdem generis*' ('of the same kind') rule of construction.
2. General words which stand independent of specific provisions have the effect of incorporating only those provisions of the charterparty which relate to the purposes and objectives of the contract of carriage: i.e. the shipment, transportation and delivery of goods, and the payment of freight. Despite judicial opinion to the contrary, 'neutral' provisions of the

charter, which do not specifically relate to carriage but are not inconsistent with it (e.g. arbitration clauses) are not incorporated in this way.

3. If the parties wish to incorporate other provisions of the charter, they must use specific and appropriate words.

4. Where a provision of the charterparty has been incorporated into the contract of carriage, a court has some licence to construe it in a way which facilitates the achievement of the objectives of the contract of carriage.

5. If the same parties are privy both to the charter and the contract of carriage, it may be possible for the one contract to feed terms into the other. Hence charterparty terms may become part of the contract of carriage by specific reference in the charterparty. Such terms will not, however, be part of the contract with subsequent holders of the bill of lading.

6. If the bill of lading purports to include a term of the charterparty which is manifestly inconsistent with other provisions of the bill, the charterparty term must be rejected. Thus, in *Gardner* v. *Trechmann* (1885) 15 QBD 154 a charterparty called for payment of freight at one rate, the bill of lading stipulated another. It was decided by the Court of Appeal that 'those clauses of the charterparty cannot be brought in which would alter the express stipulations in the bill of lading'. The incorporation provision in question was a general one, but the same result should follow even in the unlikely event that the bill of lading, having specified bill of lading freight, were specifically to refer to charterparty freight, unless there were further clear indications that bill of lading freight was to be displaced.

4.06   The extent of the carrier's liability: establishing the contractual nexus

Section 1 of the Bills of Lading Act 1855

The carrier will be responsible, in contract, to whoever engages his services. In addition, s.1 of the Bills of Lading Act 1855 (a critically important provision in the functioning of cif contracts in particular) provides that 'every consignee of goods named in a Bill of Lading, and every endorsee of a Bill of Lading, to whom the property in the goods therein mentioned shall pass upon or by reason of such consignment or endorsement, shall have transferred to and vested in him all rights of suit, and be subject to the same liabilities in respect of such goods as if the contract contained in the Bill of Lading had been made with himself'.

Only rights and liabilities relating to the goods pass to the buyer by reason of s.1, and then only if he has acquired the property in the goods 'upon or by reason of' the goods being consigned to him, under the bill, or the bill being subsequently endorsed to him. A strict interpretation of this requirement might severely limit the application of s.1, and consequently impede the free functioning of many international contracts of sale. The problem arises if we take the phrase 'upon or by reason of' to mean that s.1 only applies when property passes to the buyer at the moment, and as the sole result of, consignment or endorsement. This can never happen while the goods remain unascertained, by virtue of s.16 of the Sale of Goods Act 1979. Property cannot therefore pass where the buyer is given a bill of lading relating to a bulk cargo, and he is to draw his goods from bulk on presentation of the bill to the carrier. Nor can it happen where the usual presumption applies, that property is not to pass before payment. It is easy to imagine the large number of transactions which would be excluded from the scope of s.1 on this interpretation.

4.07   A liberal interpretation of s.1

A more liberal, and practical interpretation can be suggested, however. On this view, consignment or endorsement operates as a precondition to the passing of property, but not as the sole, or final event whereby property is transferred. Property may pass 'upon' consignment or endorsement, or 'by reason of' it, when either one has taken place, and some subsequent event, such as payment, or ascertainment, releases the contractual brake on the passing of property.

One final difficulty remains. Can s.1 ever apply where the bill of lading has been endorsed in blank, and delivered to the buyer not as endorsee but bearer?

These problems came together, but unfortunately were not finally answered, in *The Elafi* (see above [1.07]). Mustill J, having decided that the plaintiffs had a good cause of action in tort, felt it unnecessary to rule upon the alternative claim, under s.1 of the 1855 Act. He did, however, express some tentative views upon its scope.

It will be recalled that the plaintiffs had purchased six thousand tons of copra in bulk, which were covered by four bills of lading, plus an additional, undetermined quantity (arbitrarily said to be five hundred tons) for which no bill was issued at all. Some of the copra was damaged through the admitted negligence of the defendant carriers. The first question to consider in relation to s.1 is whether the damaged copra was covered by a bill of lading at all. If it were not, s.1 could have no possible application. Mustill J felt that it was for the plaintiffs to show that the damaged goods were part of the cargo covered by bills of lading. This they could not do.

Even if the plaintiffs could have discharged this burden of proof satisfactorily, a second question remained. Did property pass 'upon or by reason of' the endorsement of the bills to the plaintiffs? Mustill J expressed the provisional view that s.1 was satisfied if 'the endorsement forms an essential link in the chain of events by which title is transferred'. He omitted to notice that the bills were in fact never endorsed to the plaintiffs at all, in the sense that the plaintiffs were named endorsees. The bills were bearer bills, following their endorsement in blank by the sellers. It is indeed a liberal interpretation of s.1 which would regard holders of a bearer bill as endorsees of it, though no doubt it makes practical sense to do so.

4.08   The relationship of seller and carrier after the operation of s.1

Does the seller retain any contractual rights and liabilities under the contract of carriage after property has passed to the buyer under s.1? The answer is obviously positive, to the extent that his contract with the carrier goes beyond the transportation of particular goods. For example, the seller's contract with the carrier may be one of charter. Provided the charterparty is not assigned to the buyer, its rights and liabilities continue to affect the original parties to it.

The seller's position with regard to the goods themselves is more difficult. In *Gardano & Giampieri* v. *Greek Petroleum George Mamidakis & Co.* (1961) 2 LlR 259 a bill of lading issued under a contract between sellers and carriers named the buyers as consignees. The goods were unloaded in a damaged condition, and the sellers claimed the right to sue the carriers for substantial damages. The carriers contended that any right of action lay in the buyers alone. McNair J held that, on the facts, property had not yet passed to the buyers, and the sellers therefore retained their contractual rights. The learned judge expressed the view, however, that the sellers would have been able to sue even if property had already passed.

This part of his judgment was overruled, after extensive consideration of the relevant principles, by the House of Lords in the *The Albazero* (1977) AC 774. On facts similar to those in the *Greek Petroleum* case, sellers sought substantial damages from carriers for the loss of goods. Property had, however, already passed to the buyers at the time of the alleged breach of contract which caused the loss. The buyers failed to bring their own suit, and were eventually time-barred. Lord Diplock, with whose speech the rest of their Lordships agreed, began by restating a basic principle. The victim of a breach of contract (or tort) can only recover for such injury as he has in fact suffered. Here, since the sellers were entitled to payment for the lost goods under the contract of sale, they had suffered no loss at all. An exception to this rule was acknowledged, however. It derives from the case of *Dunlop* v. *Lambert* (1839) 6 Cl & Fin 600, an authority on which McNair J had relied in *Greek Petroleum*. This allows a party to a commercial contract concerning goods, property in which has passed to a non-contracting party after the contract was made, to sue and recover substantial damages in respect of a breach committed after property passed, even though the party suing has himself suffered no loss. This principle will operate only if (a) it was in the contemplation of the parties to the contract that property might pass to an outsider during the currency of the contract; and (b) the parties to the contract intend that the party suing is to be regarded as having made the contract on behalf of all persons who might acquire an interest in the goods. It will not apply where those persons have direct contractual rights against the carrier, as in cases where a bill of lading has been issued or endorsed to them. The Rule in *Dunlop* v. *Lambert* (under which the new goods owner would have a right to recover from the plaintiff the amount he had recovered from the defendant) was designed to protect the interests of the new owner at a time when neither the law of contract nor tort took them into account. With the development of the tort of negligence and the passing of the 1855 Act, the new goods owner's position is generally well-secured. Lord Diplock pointed to 'the complications, anomalies and injustices' which might occur if the *Dunlop* rule were extended to situations in which the new goods owner had his own contract with the carrier, but on terms different from those of the seller. It would, for example, be unjust to allow a seller to recover substantial damages on behalf of a buyer whose own rights of suit were now time-barred, as it would if the carrier were to be allowed to evade the estoppel which arises between himself and subsequent bill of lading holders regarding statements in the bill, simply because it was the seller and not the buyer who was bringing the action.

It should be noted, however, that the original contracting party's rights (and liabilities) under the contract to which the new owner has become party are not extinguished by virtue of s.1. The plaintiffs in *The Albazero* failed, not because they had no cause of action, but because they had suffered no loss as the result of the defendant's breach.

4.09 The Rule in Brandt v. Liverpool Steam Navigation Co.

The carrier might also attract contractual liability under the Rule in *Brandt* v. *Liverpool Steam Navigation Co.* (1924) 1 KB 575. It had been recognised, in *Sewell* v. *Burdick* (1884) 10 App Cas 74, that although the endorsement and delivery of a bill of lading to a pledgee does not come within the compass of s.1 of the Bills of Lading Act 1855, an implied contract might nevertheless arise between the carrier and bill of lading holder. In *Brandt's* case consignees of goods, delivery of which had been delayed by the carrier's breach, sought damages. Although on the facts s.1 did not apply, the Court of Appeal held that a contract could be implied from the fact that that the plaintiffs had presented the bill of lading to the carriers and paid the freight. The terms of this implied contract were those of the bill itself (since the carrier would be unwilling to deprive himself of the protection which the bill provided). The result, in Atkin LJ's words, is that 'the indorsee of the bill of lading is substantially in the same position as though he came under the Bills of Lading Act'. In *Cremer* v. *General Carriers* (1974) 1 WLR 341, Kerr J extended this principle to holders of delivery orders, who do not come within s.1 in any event.

In principle there is no reason why the Rule in *Brandt's* case should not apply to any interested party, since the inference of a contract, and its terms, is usually an issue of fact. The key question is whether the relevant party offered to assume a responsibility – typically, but not necessarily, to make some payment, such as freight or demurrage – in return for which the carrier agreed to extend his own liability – typically but not necessarily as defined in the bill of lading – to cover that other party.

It seems not to have occurred to the Court of Appeal in *Brandt's* case that the consideration provided by the carrier was nugatory, since he was simply performing (or agreeing to perform) a duty already owed to the shipper. No doubt three such experienced commercial lawyers as Bankes, Scrutton and Atkin LJJ (arguably the finest Commercial Court of Appeal ever to sit) were not overly concerned with such nice points of theory. More likely, the point was not raised in argument, and, in an unreserved judgment, it did not occur to them to consider it.

It was noted at the beginning of this chapter that the master of a chartered vessel usually issues bills of lading on the shipowner's behalf. As a result, the contract which s.1 of the Bills of Lading Act 1855 acknowledges is between the holder of the bill and the shipowner, not the holder and the charterer. By the same token, the master who delivers in exchange for the payment of freight creates an implied contract between the bill of lading (or delivery order) holder and the shipowner.

In exceptional cases, however, the contract in either case may be between the holder and the charterer, and the shipowner will not be a party. In *The Venezuela* (1980) 1 LlR 393, defendant subcharterers issued a bill of lading which designated themselves as carriers. The plaintiff transferees of the bill sued for damage caused to the goods during transit. Sheen J noted that the contract for carriage of goods aboard a chartered ship is usually made between the goods owner and the shipowner.

This is not, however, invariable, but is determined according to the facts of each case. Charterers are free to contract with the goods owner, and in this case had done so. The bill of lading gave no indication of who were the vessel's owners, and indicated that the defendants were the carriers. In *Tillmans* v. *SS Knutsford Ltd* (1908) 1 KB 185, a bill of lading signed by the charterers 'for the captain and owners' was held to bind the owners. The charterers had the right to order the master to sign bills. Channell J held that the effect of the charterer's signing on the master's and owner's behalf was just the same as if the master himself had signed.

4.11 The carrier's liability in contract

Two separate regimes regulate the carrier's liability in contract. It will be determined either by the common law of contract, or by the provisions of the Carriage of Goods by Sea Act 1971 where these apply. Since that Act does not set out a comprehensive code, however, the common law will continue to apply to situations in which the Act is not relevant. It is assumed that readers are familiar with the English law of contract.

Prior to 1924, contracts for the carriage of goods by sea were regulated by the common law alone. Two specific practical difficulties emerged from this. First, shipowners (who were often organised into oligopolistic cartels, or 'conferences') tended to occupy a dominant market position, enabling them to offer their services on terms which severely limited their own liabilities. Secondly, there was a lack of standardisation, in the law of trading nations, with regard to such questions as the incorporation, interpretation and legitimacy of these protective provisions. As a result, an issue litigated in one law district might well be resolved differently from an equivalent issue tried elsewhere.

In an attempt to unify or harmonise the law relating to the carriage of goods by sea, the Hague Convention of 1922–24 established a body of rules, to be incorporated into domestic law by the various signatories to the Convention. The Carriage of Goods by Sea Act 1924 represented the response of the United Kingdom, and the Hague Rules, as a result, became part of the law of this country. The 1924 Act was repealed and replaced by the Carriage of Goods by Sea Act 1971. The Schedule to this comprises the Hague Rules as amended by the Brussels Protocol of 1968. The amended provisions are known as the Hague–Visby Rules, although never actually referred to as such in the Act or Schedule.

Unfortunately, not all major trading nations were signatories to the original Hague Rules, nor have all the original signatories adopted the amendments. As a result, a plethora of different legal regimes still exists, and the problems at which the original Act was aimed are by no means resolved. The question of whether contracting parties can avoid the application of the Hague–Visby Rules is determined by that part of English law known as the conflict of laws, and will be examined in the final chapter. For the present, we will assume that the Act is potentially applicable, and proceed to examine its scope.

4.12 Application of the Hague–Visby Rules

The Act is complicated, and the provisions regulating the application of the Rules (see Figure 4.1) must be extracted both from

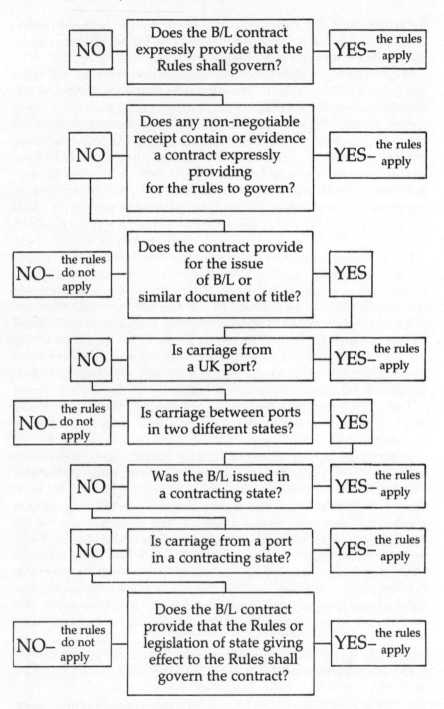

Fig. 4.1 When do the rules apply?

subsections of the Act itself, and from Article X of the Rules. There are two basic situations in which the Rules will apply. First, the use of certain kinds of documentation can be decisive. Second, if these documents are not employed, then the use of alternative documentation, coupled with other factors, will determine the matter.

The documents which suffice by themselves to bring the Act into operation are identified in s.1(6). There are two types: '(a) any bill of lading if the contract contained in or evidenced by it expressly provides that the Rules shall govern the contract'. This appears relatively straightforward. Three things should be noted, however. First, the contract must *expressly* provide for the Rules to apply. It will not be enough here for the Bill to incorporate the law of a State which has enacted the Rules. It will be sufficient as between shipper and carrier to bring the Rules into play that they make the necessary provision in a term which does not appear in the Bill itself. This, however, will not suffice as between carrier and a subsequent holder of the bill (including, *semble*, the shipper if the bill is negotiated back to him). Second, s.1(6)(a) will not apply if the parties use a document of title similar to a bill of lading, but not a bill strictly so-called. Third, the bill must actually be issued. It is not sufficient that the underlying contract contemplates that this will happen.

The second type of document to which s.1(6) applies is '(b) any receipt which is a non-negotiable document marked as such if the contract contained in or evidenced by it is a contract for the carriage of goods by sea which expressly provides that the Rules are to govern the contract as if the receipt were a bill of lading'.

If s.1(6) does not apply, then *two* requirements must be satisfied. The first is to be found in s.1(4): the contract of carriage must provide, expressly or by implication, for the issue of a bill of lading or any similar document of title. Three things can be noted here. First, provision for the issue of the relevant document may be express or implied. Implication will presumably follow the familiar rules of English contract law: e.g. because it is so obvious from the particular circumstances as to go without saying (the so-called *Moorcock* Rule); through a consistent course of dealing in which a bill has invariably been issued; or through the custom of the particular trade. Second, it is not necessary that the document actually be issued: it is sufficient that the contract provides for it. In *Pyrene* v. *Scindia Navigation*, for example, no bill was in the event issued, since the goods were damaged during loading and never shipped. Nevertheless, the Rules applied. Third, if a different type of document of title is issued, it must be 'similar' to a bill of lading. The mere fact that it is a document of title will not do. In *Hugh Mack & Co. Ltd* v. *Burns & Laird Lines Ltd* (1944) 77 LlLR 377, for example, carriers issued a non-negotiable receipt. The Court of Appeal of Northern Ireland held that, even if this were a document of title, it was not similar to a bill of lading. Just what types of document will satisfy this requirement may need to be determined from case to case. The customs of the particular trade or port will be relevant.

The second requirement, when s.1(6) does not apply, will be satisfied if shipment is from a ports in the United Kingdom: s.1(3). If it is not, then the carriage must be between ports in different states *and* either (i) the bill of lading is issued in a contracting state: Article X(a); or (ii) the carriage is from a port in a contracting state (i.e. a signatory to the Convention): Article X(b); or (iii) the contract contained in or evidenced by the Bill of Lading provides that the Rules, or legislation giving effect to them, are to govern the contract: Article X(c).

Article X(c) is superficially similar to s.1(6)(a), but on closer examination can be seen to be only partially congruent. It will apply where the contract is governed by relevant legislation, even though the contract itself does not expressly refer to the Rules, whereas s.1(6)(a) will not. On the other hand, it will not apply even if the contract expressly incorporates the Rules, unless the carriage is between two different states; s.1(6)(a) has no such limitation. Neither will apply if the bill refers to relevant legislation, but the carriage is between ports in the same state. In such an eventuality the Rules will only operate if the port of shipment is within the UK.

4.13   Scope of the Rules

The Hague–Visby Rules apply to contracts for the carriage of goods by sea 'from the time when the goods are loaded on to the time they are discharged from the ship': Art.I(e). In *Pyrene* v. *Scindia Navigation*, counsel for the shippers argued that the Rules did not come into operation until goods were actually loaded on board. Devlin J rejected this contention, holding that the Rules applied to the whole loading process.

Although the parties cannot contract out of the Rules, or provide that they shall apply in a reduced form, they may make whatever provision they choose for the period before loading and after discharge: Art. VIII. Furthermore, the parties may agree that the carrier's liabilities shall be *increased* during the period to which the Rules relate, provided that agreement is incorporated into the Bill of Lading.

4.14   The carrier's liability under the Hague–Visby Rules

(a) Seaworthiness

Under the Rules there is no absolute obligation on the carrier to provide a seaworthy vessel, such as is implied at common law. The carrier's responsibility is set out in Article III Rule 1. This provides that 'the carrier shall be bound before and at the beginning of the voyage to exercise due diligence to (a) make the ship seaworthy; (b) properly man, equip and supply the ship; (c) make the holds, refrigerating and cool chambers, and all other parts of the ship in which goods are carried, fit and safe for their reception, carriage and preservation'. In fact, (b) and (c) appear to be specific instances of seaworthiness, rather than separate obligations in their own right: see Art. IV(1).

Various aspects of this obligation, or its identical forerunner in the Hague Rules, have been the subject of judicial discussion. In *Maxine Footwear Co. Ltd* v. *Canadian Government Merchant Marine Ltd* (1959) AC 589 an under-officer on the defendant's vessel ordered that frozen pipes be thawed. An acetylene torch was used and a fire ensued, as a result of which the plaintiffs' goods on board were destroyed. The defendant carriers put forward several reasons why they should not be liable. First, under Art. IV(2)(b), a carrier is exempt from liability for loss or damage caused by fire. The Privy Council dismissed this superficially plausible contention. In Lord Somervell's words, the seaworthiness requirement in Art. III(1) 'is an overriding obligation. If it is not fulfilled and the non-fulfilment causes the damage the immunities of Article IV cannot be relied on'.

The carriers next argued that the obligation under Art.III(1) applied only at two specific moments: the commencement of loading and the beginning of the voyage. Since the fire had broken out during the interval between these two points they should not be held liable for the damage. This argument, based upon a construction of the phrase 'before and at the beginning of the voyage' and an analogy with the position at common law, was also rejected by the Judicial Committee. In their view, the obligation of seaworthiness is a continuous one, covering 'the period from at least the beginning of the loading until the vessel starts on her voyage'. Precisely when the obligation commences their Lordships felt it unnecessary to decide. Finally, the Court re-emphasised that the requirement of due diligence is not satisfied simply because no personal fault can be attached to the carrier or those acting for him in a managerial capacity. The negligence of his employees sufficed to put him in breach of the obligation.

4.15   Due diligence

The exact extent of the carrier's duty to exercise due diligence was considered by the House of Lords in *Riverstone Meat Co.* v. *Lancashire Shipping Co.* (1961) AC 807. Here the carriers seem, ironically, to have fallen foul of Article III(1) through their anxiety to comply with its requirements. The defendants put their ship into dry dock for repair and overhaul prior to sailing. They employed a reputable firm of repairers, and also engaged the services of an experienced and competent marine superinten-dent. This gentleman, acting in his turn with 'more than usual caution', caused the ship's storm valves to be opened for inspec-tion. Owing to the carelessness of one of the repairer's fitters, one valve was improperly closed. Water entered the hold during the voyage, and the plaintiff's goods were damaged.

Lord Radcliffe held that the defendants, having appointed apparently competent agents, had exercised the amount of care required at common law. Nevertheless, he decided that the com-mon law standard was inappropriate when considering liability under Article III(1). In his opinion, the key question was whether the unseaworthiness 'is due to any lack of diligence in those who have been implicated by the carriers in the work of keeping or making the vessel seaworthy'. The obligation is to use due dili-gence to make the ship seaworthy, not to use due diligence in the selection of others who appear competent to fulfil this task.

The carrier is only liable, however, for the acts of those who can be said to be acting on his behalf and when the ship is under his control. Hence he is not liable for undetectable unseaworthiness caused by the actual builders of the ship, whether or not it was built to his order or he was the first owner of it. Similarly, he ought not to be liable for latent unseaworthiness caused by the negligence of those over whom he has no control, for example, government officials acting under compulsory powers.

4.16 Seaworthiness defined

Neither the 1971 Act nor the Rules themselves contain any definition of unseaworthiness. Examples of unseaworthiness, according to that vastly experienced commercial judge, Lord Wright, may assume an almost infinite variety: see his judgment in *Smith Hogg & Co.* v. *Black Sea & Baltic General Insurance Co.* (1940) AC 997. There are, however, quite a number of judicial definitions, which in effect seem to amount to the same thing. In order to be seaworthy, a ship must be reasonably fit to carry the particular cargo on the particular voyage contemplated in the contract of carriage. Thus, not only must the vessel be sufficiently robust to withstand the exigencies which that voyage might entail: the crew must also be adequate to the task, both in numbers and competence, and the ship must be reasonably fitted to receive and carry the cargo.

4.17 Unseaworthiness and defective stowage

Difficulties have arisen, not so much in defining seaworthiness, as in determining whether the requirement is satisfied in any given situation. A number of close cases have been decided in which the connection between unseaworthiness and defective stowage in particular has been considered.

One such is *Elder Dempster & Co.* v. *Paterson Zochonis & Co.* (1924) AC 522, a decision more generally remembered (or best forgotten) for having created 'an anomalous and unexplained exception' to the doctrine of privity of contract (according to Lord Reid in *Scruttons Ltd* v. *Midland Silicones* (1962) AC 446). Here defendant carriers undertook to transport a cargo of palm oil in casks and palm kernels in bags. They loaded the oil first, and stacked the nuts on top, with the result that the casks were crushed and the oil lost. There was no suggestion that the casks were not sufficiently sturdy in themselves. The contract of carriage contained a provision exempting the carriers from liability for improper stowage but not for unseaworthiness. A majority of the House of Lords took the view that the vessel was seaworthy.

The matter was to be tested, it would appear, at the moment the cargo that was the subject of the claim was put on board. If the ship was fit to receive that cargo at that time it could not be rendered retrospectively unseaworthy by loading other cargo on top of it, with the result that it was damaged or destroyed. Lord Sumner (for once) accepted the view of Scrutton LJ in the court below, that any other decision would take the law beyond established principles and produce absurdities.

One hesitates to question such forthright pronouncements from the two contemporary masters of English commercial law. Nevertheless, the dissenting judgment of Lord Finlay does seem to address the issue with equal rationality. In his view, the carriers had undertaken to carry a composite cargo of oil and nuts. The ship was unsuitable to carry such a cargo. Therefore it was unseaworthy. In Lord Sumner's opinion, however, the master should have refused to load any further cargo that might endanger the oil. Hence the plaintiff's loss was caused by the incompetence of the captain and not the unsuitability of the ship. His Lordship gave scant attention to the possibility that this incompetence was itself sufficient to render the ship unseaworthy. Although the case was decided at common law, before the introduction of the Hague Rules, it was accepted in another 1924 House of Lords decision – *Standard Oil Co.* v. *Clan Line* (1924) AC 100 – that the inadequacy of the captain can render a ship unseaworthy. Here an otherwise competent and experienced master sank his ship by putting it through a manoeuvre to which it was not suited. He had never had charge of this particular type of vessel before and was ignorant of its peculiarities. Lord Atkinson said that there is no difference between lack of skill and lack of knowledge. 'Each rendered the master unfit and unqualified to command, and therefore makes the ship he commands unseaworthy.'

The majority in the *Elder Dempster* case accepted that a ship might become unseaworthy through bad stowage, as in *Kopitoff* v. *Wilson* (1876) 1 QBD 377. A cargo of armour plates, inadequately secured, broke loose during the voyage and smashed through the ship's side, sinking her. The ship was deemed to be unseaworthy. The House in *Elder Dempster* also agreed that a ship may be unseaworthy if her accommodation is unsuitable or insufficient to receive the cargo. Thus the decisions in *Owners of cargo on ship Maori King* v. *Hughes* (1895) 2 QB 550 (where the ship's refrigeration was defective and the cargo frozen meat) and *Queensland National Bank* v. *P & O Steam Navigation Co.* (1898) 1 QB 567 (where a ship's strongroom was not reasonably fit to resist thieves) were accepted as correct.

In the light of these decisions it seems that the question of unseaworthiness, as a matter of principle, can be resolved by looking at a situation in two stages. First, one must consider the ship in the state in which it is offered to the shipper. Is the vessel, in that condition, reasonably fit to receive and transport the cargo? In *Tattersall* v. *National SS Co.* (1884) 12 QBD 297 a ship infected with foot and mouth disease was deemed unfit to carry a cargo of cattle. In *Ciampa* v. *British Steam Navigation Co.* (1915) 2 KB 774 a ship that the carriers knew would be fumigated at an intermediate port was held unfit to carry a cargo of fruit.

The second stage is to consider the ship after loading. Is the ship now, actually or potentially, unfit to face the dangers of the voyage: i.e. is the ship itself in danger? It would seem that the differing opinions in the *Elder Dempster* case turn upon the application of these principles to the facts.

4.18 The principles in operation

A nice problem also arose from the application of these principles to the facts, in *Actis Co.* v. *Sanko Steamship Co: The Acquacharm* (1982) 1 WLR 119. A vessel was chartered to carry a cargo of coal from Baltimore to Tokyo, a voyage which would take the ship through the Panama Canal. The master was ordered to load to the level permitted by the Panama Canal Company. He, however, overloaded his ship, so that she was not safe to pass through. Delay was caused while part of the cargo was offloaded and carried through the canal on another vessel. The goods owners sought damages.

The Court of Appeal held that the ship was seaworthy. The captain's action in overloading constituted mismanagement, for which the shipowners were exempt from liability under article IV(2)(a) of the Rules. Lord Denning MR said that seaworthiness in the context of the Hague Rules 'means that the vessel – with her master and crew – is herself fit to encounter the perils of the voyage and also that she is fit to carry the cargo safely on the voyage'. Shaw LJ warned against 'any artificial extension of the concept of seaworthiness', and repudiated the suggestion that the seaworthiness of a vessel is a function of 'her ability to perform the contractual voyage without impediment'.

These brief, generalised, and unsubstantiated assertions should not be taken out of context. Clearly the ability of the vessel to perform the contractual voyage can be a factor of decisive importance in determining her seaworthiness. A ship that can safely traverse the English Channel is not necessarily suited to the South China Seas. The important point in *The Acquacharm* was that the ship was at no stage in physical danger from the sea. The ship was required to lighten in order to complete a stage of the journey, but she was never unsafe.

It has already been noticed that the master in *Elder Dempster* behaved incompetently in loading the ship as he did. Why did his incompetence not render the ship unseaworthy? It would seem that one must distinguish general incompetence from specific instances. A ship will be seaworthy if her master is generally fit to command that ship and the crew generally able to perform its duties. Instances of localised incompetence – such as causing the ship to be loaded incorrectly – may not be relevant to seaworthiness, unless they are evidence of general inability, or unless they cast the ship itself into physical danger.

A somewhat different explanation of *The Acquacharm* is suggested by Staughton J in *Empresa Cubana Importada De Alimentos 'Alimport' v. Iasmos Shipping Co. SA: The Good Friend* (1984) 2 LlR 586. The plaintiffs had purchased soya bean meal for delivery at Havana aboard the defendants' ship. Cuban officials refused to allow the cargo to be landed, because it was infested with insects. The carriers contended that the requirement of seaworthiness did not include the ability of the ship to discharge the cargo, still less to discharge it at any particular port. Staughton J felt bound by previous authority to deny this contention and to conclude that the obligation under Article III(1) comprehends the vessel's fitness to load, transport and deliver the particular cargo as agreed in the contract of carriage.

As in *The Acquacharm*, however, the cargo in *The Good Friend* was at no time in physical danger from the condition of the ship. The infestation could, in all probability, have been controlled by fumigation which (unlike that in the *Ciampa* case) would not have damaged the goods. Staughton J distinguished the earlier case on the ground that the impediment in the way of completing the contractual voyage was temporary and minor, whereas in the case before him it was major and permanent. He held that the obligation of seaworthiness was broken even though the cargo suffers no physical damage and its owner's loss is only economic.

This would seem to represent a considerable extension of the concept of seaworthiness. In *The Acquacharm* Shaw LJ indicated that, while a ship and its cargo remain in the same condition throughout a journey, its seaworthiness is a constant factor, which cannot be affected or altered by external considerations. However, if in *The Good Friend*, the goods owner had been given a choice of destinations, the seaworthiness or otherwise of the carrying vessel would (following the logic of Staughton J's decision) be determined according to whether or not the vessel was ordered to a port where discharge of the cargo was prohibited.

It is submitted that the concept of seaworthiness is circumscribed by considerations of physical suitability, is confined to the safety of the ship or cargo, and is determinable, once and for all, before the contract voyage begins. Since, under the Rules, seaworthiness is required only at the commencement of the voyage, subsequent changes will be irrelevant in any event.

4.19   Seaworthiness and causation

Even if a vessel is unseaworthy, the carrier will not be liable unless that condition is a cause of loss. As Lord Wright pointed out in *Smith Hogg & Co.* v. *Black Sea & Baltic General Insurance Co.*, however, unseaworthiness can never operate by itself as the sole cause. It will always be triggered by, or operate in conjunction with, some other causative factor. The carrier will nevertheless remain liable, unless the other factor by itself would have brought about the loss in any event. In *Smith Hogg* the carrying vessel was so overloaded as to be unstable, and therefore unseaworthy. The ship called at an intermediate port to refuel. The manner in which this operation was carried out, coupled with the instability of the ship, caused her to settle in the water, and part of the cargo was lost or damaged.

Lord Wright advocated a robust, commonsense approach to the issue of causation (as he was to do in later cases, such as *Yorkshire Dale Steamship Co.* v. *Ministry of War* (1942) AC 691, and *Monarch Steamship Co.* v. *Karlshamns Oljefabriker* (1949) AC 196). 'The question', in his opinion, 'is, would the disaster not have happened if the ship had fulfilled the obligation of seaworthiness, even though the disaster could not have happened if there had not also been the specific peril or action.' He eschewed any adjectival description of the type of cause for which one was seeking, such as 'dominant', 'effective', 'real', or 'actual'. Such words, in his opinion, added nothing. He similarly repudiated the invocation of dog Latin phrases such as '*causa causans*' and '*causa sine qua non*'. In *Metal and Ores Pty Ltd* v. *Compania De Vapores Stelvi*

SA (1983) 1 LlR 530, Neill J, while purporting to adopt the pragmatic attitude of Lord Wright, nevertheless seemed concerned
to determine whether unseaworthiness was the dominant cause
of loss.

4.20 *The carrier's duties towards the goods while in his charge*

The carrier's second obligation under the Hague–Visby Rules
is set out in Article III(2) This provides that 'the carrier shall
properly and carefully load, handle, stow, carry, keep, care for,
and discharge the goods carried'. Unlike the obligation of seaworthiness, this second duty is made subject to Article IV. This
sets out a series of specific limitations on liability, and is examined
below (see [4.21]). In *Gosse Millerd* v. *Canadian Government Merchant Marine Ltd* (1927) 2 KB 432, Wright J stated that the carrier's
obligation under Article III(2) is to deliver the goods in the same
condition in which he took them on board. This is incorrect. The
true nature and extent of the carrier's duty is explained by Lord
Pearce in *Albacora SLR* v. *Westcott & Laurence Line Ltd* (1966) LlR
62. It is not, he said, an obligation to achieve a particular result
– i.e. the safe discharge of the goods – but to perform a number
of operations in a particular way. Nor is there any obligation to
perform all of those operations. Although some of them are basic
to the undertaking to transport the goods, the carrier may agree
that another party shall load, stow, or unload them. Article III(2)
lays down the manner in which the carrier shall perform those
tasks which he has agreed to perform; it does not stipulate what
those tasks shall be. In *Ismail* v. *Polish Ocean Lines* (1976) 1 All ER
902, for example, the contract provided that the shipper should
load and stow the goods. The carriers were held not liable for
deterioration which resulted from overloading. In the *Albacora*
case, the House of Lords considered the meaning of the phrase
'properly and carefully'. Fish shipped aboard the defendant's
vessel deteriorated during the course of a voyage from Glasgow
to Genoa. The plaintiff consignees sought damages, arguing that
the duty to carry the goods 'properly' required that the carriers
provide a suitable system for transporting the particular cargo.
Since the voyage had taken place in September, the fish ought
to have been refrigerated. The carrier, however, had no means of
knowing this. The House of Lords agreed that the word 'properly'
signified that the carriers should deal with the goods in accordance with a sound system. They went on to hold, however, that

the soundness of a system must be evaluated in the light of the carrier's knowledge of the goods and their characteristics.

In *International Packers London Ltd* v. *Ocean SS Co. Ltd* (1955) 2 LlR 218 goods owners sued carriers in respect of damage incurred during a voyage from Australia to Glasgow. The damage was the result of two separate incidents. During heavy weather encountered shortly after leaving Melbourne, tarpaulins protecting the hold in which the plaintiffs' goods (cases of tinned meat) were stored, were washed away. Water entered the hold and the goods were damaged. The plaintiffs alleged that the carriers' failure to fasten the tarpaulins more securely constituted a breach of the obligation to carry, keep and care for the goods.

Following the storm, the ship put in to Fremantle, where the damage was inspected. A surveyor, engaged by the defendants, negligently concluded that there was no risk of further damage to that part of the plaintiff's goods which were stored in the lower hold. These cases were as a result left in the hold, and were attacked by rust. McNair J held that, although the defendants were in breach by failing to secure the tarpaulins properly, they could nevertheless rely upon one of the defences in Article IV: namely that their failure was an act, neglect or default in the navigation or management of the ship. They were, however, liable for the negligence of the cargo surveyor. First, a carrier is no more able to discharge his duty under Article III(2) by appointing an apparently competent expert than he is under Article III(1). The obligation in each case is put upon the carrier himself. Secondly, the obligation to care for the goods can require that the carrier takes steps to protect or relieve the goods from the consequences of an earlier mishap, even though the carrier was not responsible for it. He must do what is reasonable in the circumstances.

McNair J accepted without demur the comment in *Scrutton on Charterparties* that the carrier may have a lien on the goods for any expenses incurred. This matter has in fact never been expressly decided, and it is not altogether obvious why it should be so in regard to expenses incurred to forestall or remedy the consequences of events for which the carrier is liable. There may be a stronger case for a lien where the necessity for remedial or preventive action arises from unexpected circumstances not involving a breach by the carrier of his basic obligations.

In *The Rio Sun* (1985) 1 LLR 350 owners of a cargo of crude oil contended that it was the carrier's duty to heat and circulate the oil, to prevent deposits forming, when it became apparent that the voyage would take much longer than expected. Bingham

J seemed to accept this argument in principle (see *Notara* v. *Henderson* (1872) LR 7 QB 225) but found on the facts that the duty had not been broken. It is not the general practice to heat crude oil cargoes, and the master had no reason to suppose that this cargo, though consisting of a type of oil he had never carried before, required special treatment.

4.21   The Article IV defences: applicable generally in the absence of fault

The carrier's duties under Article III(2) are expressly subject to the provisions of Article IV. This contains a number of defences and limits of liability. One general and sixteen specific defences are itemised. Neither the carrier nor the ship is responsible for loss or damage caused by circumstances falling within any one of these categories. In *Shipping Corporation of India Ltd* v. *Gamlen Chemical Co. Pty Ltd* (1980) 147 CLR 142 defendant carriers argued, with superficial plausibility, that since some of these defences were expressly disallowed where the carrier was at fault, the rest must be available even though fault was present. The High Court of Australia had little difficulty in repudiating this contention, however. While the carrier's duties under Article III(2) are made subject to the provisos in Article IV, this says nothing of the circumstances in which those provisos will apply. An express reference to the unavailability of a particular defence in the event of negligence would be inappropriate in a number of instances. To provide, for example, for a defence of Act of God (Article IV(2)(d)) 'unless caused by the actual fault or privity of the carrier' would be patently ridiculous. Most pertinently, to uphold the carrier's contention would be to extract virtually all content from his Article III (2) duties in a great many instances.

4.22   The navigation or management of the ship

The first specific defence in Article IV(2) is '(a) Act, neglect, or default of the master, mariner, pilot, or servants of the carrier in the navigation or in the management of the ship'. The principal difficulty which this provision has presented is in determining whether the relevant behaviour was concerned with the navigation or management of the ship. Each decision seems to turn on its particular facts. Although criteria have been established in the leading cases, they are in practice rather poor predictors.

One such set of facts provoked a sharp disagreement between Scrutton LJ and Lord Sumner in *Gosse Millerd Ltd* v. *Canadian Government Merchant Marine Ltd*. The defendant's vessel, which was carrying the plaintiff's goods – a consignment of tinplates – was in dock for repairs and to discharge other cargo. During these operations hatch covers and tarpaulins were left off the entrance to the hold in which the plaintiff's goods were stored. Rainwater entered and the tinplates rusted. To the plaintiff's claim for damages the defendant pleaded that the failure to replace the covers and tarpaulins fell within Article IV(2)(a). A majority of the Court of Appeal agreed that this was so. Sargant LJ held that the defence covered operations affecting the ship as a whole carried out for the ship's purposes. Scrutton LJ felt that the defence related to the management of the ship as a physical entity unconnected with its cargo carrying function.

The House of Lords rejected both these views. In Lord Sumner's opinion, their effect would be to deprive the cargo owner of virtually the whole protection of Article III(2), and place the shipowner in, if anything, an even more favourable position than he had occupied before the Hague Rules were introduced. According to Lord Sumner, for the defence to apply the relevant behaviour must relate to the vessel as a whole, and not just to a particular part of it. It may be that only a part, perhaps a very minor part, of the ship is being employed in a way which causes the damage; nevertheless the defence will be available only provided what occurred was part of a general operation. Steering the ship, for example, is a localised operation, but it affects the whole vessel. In the *Gosse Millerd* case, the tarpaulins were specifically used for the protection of the cargo. Their removal was not required in order that tasks relating to general management could be performed.

Lord Sumner objected to Scrutton LJ's view of the law, and Sargant LJ's interpretation of the facts. The dissenting judgment of Greer LJ was accepted as correct by the House of Lords. This was also applied in the Canadian case of *The Washington* (1976) 1 LLR 453. At first sight this seems to involve a fairly clear instance of negligent navigation. The master of the defendants' ship failed to alter course to avoid heavy weather; a cargo of glass broke loose and shattered. The defendants pleaded that this constituted negligence in the navigation of the ship. Heald J held that the master had failed to use the apparatus of the ship for the protection of the cargo, and the defence was therefore not available. The decisive factor appears to be that the ship itself was in no danger, and the master's decision to stay on course was not taken primarily in the interests of his vessel.

In *Goose Millerd* Lord Sumner warned against drawing inferences between different but apparently analogous sets of circumstances. In *International Packers* v. *Ocean SS Co.*, McNair J took the view that the position of a ship in port and at sea was not the same, and ruled that tarpaulins used to cover hatches while at sea were part of the mechanism for securing the general safety of the ship.

4.23   Fire

The second defence under Article IV(2) is '(b) fire, unless caused by the actual fault or privity of the carrier'. The meaning of the requirement of actual fault or privity was considered by the House of Lords in *Lennard's Carrying Co. Ltd* v. *Asiatic Petroleum Co. Ltd* (1915) AC 705. This case concerned the application of s.502 of the Merchant Shipping Act 1894, which provides an equivalent defence. The defendant shipowners were a limited company, which, being inanimate, could not actually be at fault or privy to any knowledge. The managing director was aware of the defective condition of the ship's boilers, which caused a fire leading to the loss of the plaintiff's goods. The House of Lords held that in such cases one must look for that person, or body of persons, which is 'the directing mind and will of the corporation'. The fault, or knowledge, of that person or body is attributable to the company itself.

4.24   Perils of the sea

The third defence, '(c) perils, dangers and accidents of the sea or other navigable waters', has probably been the subject of most litigation, be it under the Hague Rules, the Merchant Shipping Act 1894 (where an equivalent defence is allowed) or at common law under a specific provision of the contract of carriage. The first difficulty is to determine just what is meant by a peril of the sea (it is doubtful whether the phrase 'dangers and accidents' extends the defence much further). In *Thames & Mersey Marine Insurance Co.* v. *Hamilton Fraser & Co.* (1887) 12 App Cas 484 Lord Macnaghten said that it was impossible to frame a definition of the words. The fact that they embrace a wide and varied range of maritime misadventures is well attested by the cases themselves. As a matter of semantics, it seems apt to cover any accidental occurrence whereby seawater is admitted into the vessel.

Whether, as a matter of law, the phrase applies to incidents which were foreseeable, and against which precautions might have been taken remains a matter of dispute. The source of conflict seems to be the judgment of Lord Herschell in the seminal case of *Thomas Wilson, Sons & Co.* v. *The Xantho (Cargo Owners)* (1887) 12 App Cas 503. Here Lord Herschell said that, in order for there to be a peril of the sea, there 'must be some casualty, something which could not have been foreseen as one of the necessary incidents of the adventure'. In Canada, this has been taken to mean that eventualities which could have been foreseen or guarded against do not constitute perils of the sea (see the judgment of Ritchie J in *Goodfellow Lumber Sales Ltd* v. *Verrault* (1970) 1 LLR 185 and the cases cited there).

In *Canada Rice Mills Ltd* v. *Union Marine and General Insurance Co. Ltd* (1941) AC 55 Lord Wright expressed the opinion that damage caused by a storm, the occurrence and ferocity of which are unexceptional, can constitute a loss by peril of the sea. In the *Goodfellow* case Ritchie J refused to regard this opinion as at odds with Lord Herschell's judgment in *The Xantho*, or to conflict with the principle that the only legally relevant perils are those which cannot be foreseen or against which precautions cannot be taken.

The approach taken in the Canadian courts seems to be based upon a misreading of Lord Herschell's judgment. Furthermore, it would seem that Lord Wright's speech in the *Canada Rice Mills* case is clearly opposed to the principle applied by Ritchie J. Lord Herschell was concerned to exclude from the concept of perils of the sea, damage or loss which inevitably results from going to sea at all: in other words, wear and tear on the vessel. He had nothing to say about foreseeable, but contingent, damage. Lord Wright, for his part, was clearly referring to incidents, which are a normal, usual – in short, foreseeable – risk of a particular voyage.

Courts in Australia have taken the opposite approach to that adopted in Canada. In *Shipping Corporation of India Ltd.* v. *Gamlen Chemical Co.*, badly stowed cargo broke loose and was damaged during heavy weather which, though unusually severe, was not unforeseeable. Four out of five judges in the High Court of Australia held that this was a peril of the sea. (The fifth reserved his opinion.) In the majority view, the availability of the defence in Article IV(2)(c) turned on the question of whether or not the peril caused the loss or damage. In the view of Mason and Wilson JJ, with whose joint judgment Aickin and Gibbs JJ concurred, where the loss would not have occurred but for the carrier's negligence, the same result is achieved as in the Canadian cases. Similarly, where loss or damage would have occurred in any event, regardless of the carrier's lack of care, he will have the defence of lack of causation, and it will not matter whether the particular peril was or was not foreseeable.

Although the majority in the *Gamlen* case equated Australian and English law on this subject, the matter cannot be regarded as free from doubt. In *Hamilton Fraser & Co.* v. *Pandorf & Co.* (1887) 12 AC 518, rats ate through a lead pipe, with the result that sea water entered a hold and damaged the plaintiff's cargo of rice. The House of Lords held that the carriers could take advantage of the exception of perils of the sea in the contract of carriage. Lord Halsbury LC said that the idea of a 'peril' involved something both fortuitous and unexpected. Others of their Lordships (including Lord Herschell) noted that the action of the rats was unforeseeable, without overtly incorporating this fact into any definition of a sea peril. Lord Bramwell, on the other hand, was content to adopt Lopes LJ's definition of a peril of the sea in the court below: 'It is sea damage, occurring at sea, and nobody's fault'. Lord Fitzgerald, having noted that the accident was unforeseen, stressed that unforeseeability was not, in his opinion, a constituent of a sea peril. Although the matter would appear to be largely semantic, the Australian approach does seem the more harmonious, and the question of foreseeability should go to the issue of causation, not to the definition of a peril of the sea.

The conclusion in the *Pandorf* case, that the damage was caused by a peril of the sea, may strike one initially as rather odd. In *Leesh River Tea Co. Ltd* v. *British India SN Co. Ltd* (1967) 2 QB 250, a stevedore employed to load and unload cargo at an intermediate port stole a storm valve cover plate. As a result, water entered a hold when the vessel put to sea, and the plaintiff's goods were damaged. The carriers raised the defence of perils of the sea. The Court of Appeal held that the availability of the defence turned upon whether or not the carriers were responsible for the actions of the thief. Thus, although a similar combination of circumstances contributed to bring about the plaintiff's loss in both cases, the issue of causation turns, not upon the factual matrix, but upon the defendant's legal responsibility for the actions of the third party. In *Pandorf* it was decided that the carriers had not been remiss in failing to exterminate the rats. In *Leesh River* the carriers were held not to be responsible for the theft of the plate. These are further illustrations of Lord Wright's observation that English law tends to adopt a practical and pragmatic approach to causation, rather than a logical or philosophical one. Where similar events conjoin to produce an end result in which goods are damaged by seawater, the law will regard that damage as caused by the sea when the defendant is not legally responsible for any of the other contributing events, but as caused by the defendant when he is.

In exceptional cases the defence may apply even though there has been no incursion by seawater at all. If a ship breaks free of her moorings and runs aground, in circumstances not involving negligence, and, before she can be refloated, the cargo perishes, the carrier should not be liable. In *The Thrunscoe* (1897) P 301 ventilators were closed during heavy weather, as a result of which the cargo was damaged. The carriers were held not liable. Similarly, in the *Canadian Rice Mills* case, it was decided that the overheating of a cargo of rice, brought about by the closing of ventilators in heavy weather in order to prevent the incursion of the sea, constituted damage caused by a peril of the sea. Though this was an insurance case, there is no difference in principle on this point between the law relating to marine insurance and that relating to contracts of carriage.

One final point: although Lopes LJ's tidy summation – 'sea damage, occurring at sea, and nobody's fault' – received strong support in *Hamilton* v. *Pandorf,* it should not be supposed from this that a peril of the sea cannot strike while a vessel is in harbour or even when berthed. Had the vessel in the *Leesh River* case sunk because, for example, she had settled in the water as cargo was loaded and the exposed valve submerged, this would constitute loss by a peril of the sea. It would have made no difference in the *Pandorf* case itself had the rats done their work while the ship was in port or on the open sea.

4.25   Other defences

The following five defences appear not to have been the subject of litigation under the Rules. They are: (d) Act of God; (e) Act of War; (f) Act of public enemies; (g) Arrest or restraint of princes, rulers or peoples, or seizure under legal process; and (h) Quarantine restrictions. Presumably, the same issue of causation might arise in these areas as in those already considered, however unlikely this might be in the first three instances. Where arrest takes place, or quarantine restrictions are imposed, because, for example, the carrier is attempting to smuggle goods, or his vessel is infected, the relevant defences will not be available. Act of God was described by Lord Esher MR in *Pandorf* v. *Hamilton* (1886) 17 QBD 670 as having a commercial, rather than a religious connotation, and meaning 'an extraordinary circumstance which could not be foreseen, and which could not be guarded against.' This bears close resemblance to one definition of a peril of the sea, and the two types of danger will clearly overlap, to some extent.

In *Kawasaki Kisen Kabushi Kaisha of Kobe* v. *Bantham Steamship Co.* (1939) 2 KB 544, a charterparty gave the parties the option to cancel in the event of war breaking out involving Japan. The Court of Appeal ruled that there was no technical definition of war, but that a commonsense approach should be adopted. It was certainly not necessary that a state of war between combatants be formally recognised as existing by HM Government. An act of war, for the purposes of the Rules, presumably bears a similar, pragmatic, meaning.

4.26   Act or omission of the shipper or goods owner

Article IV(2)(i) contains the defence of 'act or omission of the shipper or owner of the goods, his agent or representative'. In *Ismail* v. *Polish Ocean Lines* (1976) 1 All ER 902 a vessel capable of carrying fourteen hundred tons of cargo was chartered to bring potatoes from Egypt to England. In the master's opinion, one thousand tons was the maximum amount that could be properly loaded, allowing for ventilation and protective packing. The shipper's agent, claiming expert knowledge, insisted upon loading a full cargo. In his view, no protective packing (known as dunnage) was necessary. On arrival in England, a large proportion of the potatoes was found to be rotten. Two-thirds of this loss was attributable to the lack of dunnage. The shipper claimed damages.

Clauses in the contract of charter provided that the shipper was to load and stow the cargo, but that the master was to be responsible for proper stowage and dunnage. The Court of Appeal decided that the carrier's duty under Article III(2) did not arise, since the shipper had taken on the task of loading and stowing. Furthermore, the supervisory responsibility of the master set out in the charterparty was subject to the defence in Article IV(2)(i).

In any event, the court decided that the shipper would, on these facts, have been estopped from pleading a breach of the carrier's obligations.

4.27   Inherent vice

Presumably the IV(2)(i) defence will serve to protect the carrier when a shipper fails to inform him about peculiar characteristics of the goods, necessitating special treatment during the voyage. Such an omission will also entitle the carrier to invoke the defence under Article IV(2)(m). This exonerates the carrier from liability for 'wastage in bulk or weight or any other loss or damage arising from inherent defect, quality or vice of the goods'.

The same line that demarcates the carrier's liability for the seaworthiness of his vessel, in the sense of its suitability to carry the goods, also delineates the limits of this exception. In other words, seaworthiness (in the above sense) and inherent vice are reciprocally related. The one begins where the other ends. Hence, inherent vice is not simply a factual characteristic of the goods. The mere fact that they are incapable of surviving the contract voyage in suitable condition does not determine liability or lack of it. First it must be established what responsibility the carrier has undertaken with regard to these particular goods. The extent of the carrier's obligation to provide a ship capable of carrying the cargo to its destination in substantially the condition in which it was shipped is determined by reference to whatever information the carrier has regarding those goods. In *The Albacora*, fish was shipped from Glasgow to Genoa during September. The cargo deteriorated owing to lack of refrigeration. The carriers had been given no special instructions, and did not know that refrigeration was necessary. The House of Lords decided that the defendant carrier was protected by Article IV(2)(m). As Lord Reid noted, 'whether there is inherent defect or vice must depend on the kind of transit required by the contract'. Where the carrier provides the kind of transit he agreed to provide, deterioration of the goods during that transit is the result of inherent vice.

In *The Rio Sun*, Bingham J, having determined that it was not common practice to heat cargoes of crude oil, held that deterioration caused by a failure to heat was the result of inherent vice. His conclusion on this particular issue – that 'there was no breach of Article III r.2, but *in any event* [the carriers] are entitled to rely on Article IV r.2(m)' (my emphasis) cannot pass without comment, however. A breach of Article III(2) and the application of Article IV(2)(m) are mutually exclusive, because inherent vice is defined by reference to the fulfilment of the carrier's duties under Article III(1) and (2). Suppose, for example, that conditions change during the voyage, and the carrier becomes aware that the goods require additional protection. He is informed by radio, let us say, that heating or refrigeration is needed, or freak temperatures make this necessary. If he fails to turn on his heating or refrigeration unit, and the goods deteriorate, he cannot plead inherent vice. Inherent vice is a relative condition, determined by reference to the carrier's performance of his own obligations.

4.28   Insufficiency of packing

Insufficiency of packing is a defence under Article IV(2)(n). This exception is closely related to its predecessor. It may be described as the inherent vice of the packing: that is, its inability to survive the contract journey intact. By the same token, the carrier will not be liable if he is unaware that the packing is inadequate. In *The Lucky Wave* (1985) 1 LLR 80 coiled steel wire was carried from Immingham to Durban. A warehouse inspection, two days after the goods were landed, disclosed that a proportion of the goods had broken loose from its straps and was damaged. Sheen J noted that there was nothing to show that the damage had occurred during the two days when the goods were in the warehouse. Since the bill of lading acknowledged that the wire had been loaded in good order and condition, it was incumbent upon the defendant carriers to show how the damage had occurred. Cargo of this kind and packed in this way had been successfully carried for a number of years. The inference therefore was that the carriers had mishandled it on this occasion, and the defence under Article IV(2)(n) was therefore inapplicable.

4.29   Insufficiency of marks; latent defects

Article IV(2)(o) covers insufficiency or inadequacy of marks, and IV(2)(p) latent defects not discoverable by due diligence. Neither provision has been litigated, and, subject to the general causation rider outlined above, the scope and applicability of each would appear to be largely questions of fact.

4.30   The residual defence

Article IV(2)(q) is a catch-all provision covering 'any other cause arising without the actual fault or privity of the carrier, or without the fault or neglect of the agents or servants of the carrier, . . .'. In the opinion of Mason and Wilson JJ in *Shipping Corporation of India* v. *Gamlen* this defence expresses the fundamental scheme of the Rules. They impose certain obligations upon the carrier (from which he cannot free himself) but provide immunity where he, or those for whom he is responsible in the context of the specific defence have not been negligent. In *Leesh River Tea Co. Ltd* v. *British India SN Co. Ltd* Sellers LJ noted that Article IV(2)(q) can rarely be invoked, presumably because of the wide-ranging nature of the foregoing defences. Nevertheless, he regarded it as apt to cover instances of theft or malicious damage.

Article IV(2)(q) is the only defence to make specific reference to the burden of proof. It provides that 'the burden of proof shall be on the person claiming the benefit of this exception to show that neither the actual fault or privity of the carrier nor the fault or neglect of the agents or servants of the carrier contributed to the loss or damage'. The incidence of the burden of proof in Article IV(2) cases has been a matter of some controversy, but it now seems possible to set in out with some confidence. It is for the goods owner to establish a *prima facie* breach by the carrier. This he can often do by showing that the goods were delivered *to* the carrier in apparent good order and condition – which will be evidenced by the bill of lading – and delivered *by* him in a damaged state. Goods which are superficially sound may nevertheless be defective. It will then be incumbent on the goods owner to show, on balance, that the goods were inherently sound.

Once a *prima facie* case is established, the carrier must bring himself within one at least of the exceptions. It is at this point that controversy has arisen. In the course of his judgment at first instance in the *Gosse Millerd* case (1927) 2 KB 432, Wright J suggested that carriers must, in addition to establishing the specific ingredients of the relevant exception, disprove negligence. This view is now generally accepted as heterodox. It was doubted by Lord Pearce in *The Albacora* case, and specifically rejected by Lord Pearson. The goods owner must prove his loss. The carrier must then bring himself within the terms of an exception, which may, in particular instances only, require that he disprove negligence. In the other instances, the defence will be disallowed upon proof of negligence proffered by the goods owner.

4.31   *The carrier's obligation with regard to the bill of lading*

The carrier's third obligation under the Hague–Visby Rules is set out in Article III(3). This relates to the bill of lading and provides for the issue of a bill as soon as the goods are received by the carrier, if the shipper so demands. This, it will be realised, will in many cases be a received rather than a shipped bill. The bill must contain certain information. First, the leading marks necessary for identification of the goods, as provided in writing by the shipper before loading, must be indicated. This obligation only arises provided the marks are clearly shown on the goods themselves (if uncovered) or on their packing. The marks should be capable of remaining legible throughout the journey. Secondly, the bill must show either the number of packages or pieces, or the quantity or weight, again as provided by the shipper in writing. Finally, the bill must show the apparent order and condition of the goods.

The carrier is, however, under no obligation to show matters which he suspects, on reasonable grounds, not accurately to represent the goods actually received or which he has no reasonable means of checking.

The shipper is deemed, by Article III(5) to have guaranteed the accuracy of the information which he has given the carrier for the purposes of this obligation. The carrier is entitled to an indemnity from the shipper for any liability arising from any inaccuracy. There will be no indemnity, presumably, in regard to matters which the carriers had the means to check. In *Brown Jenkinson & Co. Ltd* v. *Percy Dalton (London) Ltd* (1957) 2 QB 621 shippers gave carriers an express indemnity relating to the condition of the goods on shipment. As a result, the carriers issued a clean bill of lading in relation to goods which were visibly defective. The Court of Appeal decided, by a majority, that the carriers could not enforce this indemnity, when they themselves were held liable to holders of the bill. The majority regarded the indemnity as fraudulent, and therefore illegal, even though it was apparently quite common practice for clean bills to be issued against indemnities in such circumstances.

4.32 Deviation

Article IV(4) provides that 'any deviation in saving or attempting to save life or property at sea or any reasonable deviation shall not be deemed to be an infringement or breach of these Rules or of the contract of carriage, and the carrier shall not be liable for any loss or damage resulting therefrom'. A deviation is a deliberate departure from the contractual route. Unless the route is specified expressly, a master is free to follow any course which is usual in the circumstances, that is, as they exist at the time of the voyage. The fact that the ports of departure and discharge are fixed does not of itself require the master to follow the shortest or most direct sea line. The usual route may be determined by the established practice of that particular carrier, or by prevailing commercial practice. In *Reardon Smith Line Ltd* v. *Black Sea & Baltic General Insurance Co.* (1939) AC 562 it was shown to have been the practice, for a period of five years or so, for vessels in the Black Sea to turn aside from the direct route in order to refuel at Constanza, where cheap fuel oil was temporarily available. This detour was held to be part of the usual route during that period. If there is no usual route, the master must follow a reasonable one. A ship may deviate even though the master believes that he is following the correct path. The question is whether the course, freely chosen by the master, is in fact within the tolerances allowed by the contract.

The contract may provide for alternative ports of discharge. In *Renton* v. *Palmyra* (1957) AC 149 a contract for the carriage of timber from Canada to London provided that the master might discharge at any safe or convenient port, if prevented from entering or using the nominated port of discharge. London being strikebound, the master proceeded to Hamburg and discharged there. The House of Lords ruled that there had been no deviation. The contract voyage, and the contract ports, must be determined according to the terms of the particular contract and the circumstances of the case.

4.33 Reasonable deviation

The Rules permit 'any deviation in saving or attempting to save life or property at sea, or any reasonable deviation . . .'. It may be assumed that any deviation to save life is reasonable. Deviations to save property are allowed whether reasonable or not: in other words, there seems to be no question of balancing the cost of the deviation against the benefit of recovering the particular property endangered. Whether any other deviation is reasonable is a question of individual circumstances. The leading case is *Stag Line* v. *Foscolo Mango* (1931) AC 328. A ship taking coal from Swansea to Constantinople left port carrying two engineers who were running a test on certain equipment. When the test was completed the ship turned off course to drop the engineers at a nearby port. Having accomplished this, the ship failed to return immediately to the regular route and, while off course, ran aground, Goods owners sought damages for loss of cargo.

Though the question of reasonable deviation seems to have been treated largely as a question of fact, an important difference of principle emerges from the judgment of Lord Buckmaster, on the one hand, and Lord Atkin on the other. According to Lord Buckmaster, a reasonable deviation is one 'which, where every circumstance has been duly weighed, commends itself to the commonsense and sound understanding of sensible men'. This requires that the deviation be reasonable in relation to both parties to the contract of carriage. In Lord Atkin's opinion, however, 'the true test seems to be what departure from the contract voyage might a prudent person controlling the voyage at the time make and maintain, having in mind all the relevant circumstances existing at the time, including the terms of the contract and the interests of all parties concerned, but without obligation to consider the interests of any one as conclusive'. According to Lord Atkin, a deviation may be reasonable, though made exclusively in the interests of one party to the contract of carriage, or, indeed, of neither, as for example where a passenger or crew member is urgently required on shore.

A deviation which is reasonable in itself, for example a deviation to effect essential repairs to the vessel, may nevertheless be necessitated by a previous breach by the carrier. Although Article IV(4) declares that reasonable deviations are no breach, this should not be taken to mean that the carrier is exonerated from previous, independent breaches. In *Kish* v. *Taylor* (1912) AC 604 an unseaworthy vessel deviated in order to effect repairs, then proceeded to deliver the cargo. The carriers claimed a lien for dead freight in respect of the shipper's failure to load a full cargo. The defendant holders of the bill of lading claimed that the effect of the deviation was to deprive the carriers of this right. The House of Lords ruled that the deviation was reasonable and the right to dead freight remained. In Lord Atkinson's words, '[it is] the presence of the peril and not its cause which determines the character of the deviation'. This, however, should not be taken to mean that the earlier unseaworthiness is in any way excused. The defendant, had he so chosen, might have repudiated the contract for breach of the condition of seaworthiness. The right to dead freight arose before the ship became unseaworthy, however, and would therefore have been unaffected by any such repudiation.

4.34   Effects of wrongful deviation

It was assumed in *Kish* v. *Taylor* that (again in the words of Lord Atkinson) 'voluntary or unwarranted deviation may render the contract of affreightment void *ab initio*'. For this proposition the decision of the Court of Appeal in *Thorley* v. *Orchis* (1907) 1 KB 660 was given. Here Fletcher Moulton LJ considered the position of a carrier who, having deviated, proceeded to carry the goods to their destination. In his opinion, 'the most favourable position which he can claim to occupy is that he has carried the goods as a common carrier [i.e. one with no special contract] for the agreed freight'. He went on to state that, in some cases, the carrier would not even be entitled to this status.

In *International Guano* v. *McAndrew* (1909) 2 KB 360 Pickford J held, on the authority of *Thorley* v. *Orchis*, that a contract of charter is made void from its outset by a deviation occurring during the voyage, even though the point did not arise for decision in the case before him. He ruled, however, that, on the present facts, the carrier's position could be no worse than a common carrier, and he was therefore entitled to one of the defences available to a common carrier: that of inherent vice. (The others are Act of God and Act of the Monarch's enemies.)

A more extreme position was taken by the Court of Appeal in *James Morrison* v. *Shaw, Savill* (1916) 1 KB 783. Here a deviating vessel was torpedoed and sunk during the First World War. The defence of loss occasioned by the King's enemies was denied to the carriers. Swinfen Eady LJ ruled that the defendants were liable in damages to the goods owners unless they could establish that the loss would have occurred in any event, whether the ship had been deviating or not.

The law relating to the effects of a wrongful deviation received its most extensive and authoritative review in *Hain SS Co.* v. *Tate & Lyle Ltd* (1936) 2 All ER 597. A ship was chartered to carry a cargo of sugar from ports in Cuba and San Domingo. By an oversight the master was not informed of the San Domingan port. Having loaded the Cuban sugar he therefore set off for home. The mistake was quickly spotted and the master redirected to San Pedro, in San Domingo. The ship ran aground in this harbour. Part of the cargo was lost, the rest transshiped and eventually carried to its destination.

The shipowners claimed a contribution from the goods owners in respect of the damage to the ship (so-called general average) and for the balance of the freight, to both of which they would in normal circumstances be entitled. The goods owners, in ignorance of the deviation, made a general average payment to the carriers, in order to obtain the release of the sugar. They sought the return of this sum. The House of Lords held that the carrier was not deprived of his right to a general average contribution in these circumstances. Lord Atkin said that an unjustified deviation does not automatically cancel the contract of carriage, leaving the shipowner in the position of common carrier. Nor does it automatically deprive the carrier of the protection of certain of its terms while leaving the rest intact. Its effect, in his view, was no different from the effect of any other serious breach. In other words, the innocent party is given the option to terminate further performance of the contract. On the particular facts, this right had not been exercised.

Observations in the judgment of Lord Wright appear at first glance to contradict both points made by Lord Atkin on the effect of a wrongful deviation. Thus Lord Wright states, first of all, that deviation deprives the carrier of the right to rely upon exceptions and, later in his judgment, that the effect of deviation is to abrogate the contract of carriage or charter. Lord Maugham, on the other hand, expressed himself in agreement with the reasoning in both judgments.

4.35 Summary

The cases on unjustified deviation are far from consistent, but the following propositions are suggested as the soundest view:

(a) An unjustified deviation, even of the most brief and minor kind, constitutes a major breach of contract, giving the innocent party the right, when he learns of the deviation, to cancel the contract of carriage or charter.

(b) The shipper's waiver of this right does not without more bind an indorsee of the bill of lading, who may cancel the contract of carriage contained in the bill of lading within a reasonable time of learning of the deviation.

(c) Cancellation does not operate retrospectively, so as to avoid the contract from the beginning, but prospectively, from the date of deviation. Rights and liabilities accruing before that date remain intact.

(d) If the contract is cancelled, the carrier cannot rely upon any terms in the contract which would have applied after that date.

(e) If the contract is not cancelled, his right to rely upon particular terms in the contract will be a matter of construction. Generally speaking, protective clauses will not apply to events occurring during deviation, following the so-called 'four corners' rule of construction that such provisions only protect the carrier when he is performing the contract in the stipulated manner.

(f) If the contract is cancelled, but the carrier nevertheless continues to carry and discharge the goods, his right to payment will depend upon whether or not a contract to pay for these services can be implied. Scrutton and Greer LJJ's suggestion, when the *Hain* case was before the Court of Appeal, that the carrier in no circumstances may claim payment, was emphatically rejected by the House of Lords.

In *Suisse Atlantique SA* v. *Rotterdamsche Kolen Centrale* (1967) 1 AC 361 Lord Wilberforce expressed the view that the deviation cases should be decided according to the normal principles of the law of contract. In Lord Reid's opinion in the same case, 'it was made clear in *Hain SS Co.* v. *Tate & Lyle Ltd* that there is no special rule applicable to deviation cases: the ordinary principles of the law of contract must be applied'. Unfortunately, Lord Wilberforce saw fit to renege from this position, in *Photoproductions Ltd* v. *Securicor Transport Ltd* (1980) AC 827. He observed, without further elaboration, that 'it may be preferable that [the deviation cases] should be considered as a body of authority *sui generis* with special rules derived from historical and commercial reasons'. The principal justification for treating deviation cases differently from the norm is that a wrongful deviation may have the effect of invalidating any marine insurance covering the vessel or the goods. However, it is submitted that the position of innocent parties is adequately protected by the application of the principles listed above.

4.36   *The extension of the defences to third parties*

By virtue of Article IV *Bis*(1) 'the defences and limits of liability provided for in these Rules shall apply in any action against the carrier in respect of loss or damage to goods covered by a contract of carriage whether the action be founded in contract or tort'. Although judges frequently remind us that the Rules are to be construed as if they were part of the contract of carriage, their protection in fact extends beyond contractual liability to cover tortious liability also. It will be recalled, however, that the majority of the Article IV(2) defences only apply provided there has been no negligence on the part of the carrier or those for whom he is responsible. Hence proof of actionable negligence will automatically rule these defences out. The monetary and time limits on liability laid down in Article III(6) and IV(5) will continue to apply, however. Article IV *Bis*(2) makes the defences and limits of liability available to servants and agents of the carrier, provided the defendant is not an independent contractor, and (IV *Bis*(4)) provided that damage was not intentionally or recklessly inflicted. Article IV *Bis*(4), unlike *Bis*(1) expressly and *Bis*(2) by implication, does not apply to loss, as distinct from damage, relating to goods. Presumably this omission is an oversight, and a servant who deliberately converted goods in circumstances involving no damage to them would not be able to take advantage of the limits of liability laid down elsewhere in the Rules.

Article IV *Bis*(2) is not, as might be first thought, a statutory exception to the doctrine of privity of contract, since the Rules, of which the servant or agent is allowed the benefit, are not part of a contract, but simply come into operation provided a particular type of contract exists. Nevertheless, it achieves, to a limited extent, an objective sought by carriers through specific contractual provisions designed to protect third parties. This objective was eventually gained, with the active cooperation of the courts, who were prepared to strain basic common law principles in order to meet the needs of commerce. An examination of the cases in which this occurred will be postponed until the carrier's common law position is examined: see below [4.42].

4.37   *The carrier's position at common law*

If the statutory regime discussed above does not apply, a carrier is free to make whatever contract he can, subject to the principles of the common law relating to such matters as misrepresentation, duress, privity, and illegality. In practice, even if the Rules are not incorporated, a common law contract for the carriage of goods by sea will include most, if not all, of the exceptions listed in Article IV(2). Indeed, these exceptions originated in common law contracts. As we have already seen, many of the seminal cases on, for example, the nature of a peril of the sea and the scope of that particular exception were decided at common law.

4.38   Seaworthiness

To the extent that the carrier is not protected by specific exceptions or limitations of liability, he is a so-called common carrier. As such, his position has been well established since the beginning of the nineteenth century. With regard to the seaworthiness of his ship, his obligation is analogous to that of a seller under s.14(3) of the Sale of Goods Act 1979. In other words, the vessel must be reasonably fit for its purpose. This obligation, unlike that under Article III(1), is not circumscribed by the exercise of due diligence. As Sellers LJ put it in *John Carter* v. *Hanson Haulage* (1965) 1 All ER 113, 'the shipowner [is] liable at common law for failure to make the ship seaworthy in fact, although he may have taken all reasonable care to do so'. The definition of seaworthiness is the same at common law as under statute, and comprehends the suitability of the vessel to carry the contract cargo. The carrier is not, however, liable merely because the ship is in fact unsuitable. Just as the seller is entitled, under s.14(3), to be given sufficient information regarding the buyer's requirements to be able to make a suitable selection of goods, so too is the carrier entitled to be informed of the special needs of the cargo. The result in *The Albacora* (where the carrier was not told, and could not be expected to know, that the cargo required refrigeration) would have been just the same had the case arisen at common law. As Lord Sumner succinctly put it in *FC Bradley & Sons Ltd* v. *Federal Steam Navigation Co. Ltd* (1927) 27 LILR 395: 'the carrier answers for his ship and men, the cargo owner for his cargo'.

4.39   Care of the goods

The carrier's responsibility for the goods, once in his charge, is summarised by Lord Wright in the *Smith Hogg* case: 'Apart from express exceptions, the carrier's contract is to deliver the goods safely'. It may be recalled that the same judge laid the same responsibility on the statutory carrier in the *Gosse Millerd* case, and was criticised for having done so by the House of Lords in *The Albacora* (see above, [4.20]). However, the carrier's common law obligation is to achieve a result, rather than to perform certain tasks in a certain way.

Nevertheless, the duty is not absolute. The common law recognises three implied exceptions to the obligation to deliver the goods in the condition in which they were received. These relate to loss or damage caused by Act of God; Act of the Monarch's enemies; and inherent vice. These presumably bear the same connotations as under the Rules, with the second exception being represented by IV(2)(e) and (f): Act of War, and Act of public enemies.

4.40   Deviation

A carrier's right to deviate is more circumscribed at common law than under the Rules. (Scrutton LJ in *Stag Line* v. *Foscolo Mango* was of the opinion that the statutory right went no further than the common law, but received no support for this view from the House of Lords.) It is a right to deviate to save life, which includes the right to deviate in order to ascertain whether life is in peril. It does not cover deviation in order to save property. In *Scaramanga* v. *Stamp* (1880) 5 CPD 295 the defendant's ship deviated in order to go to the assistance of a helpless vessel. The master agreed to tow the stranded ship into port. While doing so, the defendant's ship went aground, and the plaintiff's goods on board were totally lost. The Court of Appeal held that the deviation after the tow was taken up was unjustified, as the distressed ship's crew could have been rescued by taking them on board the defendant's vessel. Whether the master would then be justified in a further deviation in order to drop those rescued at a convenient point is not discussed.

Deviation in the interests of safety is further exemplified in *The Teutonia* (1872) LR 4 PC 171, in which a master was misinformed that the port for which he was heading was in enemy hands, and so turned away from it. The deviation was held to be justified. Brett J regarded it as 'obvious that, if a Master receives credible information that, if he continues in the direct course of his voyage, his ship will be exposed to some imminent peril . . . he must be justified in . . . deviating from the direct course'. In *Kish* v. *Taylor*, as we have seen, deviation to alleviate a self-inflicted danger was held to be justified. The unseaworthiness which caused that danger was not itself excused, however.

4.41   *The extension of defences to third parties*

The availability of contractual defences to non-contracting parties – typically the carrier's employees or agents – is determined by the doctrine of privity. This is relatively easy to state and simple to justify, at least in terms of the theory of contract law out of which it springs. Unfortunately, it is less easy to justify in practice, and has frequently proved an obstacle to efficient commercial intercourse. The English law of contract is based upon the notion of the freely negotiated bargain. Each side pays – or agrees to pay – for what it wants from the other. It follows, with some logic but less sense, that only those who have agreed to pay into the bargain should be entitled to take anything out of it. This is the doctrine of privity: an exclusionary rule which denies third parties any right to the benefits or protection of the contract just as it saves them from its liabilities. This follows, even though the contract in terms purports to confer its benefits and protection or impose its liabilities, upon the outsiders.

This means that, although a contract of carriage may attempt to extend protective provisions to those who perform the contract on the carrier's behalf, those third parties will remain fully liable. Not being parties to the contract, they cannot be sued for breach of it, but if the requirements of a tort are made out, the contract cannot protect them. Such an approach often flies in the face of commercial reality, where, in particular, the price of the carrier's services will have been calculated on the assumption that the liability of third parties is effectively limited. In *Scruttons Ltd* v. *Midland Silicones* (1962) AC 446 consignees sued stevedores for negligently damaging their goods while unloading them. The carriers had limited their own liability to an amount substantially below the true value of the goods. The plaintiffs therefore sued the stevedores for the full amount. Lord Reid prefaced his judgment by expressing regret that the doctrine of privity was part of English law. He nevertheless felt bound to apply it, since the doctrine had been entrenched by an earlier House of Lords decision, in *Dunlop* v. *Selfridge* (1915) AC 79. The stevedores were therefore unable to take advantage of the limitation of liability. Lord Reid did suggest a roundabout way of protecting stevedores in a similar situation. This involved an indemnity from the carrier to the stevedores. The carriers would in turn extract a contractual promise from the shippers not to sue the stevedores, thereby rendering the shippers liable to the carriers, and the carriers to the stevedores, should the shippers break their promise and sue. Such a device is perfectly sound in theory, but so clumsy and cumbersome in practice that it appears never to have been put to much use.

4.42   The Eurymedon

Instead, a theoretically questionable, but practically straight-forward path around the doctrine of privity was revealed by the Privy Council in *New Zealand Shipping Co. Ltd* v. *Satterthwaite & Co. Ltd; The Eurymedon* (1975) AC 154. Here a similar problem to that in the *Midland Silicones* case arose, with stevedores this time seeking to take advantage of the time limits for bringing suit contained in Article III(6) of the Rules. A clause in the contract of carriage purported to extend the protection of the contract to the stevedores. A majority of the Privy Council advised that the steve-dores were duly protected. In their view, the clause constituted an offer by the goods owner to the stevedores (using the carrier as agent to convey the offer) to exonerate the stevedores from liability, beyond the period of limitation in the Rules. That offer was accepted by the stevedores unloading the ship, in reliance on the offer. A unilateral contract was thereby formed, with no communication of acceptance being required. The stevedores provided consideration by carrying out their contract with the carriers to unload the ship. As Lord Wilberforce, for the majority, said: 'an agreement to do an act which the [stevedore] is under an obligation to a third party [i.e. the carrier] to do, may quite well amount to valid consideration'. The reason for this is that 'the promisee [i.e. the goods owner] obtains the benefit of a direct obligation which he can enforce'. In other words, he can sue the stevedores for breach of contract should they fail to unload the ship, or perform this task badly.

A moment's thought should be enough to expose the fallacy of this explanation. The goods owner can only sue the steve-dores in contract if they have a contract with them. One cannot construct a contract on the foundation of a right to sue which only exists if the contract is already there in the first place. The supposition is literally preposterous.

But, as Lord Wilberforce makes plain, it is only a means to an end, and theoretical consistency should give way to the demands of commercial necessity. It is clear that all three participants – carrier, goods owner and stevedores – are mutually engaged in a common enterprise – getting goods from one place to another – for reasons of profit, and that each requires the others in order to realise that profit. In such circumstances, to quibble about strict compliance with the theoretical imperatives of the law of contract seems niggardly and pedantic. Two members of the Privy Council nevertheless dissented.

In *Port Jackson Stevedoring Pty Ltd* v. *Salmon & Spraggon Pty Ltd*; *The New York Star* (1980) 3 All ER 257 Lord Wilberforce, speaking for a unanimous Privy Council, said that *The Eurymedon* approach should be treated as typical rather than exceptional, and that stevedores should be regarded, as a rule, as within the pale of the contract of carriage. The needs of commerce, he suggested, were not best served by drawing fine distinctions from case to case. Nonetheless, in *The Suleyman Stalskiy* (1976) 2 LIR 609 the Supreme Court of British Columbia distinguished *The Eurymedon* on the facts, and held the stevedores liable.

4.43   The carrier's right to freight

A carrier is entitled to be paid freight provided he delivers the contract cargo. This basic rule was established by the judgment of the Court of Common Pleas in *Dakin* v. *Oxley* (1864) 15 CB (NS) 646. There Willes J said that the question was whether the carrier had substantially performed the service for which the contract provided that freight should be paid. He went on: 'As a rule, freight is earned by the carriage and arrival of the goods ready to be delivered to the merchant'. It makes no difference to the right to freight that the goods are damaged. If only a part of the cargo is delivered, the carrier will be entitled to a proportionate part of the freight. In *The Mutula* (1978) 2 LIR 5 Roskill LJ described this as a basic rule of English commercial law.

Nevertheless, it can be displaced by the contrary agreement of the parties themselves. In *The Metula*, a contract of charter called for freight to be paid according to the amount of cargo loaded, rather than the amount discharged. The Court of Appeal held the carriers entitled to the full amount of freight, even though a substantial quantity of freight had been lost in transit. Furthermore, if the contract provides for the payment of a single amount not calculated according to the weight of the cargo (so-called lump sum freight), the carrier is, generally speaking, entitled to this payment in full, no matter how much cargo is actually delivered: see *The Norway* (1865) LT 50.

Since freight is payable against delivery of the contract cargo, in the absence of contrary agreement, it is necessary to know just what constitutes 'the contract cargo'. In *The Caspian Sea* (1980) 1 LLR 91 freight was withheld because the goods were delivered in a deteriorated condition. Donaldson J reiterated that the carrier's right to freight is not affected by the fact that the goods are damaged on delivery. The crucial question is whether they are substantially the same goods. Does the description applied to the goods on shipment still apply, albeit now qualified by some pejorative adjective, or are the goods so badly affected as to be something different? *Duthie* v. *Hilton* (1868) LR 4 CP 138 provides a good illustration. Bagged cement was wetted during transit and solidified. It was decided that the cement had ceased to exist, and had become a different substance. Similarly, in *Asfar* v. *Blundell* (1896) 1 QB 123 dates had been so contaminated with sewage as to cease to be the commercial entity, dates. The criterion is a mercantile, rather than a biological, chemical, or philosophical one, however.

The carrier is not entitled to freight unless he completes the contract by tendering the goods at the port of discharge. However, it seems that in certain circumstances the carrier will be able to claim freight even though the goods are not brought to port by ship. In *Thomas* v. *Harrowing Steamship Co.* (1915) AC 58 the carrying vessel ran aground while waiting to enter the home port, and a large part of the cargo was washed ashore. This the carriers collected and tendered to its owners. The House of Lords decided that the carriers were entitled to their freight.

This decision should not be regarded as an authority of general relevance to international sales, however. Unless the carrier is authorised to transship the goods, his inability to carry them in the designated vessel effectively brings the contract of carriage to an end.

In *Aktieselkabet Olivebank* v. *Dansk Svovlsyre Fabrik* (1919) 2 KB 162 charterers, who had the option to nominate the port of discharge, named a port to which, as they knew, it was illegal for the ship to go. The carriers accordingly discharged the cargo elsewhere. The Court of Appeal held that it was an implied term that the carrier should have an opportunity of earning his freight. According to the Headnote to the Report of this case, the carriers claimed, and were awarded their freight. This is incorrect; and, had the Court of Appeal so decided, would have been wrong in principle. The plaintiffs were awarded damages for breach of the implied term outlined above. This is a case, like *Colley* v. *Overseas Exporters* (1921) 3 KB 302 in which one party can effectively prevent the other from earning his contractual remuneration. In *Colley's* case, the right to payment for goods sold arose upon their being loaded onto a ship nominated by the buyer. The buyer refused to name a ship. The seller was unable to recover the price of the goods. So here, the carrier could not claim freight unless the agreed transit had been completed. There is no suggestion that the carrier had the right to choose the port of discharge upon the defendant's effective refusal.

At first instance, Bailhache J found the contract to be frustrated, a conclusion with which Bankes LJ in the Court of Appeal agreed. It is difficult to perceive how this can be correct. The inability of the carrier to complete the voyage was caused by the defendant's breach of contract. Any frustration was self-induced, and the doctrine cannot apply.

Finally, a goods owner to whom cargo is delivered in a damaged condition cannot set off any claim for damages against the claim for freight, but must bring a separate counter-claim. This is contrary to general principle, but justified, according to Lord Denning MR in *The Brede* (1973) 2 LlR 333, by commercial necessity. In his opinion, 'the good conduct of business demands that freight should be paid according to the terms of the contract'. The alternative would, in his view, lead to undesirable delay, as questions regarding the precise amount of damage were disputed, with the carrier all the while kept out of his money. In the view of Cairns LJ in the same case, there is no need to justify this exception to the general rule. It is well-established, and has formed the basis of countless transactions.

Chapter 5

Marine Insurance

5.01 *Introduction and Definition*

A cif buyer is entitled to receive from the seller a current policy of insurance offering the level of protection which is usual at the time the cif contract of sale was made. An fob buyer, unless he is risk-happy, will himself effect insurance on the goods he has purchased. Contracts of insurance are, typically, negotiated by brokers, on behalf of a client, with underwriters. Underwriters derive their name from the fact that they subscribe to an agreed amount of cover, of the total sum required in any particular case. This is known as 'writing a line'. A policy of insurance may be underwritten (i.e. insurance cover provided) by a single underwriter or by several. If several underwriters have each accepted a proportion of the risk, a series of separate contracts will come into being, between the insured and the individual underwriter, as he subscribes for the agreed amount. The process of effecting insurance in this manner is well described by Kerr LJ in *General Re-insurance Corp* v. *Forsakringsaktiebolaget Fennia Patria* (1983) QB 856: 'each line written on a slip gives rise to a binding contract *pro tanto* [i.e. for that amount] between the underwriter and the insured . . . The underwriter is therefore bound by his line, subject only to the contingency that it may fall to be written down on "closing" to some extent if the slip turns out to have been over-subscribed'. There is therefore no question of liability attaching to the underwriter only if and when the policy has been fully subscribed.

The policy of which the buyer has the eventual benefit will be one of marine insurance, and therefore subject to the Marine Insurance Act 1906. In practice, the majority of marine insurance policies effected in the United Kingdom are on one of the Institute of London Underwriters' sets of standard terms, known as Institute Cargo Clauses A,B, and C. In addition, extra insurance covering war or strikes (neither of which is covered in the Cargo Clauses) can be effected, using the Institute War Clauses, or the Institute Strikes Clauses.

The definition of a contract of marine insurance which the Act provides is, unfortunately, far from clear. Section 1 says that it is a contract 'whereby the insurer undertakes to indemnify the assured . . . against marine losses, that is to say, the losses incident to a marine adventure'. Further detail, but little light, is added by s.3(2), which explains that 'there is a marine adventure where (a) any ship goods or other movables are exposed to maritime perils'. 'Maritime perils' are 'perils consequent upon, or incidental to, the navigation of the sea'. This would be reasonably comprehensible (albeit not a model of draftmanship) but for the fact that the definition of 'maritime perils' in s.3(2) includes a list of the types of peril comprehended by the expression. They are: 'perils of the seas, fire, war perils, pirates, rovers, thieves, captures, seizures, and detainment of princes and peoples, jettisons, barratry, and any other perils, either of like kind or which may be designated by the policy'. In *Continental Illinois NB* v. *Bathurst; The Captain Panagos DP* (1985) 1 LlR 625, Mustill J experienced an excessive amount of difficulty in making sense of these provisions. He was satisfied, however, that the list in s.3(2) was not intended to be comprehensive, and, equally, that a peril was not a maritime peril simply because it was designated in the policy. In his opinion, no single set of terms could be regarded as the archetype of a marine policy. The determinative factor is whether or not the perils insured against are, in the main, 'consequent on or incidental to the navigation of the sea'. The fact that the policy insures against other types of peril will not then prevent the contract being for marine insurance. Indeed, s.2(1) expressly provides that a contract of marine insurance may be extended 'so as to protect the assured against losses on inland waters or on any land risk which may be incidental to any sea voyage' [*sic*].

5.02   *The nature of an insurable interest*

A contract of marine insurance will be totally invalid, unless the party for whose benefit it is made has, or expects to acquire, an insurable interest in the subject matter insured. Furthermore, the parties cannot agree that such an interest is to be assumed or conceded. Although in practice this is done, through the 'ppi', or 'policy proof of interest' clause, and reputable insurers do pay out on claims made under such contracts, they are technically void as gaming or wagering contracts under s.4(2)(b).

The tender of such a policy in performance of a cif contract is bad.

An insurable interest is defined in s.5, which says that 'every person has an insurable interest who is interested in a marine adventure'. This is not a particularly happy effort; indeed, it seems to be tautologous. It is, however, developed in s.5(2), which provides that a person has an insurable interest where he stands in any legal or equitable relation to the adventure or to any insurable property at risk therein', as a result of which he may gain or lose according to the safe and prompt arrival of that property, or the successful conclusion of that adventure.

Though the assured must have an insurable interest, it is sufficient if he has acquired it by the time of the loss. In such a case, however, he must have expected to acquire an insurable interest when the contract of insurance was made, otherwise it is void under s.4(2)(a).

A legal or equitable interest in the subject matter of the insurance is therefore crucial. It is not enough that the assured has a financial stake in the success of a particular enterprise. For example, stevedores or warehousemen who expect to make a profit from the use of their services when a vessel arrives in port lack the necessary direct involvement to have an insurable interest in the transit, or the goods being carried.

To have an insurable interest in goods, those goods must be identified with sufficient particularity. It is not necessary that they be identified as the subject matter of the contract of sale, however. It is sufficient that they constitute the source from which that subject matter will be drawn, in the sense that the seller has irrevocably committed goods to the performance of the contract, though he may not have made the final selection or allocation which will pass property. In *Inglis* v. *Stock* (1885) 10 App Cas 263, for example, an fob buyer was held to have an insurable interest in a cargo of sugar in bulk, half of which he had bought from the shippers, and half from another buyer from the shippers. No separation of cargo was ever made between the two contracts. Although, following *The Elafi* (above [1.07]) we might now conclude that property passed to the plaintiff upon his second purchase, he would still have had an insurable interest even if he had not bought the rest of the shipment.

It is not sufficient to give rise to an insurable interest, however, that the goods have been identified in this way. The assured must stand to gain or lose according to whether or not they are delivered safely and promptly. In other words, he must be contractually at risk of these events. According to a leading work on marine insurance (Arnould: *The Law of Marine Insurance and Average*,) 16th Edn, p 366) an insurable interest depends *prima facie* on having property in goods. However, it is submitted that property is relevant only as an indicator of risk. Since property and risk normally travel together, property is, as Arnould suggests, *prima facie* proof of an insurable interest. If, however, property and risk have been severed (as happens typically in cif contracts upon shipment), it is the party at risk, rather than the one with property in the goods, who has the insurable interest.

5.03 A *contract* uberrimae fidei

A contract of marine is a contract *uberrimae fidei*, that is, of the utmost good faith. As a result, the assured is required to make certain disclosures. Failure to do so will entitle the insurer to cancel the contract from its very commencement, and no liability will accrue. This is an exception to the normal contractual principle, which allows contracting parties to remain silent, even if they possess information which they know would affect the judgment of the other side. As Blackburn J says in *Ionides* v. *Pender* (1874) LR 9 QB 531: 'it is perfectly well established that the law as to a contract of insurance differs from that as to other contracts, and that a concealment of a material fact, though made without any fraudulent intention, vitiates the policy'. This rule is now encapsulated in s.18 of the Marine Insurance Act 1906. Here 'material circumstances' are defined as those 'which would influence the judgment of a prudent insurer in fixing the premium, or determining whether he will take the risk'. Materiality is a question of fact.

The rule set out in s.18 was criticised in *Lambert* v. *Cooperative Insurance Society Ltd* (1975) 2 LIR 485, on the basis that a layman is unlikely to know just what information is liable to influence the judgment of the average insurer. This criticism was offered in the context of a case involving domestic insurance, however, and has much less force with regard to commercial marine insurance.

If the policy is effected by an agent, he must disclose every material circumstance known to himself, as well as every material circumstance known to the assured. It is sometimes said that the agent is deemed to know what the principal knows, and *vice versa*, but this idea should not be carried too far. In *Blackburn Low & Co.*

v. *Vigors* (1887) 12 App Cas 531 a previous agent had acquired
material information which he did not pass on to his principal.
A later agent, who was ignorant of this information, effected a
policy of insurance for the principal. The House of Lords sensibly
concluded that the principal was not deemed to know what his
first agent knew, and the second agent therefore was also deemed
not to possess the relevant knowledge.

A policy may be vitiated for non-disclosure of information
of which the assured (or his agent) ought to have been aware,
even if he was in fact ignorant of it. In *London General Insurance
Co.* v. *General Marine Underwriters Association* (1921) 1 KB 104,
for example, plaintiffs insured a cargo which, as they had the
means at hand to discover, had already been lost. The Court
of Appeal held that the defendant insurers were not liable on
the policy, even though the same information was also available
to them. Although s.18 entitles the assured to withhold certain
information, including anything which the insurer ought already
to know, it was decided that the insurers could not be expected
to remember information which, at the time it was made available
to them, was of no particular relevance.

In *C.T.I.* v. *Oceanus* (1984) 1 LlR 476 the criterion of materiality
adopted by the judge at first instance attracted a most severe
rebuke from Kerr LJ in the Court of Appeal. Lloyd J had decided
that a plea of non-disclosure should succeed only where it is
shown that a prudent underwriter would have declined the risk
altogether or charged a higher premium, if he had been aware of
the undisclosed circumstances. This is indeed what s.18 would
appear, at first glance, to say. The Court of Appeal, however, held
that 'this conclusion distorts and erodes the scope of the duty of
disclosure'. What must be shown is that the information withheld
would have influenced the insurer in forming his judgment, not
that that judgment would necessarily have been a different one.
Furthermore (although s.18 does not expressly say so) a fact will
be material if it would have affected terms other than the premium
on which the insurer would have been prepared to accept the
risk. This requires that we read the closing words of s.18(2) as
'whether, and if so, on what terms, he will take the risk'.

The information revealed to the insurer must be true. Insofar
as it consists of representations of expectation or belief these
must be made in good faith. Insofar as it consists of statements
of fact these must be substantially correct. A statement of fact is
substantially correct if the difference between it and the actual
truth 'would not be considered material by a prudent insurer':

s.20(4). The contract may provide that cover is to continue, at an additional premium, should the assured wish to effect certain changes in the insured voyage, or should it transpire that certain information regarding the subject matter was withheld or inaccurate. The exact amount of the additional premium is typically to be arranged after the event. Such a provision is known as a 'held covered' clause. The Institute Cargo Clauses, for example, contain such a clause, relating to a change of destination.

In *Liberian Insurance Co.* v. *Mosse* (1977) 2 LlR 560 Donaldson J had occasion to consider a much wider 'held covered' clause, contained in an earlier version of the Institute Clauses. This provided that the assured should be held covered for any omission or error in the description of the subject matter. Donaldson J decided that the effect of this provision was to deprive the insurer of the right to avoid the contract for non-disclosure or misdescription, but only if a fully informed insurer would merely have increased his premium by a 'reasonable commercial amount'. The clause will not apply if other terms than the premium would be altered, or if the new premium would be excessively high. As can be seen, the new Institute 'held covered' clause is much reduced in scope, but it remains possible for particular insurers to include clauses which apply to a much wider range of changes.

5.04 Liability for the premium

By a peculiar custom of the marine insurance business, the broker, and not the assured, is liable to the insurer for the premium. This exception to the usual principles of the law of agency can be found in s.53(1) of the Marine Insurance Act 1906. It was explained by Chitty J in *Universal Insurance Co. of Milan* v. *Merchants Marine Insurance Co.* (1987) 2 QB 93 on the basis that the underwriter will only be willing to give credit to the broker, with whom alone he will usually be familiar.

5.05 Types of policy

A policy of marine insurance will either be a time policy, a voyage policy, or a hybrid. As the names suggest, a time policy will provide cover for a particular period of time, while a voyage policy will insure for a particular voyage. A hybrid will cover a particular voyage, to take place within a designated time. In *The*

Eurysthenes (1976) 3 All ER 243 the Court of Appeal held that a policy which was automatically renewed from year to year, unless determined by either side, was a time policy. The period for which it was to endure was sufficiently precise to satisfy the definition in s.25.

The principal difference between time and voyage policies is laid out in s.39. In a voyage policy there is an implied warranty that the ship shall be seaworthy at the commencement of the voyage. In a time policy there is no implied warranty that the ship shall be seaworthy at any time, unless the ship is sent to sea in an unseaworthy state with the privity of the assured. In *The Eurysthenes*, cargo was lost or damaged owing to the unseaworthiness of the carrying ship. The carriers settled the goods owners' claim, and sought indemnity from their insurers. The Court of Appeal decided that the ship had been sent to sea in an unseaworthy condition, with the privity of the plaintiffs. The shipowners contended that only actual wilful misconduct would deprive them of the protection of their insurance. The insurers countered that negligence in not knowing the true condition of the vessel would suffice.

The Court of Appeal found a middle ground. Mere negligence was not enough to disentitle the shipowners, but either actual knowledge or deliberate evasion – turning a blind eye to the true situation – would be enough. Both sides were agreed that the party whose knowledge was to be assessed was the shipowner personally or, in the case of a limited company, its *alter ego* in the sense described in *Lennards* v. *Asiatic Petroleum Co.* (above [5.05]).

A cargo owner may well be in an invidious position with regard to his insurance. He is unlikely to be aware of the condition of the carrying ship, yet he may lose his cover if the ship is unseaworthy. However, the Institute Cargo Clauses now waive any breach of the warranty of seaworthiness unless the assured or his servants are privy to it.

In a voyage policy there is an implied condition that the voyage shall begin within a reasonable time (presumably, of taking out the insurance) and that it will be prosecuted with reasonable dispatch: s.42(1) and s.48. Failure to start timeously gives the insurer the option to avoid the contract. A failure to proceed timeously would seem, from the wording of s.48, to terminate the contract automatically from the time the delay becomes unreasonable. Whether or not this is the correct interpretation of this provision remains to be seen.

According to s.26(1), the subject matter insured must be designated with reasonable certainty. The policy may, however, leave the insured free to provide specific details, not of a kind to alter the risk, later. In this case the policy is a floating policy, and the provisions of s.29 will apply. In such cases the insured party must declare the relevant details promptly. If the policy covers successive shipments, the details must all be declared in sequence. However, omissions or erroneous declarations made in good faith may be rectified, even after loss of goods or their safe arrival. The usual detail not specified at the outset of a floating policy is the name of the carrying ship.

5.06   Valued and unvalued

Policies of insurance may be valued or unvalued: s.27(1). A valued policy is one in which the value of the subject matter is agreed, or in which an appropriate formula for the calculation of that value is provided. In the absence of fraud, this valuation is conclusive evidence of the insurable value of the goods as between the parties to the contract of insurance. In a floating policy, the assured may declare the value of goods prior to loss or arrival, in which case the total amount of the cover will be adeemed, or reduced, by the amount declared. If, however, the value is not declared until after loss or arrival, the policy will be treated as unvalued, and the actual value must be calculated in accordance with the formula in s.16(3). This provides that the insurable value of goods in an unvalued policy is the prime cost of the goods, plus shipping and insurance charges.

If the assured suffers a total loss, he may claim the sum agreed in a valued policy, or the insurable value in an unvalued policy. Where a part of the goods is lost, the insurable value of that part must first be calculated. In an unvalued policy, the assured will recover that amount. In a valued policy it must first be determined what ratio that amount bears to the full insurable value of the goods. The assured will then recover the proportionate sum. For example, suppose goods with an insurable value of £100,000 are insured for £80,000 out of which goods with an insurable value of £75,000 are lost by an insured peril. The assured will recover three-quarters of the sum valued: i.e. £60,000. Where goods arrive damaged, a similar formula is applied, except that the assured will recover that fraction of the valued sum or insurable value which is represented by the actual wholesale value of the goods on arrival divided into its wholesale value in sound condition. Thus, if goods are insured for, or have an insurable value of, £80,000, which on arrival in sound condition would be worth £100,000 but which, owing to damage, are actually worth £60,000, the assured will recover two-fifths of the insured sum: i.e. £32,000. If there is no wholesale price, the value must be estimated.

The meaning of the key phrase 'prime cost', on which the insurable value of goods in an unvalued policy is based, was considered by the Court of Appeal in *Williams* v. *Atlantic Assurance Co.* (1933) 1 KB 81. Scrutton LJ pointed out that the ordinary meaning, signifying the original manufacturing cost, is not always appropriate. In his opinion, where the assured is not the manufacturer, and has acquired the goods some time before risk attaches, the market value of the goods at or near the time of shipment constitutes the prime cost. If he has recently bought or agreed to sell the goods, then the invoice price will provide a useful guideline. In *Berger* v. *Pollock* (1973) 2 LlR 442, Kerr J felt that a court must do its best to ascertain the true value of the goods at the commencement of the insured adventure. This amount he felt was best summarised by the phrase 'commercial value'.

5.07 *Promissory and non-promissory warranties*

The protection offered by a contract of marine insurance may range from the virtually comprehensive (although even a so-called 'all risks' policy may contain exceptions) to the particular, as in the Institute Strikes or War Clauses. But in any event the policy may indicate certain requirements that must be satisfied as a condition of cover attaching or continuing.

These requirements may take a promissory or non-promissory form. The Act, somewhat confusingly, designates promissory conditions as warranties – an expression normally associated in modern contract law with terms of minor importance. (The word 'warranty' has a second unusual usage in marine insurance law: to indicate an exception to cover, as in the phrase 'warranted free of capture and seizure', which means that the insurance does not apply to this particular risk.)

According to s.33(1) a promissory warranty is 'a warranty by which the assured undertakes that some particular thing shall or shall not be done, or that some condition shall be fulfilled, or whereby he affirms or negatives the existence of a particular state of facts'. The Act itself implies six such terms. In all policies there is an implied warranty that the adventure is lawful and, so far as it is within the control of the assured, will be carried out in a lawful way. In voyage policies there are implied warranties that the ship is seaworthy at the beginning of the voyage, that she is reasonably fit to carry the goods to their destination, reasonably fit to encounter the ordinary perils of the port (if the policy attaches while the ship is in port); for voyages to be completed in stages requiring different preparation or equipment, that at the commencement of each stage she will be seaworthy with regard to that preparation or equipment; and, finally, an implied condition (which is presumably, although not stated to be, a promissory warranty) that the adventure will begin within a reasonable time. By virtue of s.87 the parties can contract out of any or all of these provisions, although they cannot, of course, prevent the principles of the doctrine of illegality applying.

If a warranty is not strictly observed, the insurer is discharged from liability from the date of breach, even though the breach has caused him no loss, and even though the assured may have remedied it fully before an insured peril arose. However, circumstances may so change during the lifetime of the policy that compliance is no longer necessary, as, for example, where the assured is required to take precautions against a particular danger (such as war) which has been removed before the risk attaches.

In addition to promissory warranties, there are certain non-promissory requirements which the assured must meet. Although failure to satisfy them will not constitute a breach of contract on his part, it will nevertheless deprive him of cover. Thus s.43 provides that departure from a place other than that specified in the policy will prevent the risk attaching. So too, under s.44, will departure for a different destination from that specified. If, having left for the agreed destination, the ship voluntarily heads for a different one, there is a so-called change of voyage. In such an event, the insurer's liability ceases from the time the intention to change is made apparent, not from the time of actually changing course. Similarly, if the ship deviates without lawful excuse, liability ceases, but in this case only from the time of actual deviation. It is irrelevant that the ship has regained her original course before an insured loss occurs. In a time policy, where no route is specified, the ship must follow the customary one. A list of excuses for deviation is given in s.49(1). This is more extensive than that provided by the Hague–Visby Rules or, *a fortiori*, the common law.

5.08 Proximate loss

The insurer's liability, in the event that these preconditions are satisfied, is 'for any loss proximately caused by a peril insured against', within the terms of the policy itself: s.55(1). The idea of proximate causation has plagued cases of both marine insurance and carriage of goods by sea. In carriage of goods cases it has enjoyed a schizophrenic existence, with judges alternatively referring to, or rejecting it as a useful analogy from the law of marine insurance. Indeed, one judge, Lord Wright, has at different times done both (see his judgment in the *Smith Hogg* case, where he criticises the usage, and his judgment in *Monarch Steamship* v. *Karlshamns*, where he employs the expression uncritically). Nevertheless, it would seem that in both areas of the law, judges are utilising the same ideas of causation, by whatever name it is called.

However, if this be so, then some of the leading decisions seem difficult to harmonise. To these we must now turn, in order to decide whether there are in fact certain constant principles relating to causation.

The decision of the House of Lords in *Leyland Shipping Co. Ltd* v. *Norwich Union Fire Insurance Society Ltd* (1918) AC 350 provides a useful focus. Here a shipowner claimed for a loss caused by perils of the sea. The insurers countered that the loss was in fact a consequence of war, against which the shipowners were not protected. The ship had been torpedoed, but managed to make safe harbour, where repairs might have been effected. However, she was required to move to a more exposed part of the beach by the harbour authorities. There she grounded and was so buffetted by the sea that she eventually broke up. The House of Lords ruled that the effects of the torpedoing had continued throughout, despite the ultimately futile attempts to save the ship, and caused her loss. All their Lordships were agreed that the issue was essentially one of fact. Lord Shaw stressed that too much emphasis should not be given to the word 'proximate'. Where causes combine, the 'proximate' cause is not the latest in time, but 'that which is proximate in efficiency'. By what criteria one identifies such a cause is not explained.

In the court below, Scrutton LJ had difficulty in reconciling two earlier decisions in this area, which the House of Lords eventually decided were harmonious. In *Hamilton* v. *Pandorf* (above [4.24]) damage caused to a cargo when seawater entered a hold through a hole gnawed by rats was held attributable to a peril of the sea. In *Reischer* v. *Borthwick* (1894) 2 QB 548, on the other hand, damage caused by seawater entering through a hole caused by a collision was held by the Court of Appeal to be the result of that collision (for which the plaintiff was insured) and not a peril of the sea (for which he was not covered.)

The picture is blurred even further when two additional cases are considered. In *Cory* v. *Burr* (1883) 8 App Cas 393 ship-owners were insured against losses caused by barratry (i.e. the fraudulent behaviour of the master or crew, to the prejudice of the owner and without his consent). They were not, however, insured against 'capture and seizure'. The master, in attempting to smuggle tobacco in Spanish waters (a barratrous act), was caught by Spanish revenue officers. The ship was impounded. The shipowners sought to recover from their insurers the amount of the fine they had to pay for the ship's release. The House of Lords held that the loss was caused by the seizure, and not the act of barratry. Barratry, it was said, created the occasion for the ship to be seized, but the seizure took place in consequence of a violation of Spanish law. Finally, in *Smith Hogg* v. *Baltic & Black Sea Insurance Co.* (1940) AC 997, an overloaded and therefore unseaworthy ship capsized when her master negligently refuelled her. The House of Lords held that the resultant damage to cargo was caused by the unseaworthiness (for which the defendant insurers were liable) rather than the act or default of the master (for which they were not.)

5.09   Are the cases consistent?

At a distance of time these cases seem difficult to reconcile. They are often explained as turning on their particular facts, but the potentially decisive facts are not always apparent. In *Hamilton* v. *Pandorf*, for example, the fact that the shipowners were not at fault for the activities of the rats seems to have been regarded as important. But, in the *Leyland* case, a tantalisingly oblique alternative explanation is suggested in the judgment of Lord Finlay LC. Referring to a point made by Lord Dunedin during argument (but not repeated in his speech) the Lord Chan-cellor indicated that the hole made by the rats was above the waterline. Hence water was let into the ship, not as a direct consequence of the hole, but by the rolling of the ship under

the action of the waves – in other words, by a peril of the
sea.

This is a fascinating explanation, which turns on a fact not
mentioned in the report of the case itself. Lord Dunedin, however, explained *Hamilton* v. *Pandorf* quite differently. In his view,
damage by seawater constituted damage by a peril of the sea, and
the precise way in which the seawater was admitted was, generally speaking, irrelevant. It was perfectly possible, however, for the
parties to agree that particular manifestations of sea peril should
not be covered by the insurance: for example, seawater admitted
as the result of collisions, or the actions of rats. In *Reischer* v.
Borthwick a particular instance of sea peril had alone been the
subject of the insurance; all others were excluded. In *Hamilton's*
case the parties might have, but did not, exclude from the range
of sea perils covered by the insurance sea damage caused as the
result of the activities of rats.

This does not, however, serve to reconcile *Cory* v. *Burr* and
the *Smith Hogg* case. In each a prior event created the occasion
for, but not the inevitability of a later occurrence from which loss
flowed. Lord Wright's speech in *Smith Hogg* suggests (contrary
to the opinion of Lord Shaw in *Leyland Shipping*) that the doctrine
of causation does mean different things in marine insurance and
carriage of goods by sea cases. In carriage cases it is enough, in
order to hold a carrier liable, that his act or default has been one
contributing cause, among the web of causes out of which a loss,
or damage, has emerged. In insurance cases, the insurer is liable
if the insured peril is the principal, dominant, in short proximate,
cause, rather than one among several.

If this is the correct explanation of Lord Wright's speech in
the *Smith Hogg* case it will not do. There is no need to distinguish
between the two sets of cases; indeed, it does not make good
commercial sense to do so. The only point at which they differ
is that covered by s.55(2) of the Marine Insurance Act 1906. This
provides that the insurer 'is liable for any loss caused by a peril
insured against, even though the loss would not have happened
but for the misconduct or negligence of the master or crew'.

5.10   The underlying principles

This provision gives us the clue to harmonising the foregoing
cases. The following principles emerge. First, an event may
have no causative relevance whatsoever. If so, whether or not

it constitutes a breach of contract or falls within an excepted or insured peril will be irrelevant, unless it forms the subject of a precondition on the occurrence of which liability ceases. For example, an unseaworthy vessel may be overtaken by a catastrophe which it would have encountered, and which it would not have been able to withstand, even if it had been in a seaworthy state. A carrier, or a party insured under a time policy, will not be prevented from attributing loss to the particular peril represented by the catastrophe. A party insured under a voyage policy, on the other hand, will lose the protection of his insurance, not because unseaworthiness has caused the loss, but because seaworthiness is a condition precedent to the insurer's liability.

Similarly, damage or loss which has already been inflicted will be attributed to whatever circumstance brought it about, even though a subsequent event accelerates or exacerbates that loss or damage. If, for example, a ship is sinking because it is unseaworthy, the fact that a heavy sea, which a seaworthy ship could have ridden, hastens the event does not mean that the loss was caused by a peril of the sea and not unseaworthiness. As has often been said, however, loss or damage is rarely if ever caused by a single event, but is usually the outcome of a combination of causes. Here two situations must be carefully distinguished. First, out of a general peril, for example peril of the sea, a contract of insurance may cover (or alternatively exempt the insurer from liability for) one or more particular instances. If that instance arises, liability will attach (or the exception apply) if loss or damage would not have happened but for that event. This will be the case even though, literally speaking, the actual loss or damage was inflicted by the general rather than the specific peril. Secondly, distinct and separate perils may be at the risk of the different contracting parties. Thus the insurer may be at risk for barratry, and the insured for capture and seizure. In a case like *Cory* v. *Burr* loss is caused by both perils, in the sense that it would not have come about but for them both. In these cases the law selects as the proximate cause that for which the insured party (in marine insurance) or the carrier (in carriage cases) is at risk. In a number of cases this approach is justified on grounds of construction, where the alternative would give little or no scope to one of the allocations of risk. In a case like *Cory* v. *Burr*, however, where each party's interpretation of the contract left ample scope for both provisions to operate, it is difficult to see any particular justification for the outcome eventually favoured by the House of Lords.

5.11   Exceptions: delay; inherent vice; inevitable loss

Under s.55(2)(b) the insurer is not liable for loss proximately caused by delay, even though the delay itself is caused by an insured peril. So if, for example, a ship runs aground and in consequence a cargo owner misses a favourable market, he will be unable to claim for the loss. Under s.55(2)(c) the insurer is not liable for ordinary wear and tear, ordinary leakage and breakage, inherent vice or nature of the goods insured, or for any loss proximately caused by rats or vermin. Under this provision *Hamilton* v. *Pandorf* would be differently decided, since the behaviour of rats is now put at the risk of the insured party. Both these provisions are made expressly subject to contrary stipulations in the policy. Despite this, however, it would seem impossible for a party to insure himself against a loss which is bound to occur. As Cockburn CJ in *Paterson* v. *Harris* (1861) 1B & S 336 and Lord Sumner in *British & Foreign Marine Insurance Co.* v. *Gaunt* (1921) 2 AC 41 emphasise, insurance provides protection against contingencies, not inevitabilities. In *Sassoon* v. *Yorkshire Insurance Co.* (1923) LIR 129 cigarettes being shipped to Baghdad were insured against damages by mould and mildew. On arrival they were found to be damaged in this way. Atkin LJ expressed a doubt whether a loss which was bound to manifest itself as a result of the journey undertaken could ever be the subject of insurance. In *Berk* v. *Style*(1955) 3 All ER 625 goods were shipped in bags which were too weak to withstand the ordinary incidents of sea carriage, and which burst on unloading. The plaintiff owners were insured against all risks 'howsoever arising', but subject to Institute Cargo Clauses which excluded liability for loss or damage caused by inherent vice. Sellers J was therefore able to hold that the plaintiffs could not recover the cost of rebagging, without having to decide whether an appropriately worded policy could in fact extend to inevitable losses.

In *Soya GmbH Mainz* v. *White* (1983) 1 LIR 122 the House of Lords held, as a matter of construction and commercial common sense, that loss from inherent vice could be insured against, and s.55(2)(c) displaced, even though the relevant clause did not expressly impose liability for inherent vice and was capable of applying to losses from other causes. Here soya beans were insured against heat, sweat, and spontaneous combustion (so-called HSSC cover). It was inevitable that beans with a moisture content of over fourteen per cent would suffer such damage and below twelve would suffer none. Beans with a moisture content of between twelve and thirteen per cent arrived damaged. The House of Lords held the HSSC clause apt to cover damage caused by inherent vice in these circumstances. Lord Diplock, who delivered the only speech, left open the question whether the clause would have imposed liability on the insurers if, unknown to the assured, the beans had been shipped with a moisture content so high as to make deterioration inevitable. The *Gaunt* case was not referred to.

In keeping with the assumption that one cannot insure against inevitable loss or damage, the Court of Appeal in *Sassoon* v. *Yorkshire Insurance Co.* held that the assured must prove that the loss or damage was brought about by some fortuitous cause. Where similar journeys have been successfully made in the past, this may raise a presumption that the loss or damage was the result of a chance occurrence.

5.12   Burden of proof

The claimant has the burden of proving that the loss or damage was caused by an insured peril. Furthermore, where the claim is that loss or damage resulted from a peril of the sea, the claimant cannot 'rely on a ritual incantation of the generic expression "perils of the sea" but [is] bound, if [he is] to discharge successfully the burden of proof . . . to condescend to particularity in the matter', according to Lord Brandon, delivering the only speech in *Rhesa Shipping Co. SA* v. *Edmunds; The Popi M* (1985) 2 All ER 712. Here a ship sank in calm seas, when water flooded through a large hole in her side. There was no explanation of how the hole came to be there, but both the shipowner and the insurer put forward contending suggestions. The House of Lords decided that it was for the shipowner to show how the hole was caused. If the court was unconvinced by either suggestion, it was not bound to prefer one over the other, but could decide that the burden of proof was not discharged.

The sinking of a ship as a result of water entering through a hole in her side is, without more being shown, a loss through a peril of the sea. As *Hamilton* v. *Pandorf* demonstrates, it is not necessary that the hole itself be caused by a peril of the sea, but simply that it come about through circumstances for which the assured is not responsible. In *The Popi M*, the House of Lords are in fact placing the burden on the assured of proving, not only that the loss was caused by an insured peril, but that the insured peril did not operate in conjunction with other causative factors for which the assured was at risk.

This approach is endorsed by the judgment of Bingham J in *The Zinovia* (1984) 2 LIR 264. The plaintiff shipowners claimed for a loss of their vessel, which had run aground. The defendant insurers resisted the claim, alleging that the ship had been deliberately wrecked. The learned judge held that stranding was a peril of the sea, if it occurred fortuitously, and that it was for the insurers to show that it did not. He contrasted the present case with those in which a ship is lost as a result of water entering into it when, he said, 'it is necessary to identify the cause of the ingress in order to decide whether that cause was a peril of the sea'.

It is submitted that this approach confuses two separate matters: the nature of a peril of the sea and the issue of causation. The reason why a claimant for loss caused by peril of the sea should be required to go further than claimants for loss from other causes and demonstrate the precise nature of the peril is because sea perils take so many different forms and can – as the cases demonstrate – operate so frequently in conjunction with circumstances for which the assured is responsible.

5.13   Types of loss

As s.56(1) states, a loss may be either total or partial. The policy may relate to either or both types of loss. If cover is for total loss only, the policy will generally contain a warranty (in the peculiar sense of an exception) 'free from particular average'. This rather strange expression relates to partial loss. The word 'average' in this context has no mathematical connotation, but derives from the French 'averie' and signifies a charge, expense, or loss (see *Kelman* v. *Livanos* (1955) 2 All ER 239, and s.64(1)). (A general average loss, on the other hand, does not connote a total loss of insured goods but, somewhat incongruously, a loss deliberately and reasonably incurred in order to safeguard property which is also involved in the same adventure. The subject of general average is beyond the scope of this work.)

A total loss may be actual or constructive, according to s.56(2). An actual total loss is defined in s.57(1) and covers three instances. These are: (a) the destruction of the subject matter; (b) damage to the extent that the subject matter ceases to be 'a thing of the kind insured'; and (c) the assured's being permanently deprived of the subject matter. A constructive total loss is defined in s.60(1) and (2). Section 60(1) covers two situations – that in which an actual total loss appears unavoidable and that in which the subject matter cannot be preserved from actual total loss without expenditure which would exceed the value of the property preserved. Although the subsection appears to include, as a part of the definition of a constructive total loss in these two instances the abandonment of the subject matter by the assured, the House of Lords in *Robertson* v. *Petros M. Nomikos* (1939) AC 371 held that notice of abandonment to the insurer is not an element of the definition, but a prerequisite of the right to claim. As a result the respondent was able to claim on secondary insurance which was triggered by a constructive total loss, even though no notice of this loss was ever given. Indeed, Lord Wright seemed to come close to saying that abandonment itself was not necessary.

Certainly it is not required in the three instances of constructive total loss given in s.60(2). Although this provision reads as if it were composed simply of examples of the categories in the preceding subsection, the House of Lords in *Robertson* v. *Petros M. Nomikos* determined that the two parts of s.60 provided a composite definition of a constructive total loss. The three further instances are: where the assured is deprived of possession and (a) it is unlikely that he will recover it; or (b) the cost of recovering it would exceed the value of the goods when recovered; and (c) where the cost of repairing damage and forwarding the goods to their destination would exceed their value on arrival. Although, under (a) above, recovery must be unlikely rather than uncertain, no particular degree of unlikelihood is required. As Lord Wright points out in *Rickards* v. *Forestal* (1942) AC 50, although unlikelihood indicates that the chances are against an event occurring, even the slightest imbalance will suffice here.

5.14 Notice of abandonment

The principal difference between the two types of loss is that the assured must give a notice of abandonment if he wishes to claim for a constructive total loss. (No notice need be given, however, where it would be of no benefit to the insurer. An example is where there is no possibility of salvage.) Upon a valid abandonment, the insurer takes over the interest of the insured. The House of Lords determined in the *Forestal* case that the existence of a constructive total loss is to be ascertained at the date of issuing the writ in the action. A notice of abandonment can therefore be justified even if a constructive total loss could not be shown at the time the notice was given. If, however, a constructive total loss appears to have occurred at the time notice is given, a claim will succeed, even though a later change of circumstances takes the situation out of s.60. In *Smith* v. *Robertson* (1848) 2 Dow 474, for example, an insured vessel was captured. Notice of abandonment was given. The ship was later recaptured. The underwriters were nevertheless obliged to pay for a constructive total loss.

The general necessity of notice has been explained in several cases. In *Knight* v. *Faith* (1850) 15 QB 649 it was said to be to protect the insurer against the possibility of a fraudulent claim, and to enable the insurer to secure all remaining benefits attaching to the abandoned property. Notice need not be in any particular form provided it gives a clear indication of the intention to abandon. It must be given within a reasonable time of the assured becoming acquainted with the facts from which his claim arises, and in any event within a reasonable time of the claim arising. In *Fooks* v. *Smith* (1924) 30 Com Cas 97 notice was not given until seven years after the event. Although Bailhache J held that the claimant might have discovered the relevant facts earlier, he seems to have been of the clear opinion that the notice was too late, regardless of whether the facts were discoverable.

It is possible for a constructive total loss to become an actual total loss, in which case no notice of abandonment need be given. In *Fooks* v. *Smith* the plaintiff's goods were being carried on board an Austrian vessel. On the outbreak of the First World War this became an enemy ship. In anticipation of hostilities the Austrian government ordered the ship to a safe port. Some considerable time later the goods were sold. Bailhache J held that a constructive total loss (which the goods became when the ship was diverted, since their recovery was unlikely) could become an actual total loss, but had not done so in this instance. For this to happen, it was necessary that the actual total loss follow as an ordinary and natural consequence of the constructive total loss. In his opinion, the eventual sale of the plaintiff's goods was not the natural result of their initial seizure. The point will only be important, however, where the event causing the constructive loss is covered by the insurance and the event causing the actual loss is not, and the assured has failed to give notice in time.

5.15   Partial loss followed by total loss: the doctrine of merger

If loss or damage is suffered as a result of an insured peril, and the goods are then totally lost during the currency of the insurance through an uninsured peril, the assured will be unable to recover for the partial loss unless he has incurred expense in rectifying it. This result follows from the so-called doctrine of merger. It was fully considered by the House of Lords in *British & Foreign Insurance Co. Ltd* v. *Wilson Shipping Co. Ltd* (1921) 1 AC 188. A shipowner insured his vessel against marine risks only. The ship was chartered to the Admiralty during the First World War on terms which provided that the Admiralty would pay the owners the value of the vessel, should she be lost through war risks. The vessel was sunk by an enemy submarine at a time when she was worth £1770 less than her full value, owing to unrepaired sea damage. The Admiralty paid the owners the unrepaired value of the ship, as agreed, and the owners claimed the balance from their insurers. The House of Lords, reversing the Court of Appeal, ruled that the plaintiff had no claim. Their Lordships were clearly influenced by two principal considerations. The first was that the concept of indemnity, which is the basis of insurance law, should not be contravened. The assured should not recover more than the amount of his loss. Secondly, the extent of the insurer's liability should be determinable from the face of the policy, and not depend upon private arrangements made by the assured with third parties subsequent to the contract of insurance. The plaintiff suffered loss because he had not agreed with the Admiralty that they should pay him the value of the ship as at the commencement of the charter.

The doctrine of merger was traced to the decision of Lord Ellenborough in *Livie* v. *Anderson* (1810) 12 East 648. Here his Lordship said that 'where the property deteriorated is afterwards totally lost to the assured, and the previous deterioration becomes ultimately a matter of perfect indifference to his interests, he cannot make it a ground of claim upon the underwriters'. The Court of Appeal in *Wilson Shipping* had decided that on the present facts the original damage had not become a matter of indifference to the assured, and they could therefore recover for it. It was left to Lord Sumner to make it clear that Lord Ellenborough had not been distinguishing between two situations – in one of which the assured is not damnified by the earlier loss and in the other of which he is – but that in all cases the original partial loss inevitably becomes irrelevant.

5.16   *The doctrine of subrogation*

The fundamental principle of indemnity also finds expression in the doctrine of subrogation, which is set out in s.79 of the Act. This provides that, upon settling a claim, the insurer is subrogated to all the rights and remedies of the insured in respect of the subject matter. Cases decided both before and after the passing of the Marine Insurance Act 1906 have established the implications of this doctrine in some detail. The starting point is the decision of the Court of Appeal in *Castellain* v. *Preston* (1883) 11 QBD 380. This was described by Diplock J in *Yorkshire Insurance Co. Ltd* v. *Nisbet* (1962) 2 QB 330 as 'the *locus classicus* of subrogation in insurance'. *Castellain* v. *Preston* concerned fire insurance on real property, but its principles are of general relevance.

The defendant owners of property, which was insured against fire, contracted to sell it. Before the property was conveyed to the purchasers a building on it burnt down. The defendants' claim was met by their insurers. They then received the full purchase price for the property, to which they were entitled under the contract of sale. The insurers sought to recover a sum equivalent to the amount paid under the insurance. At first instance, Chitty J held that they could not do so. In his opinion, the doctrine of subrogation was confined to the enforcement of claims which the assured might have against third parties, or receipt of the proceeds of such enforcement. The Court of Appeal reversed this decision. Brett LJ stressed that subrogation 'is a doctrine in favour of the underwriters in order to prevent the assured from recovering more than a full indemnity'. He went on: 'in order to apply the doctrine of subrogation, it seems to me that the full and absolute meaning of the word must be used, that is to say, the insurer must be placed in the position of the assured . . . [T]he underwriter is entitled to the advantage of every right of the assured, whether such right consists in contract, fulfilled or unfulfilled, or in remedy for tort capable of being insisted on or already insisted on, or in any other right . . .'

One must be careful to keep this sweeping statement in context. It must not be separated from the underlying object of subrogation which, as we have seen, is to ensure that the assured receives a full indemnity, but no more. In other words, he must

not be overcompensated at the expense of the insurer for the loss
he has suffered. He is entitled to receive such sum as represents
the value of the property at the time of the loss. Insofar as he
has received, or can obtain, monies from sources other than the
insurer to reduce the loss, he must account for these sums to
the insurer. They serve to reduce the amount which he has lost.
If, however, the assured happens to receive or become entitled
to payments which do not represent the loss suffered or are not
intended to reduce that loss, he need not account to the insurer
for them.

In *Burnand* v. *Rodocanachi* (1882) 7 QBD 333 the defendants were
owners of property on board a ship sunk during the American
Civil War by the Confederate raider, *The Alabama*. The plaintiff
insurers paid out on a valued policy for the loss. Later the United
States Government made an *ex gratia* payment to the defendants
covering the amount by which the true value of the goods
exceeded their insured value. The plaintiffs claimed this amount
under the doctrine of subrogation. The House of Lords denied the
claim. Lord Blackburn pointed out that the gratuitous payment
was expressly confined to sums *not* covered by insurance, and
was therefore not paid with the purpose of reducing the insured
loss. Although Brett LJ took the view, in *Castellain* v. *Preston*, that
this decision turned on the fact that the payment was in the
nature of a gift, rather than something to which the defendants
were entitled, it is clear from Lord Blackburn's speech that it is the
purpose, and not the nature, of such payments which is decisive.
This is borne out by the decision of the Court of Appeal in *Stearns*
v. *Village Main Gold Mining Co.*(1905) 10 Com Cas 89, where the
Transvaal Government made a similar payment in respect of
property which they had expropriated. In this instance, however,
the object of the payment was to compensate the defendants for
the very loss to which their insurance related, and therefore
served to reduce the insured loss.

When the true function of subrogation is borne in mind,
it will be appreciated that the insurer does not simply step
into the assured's shoes, becoming entitled by virtue of having
paid a claim to everything the assured may receive or become
entitled to in respect of the insured property. In the light of this,
the insurer's claim in *Yorkshire Insurance Co.* v. *Nisbett Shipping
Co. Ltd* seems not only bold, but fundamentally misguided. Here
a ship insured by the plaintiff company had been sunk by the
tortious act of the Canadian Government. The plaintiffs paid out
the defendant owner's claim for a total loss. When, some years

later, the owner's action against the tortfeasor was successful, they received in damages an amount which (because of devaluation) greatly exceeded the sum paid under the insurance. The defendants repaid what they had received from the insurers. The insurers, however, claimed to be entitled to the windfall. Diplock J held that the doctrine of subrogation is simply a shorthand method of referring to those terms which must be implied into a contract of insurance in order to make it work as the parties intended. The learned judge decided that the only terms necessary were such as guaranteed that the assured did not recover from the insurer an amount greater than his actual loss. Here the insurers had been reimbursed all monies which they had paid out and their interest was consequently at an end.

Diplock J also pointed out that an insurer has no direct rights against third parties under the doctrine of subrogation. (Brett LJ's dictum in *Castellain* v. *Preston* would seem to suggest that he has.) This is borne out by the decision of the House of Lords in *Simpson* v. *Thomson* (1877) 3 App Cas 279, in which two ships of the same line collided and one was sunk. It was decided that the insurers of the lost vessel had no direct right of action against the owner of the other ship. Nor was there any action which the owner of the lost ship could take to protect the insurer's interests, since he could not sue himself.

It is, however, an implied term that the assured will take whatever action is within his power to reduce the loss. In *West of England Fire Insurance Co.* v. *Isaacs* (1897) 1 QB 226 the owners of property damaged in a fire were held liable to their insurers for failing to enforce a claim against a third party which would have reduced the loss. According to Diplock J in the *Nisbett* case, the assured is entitled to be indemnified by the insurer for any costs incurred in pursuing claims against third parties.

5.17   The suing and labouring clause

It remains to notice one final familiar provision in contracts of marine insurance. This is the so-called suing and labouring clause, which is referred to in the Institute Cargo Clauses as the 'Duty of Assured' clause. This entitles (and, indeed, requires) the assured to take such measures as are reasonable to safeguard or protect property from an insured peril, or to minimise loss following damage from an insured peril.

Until recently, there has been relatively little authority on the meaning and scope of the suing and labouring clause. However, the decision of the Court of Appeal in *Integrated Container Service Inc.* v. *British Traders Insurance Co. Ltd* (1984) 1 LlR 154 exposes and resolves several issues to which the clause can give rise. Owners of freight containers, insured under an all-risks policy, leased them to another firm for use in the Far East. The lessees went bankrupt, leaving the containers scattered throughout the region. The owners incurred expense in recovering them, including the payment of legal fees and sums to release some containers from third party liens. The insurers contended that they were not liable to reimburse this expenditure under the suing and labouring clause. Basing themselves on a dictum by Brett LJ in *Lohre* v. *Aitchison* (1878) 3 QBD 558, they alleged that the assured must show that the loss which the assured acted to avert would 'very probably' have occurred. The Court of Appeal rejected this contention. The assured's duty is to take reasonable steps to avert or minimise loss; there is no further requirement that the loss be shown to be 'very probable'.

The defendants also relied upon s.78(3) of the Marine Insurance Act 1906. This provides that 'expenses incurred for the purpose of averting or diminishing any loss not covered by the policy are not recoverable under the suing and labouring clause'. Eveleigh LJ seems to have interpreted this to mean that the assured can recover expenses reasonably incurred to avert a risk which, if it had occurred, would have given rise to a recoverable loss. The assured does not need to show that such a loss would in fact have occurred. The learned Lord Justice left open the question whether an assured can recover where the threatened loss is of a kind which the policy is designed to cover but which might or might not give rise to liability on the insurer in the particular circumstances. (It is difficult to make complete sense of this particular part of Eveleigh LJ's judgment since, as reported, it contains apparently contradictory statements, refers to irrelevant sections of the Act, and omits a vital negative from s.78(3).) Also left open was the question whether an assured can recover expenses incurred during the period of cover in order to avert losses which would only arise after cover had ceased. The better view would appear to be that he cannot. Dillon LJ was quite clear, however, that expenses incurred after the policy term had expired, in order to minimise losses which had occurred within it, were recoverable. Since the purpose of the suing and labouring clause is to protect the insurer's interest by averting or reducing his liability, it would seem to follow that expenditure is reasonable only to the extent that the assured takes steps to achieve this objective.

5.18 Assignment

In order for international trade to function efficiently, it is essential that policies of marine insurance be assignable. The cif contract, in particular, could not have evolved fully had assignment from seller to buyer not been possible. The present law is contained in s.50(1) of the Act, which provides that 'a policy of marine insurance is assignable unless it contains terms expressly prohibiting assignment. It may be assigned either before or after loss.' The loss, however, must occur while the policy is still current. *North of England Oil-Cake Co.* v. *The Archangel Maritime Insurance Co.* (1875) LR 10 QB 249 establishes that a policy can only be assigned at a time when the assignor still has an interest in the subject matter of the insurance. In this case linseed was sold under an arrival contract, and insured with the defendant for the benefit of the sellers and their assigns. The plaintiff buyers took delivery of the linseed into lighters, one of which sank. Some time later the sellers purported to assign the policy to the plaintiffs. Since both property and risk had passed to the buyers before the loss occurred the seller's interest in the linseed had ceased. It was decided that they could not make an effective assignment. To assign while still at risk themselves, however, would simply expose them to loss. The law therefore allows an effective assignment to take place after the assignor has lost his interest in the subject matter, if the assignment is in consequence of an agreement to assign made while his interest still subsisted. This rule is now encapsulated in s.51 of the Act.

The assignee may sue on the policy in his own name, but is subject to any defences which the insurer might have raised against the original party. In *Pickersgill* v. *London & Provincial Marine & General Insurance Co. Ltd* (1912) 3 KB 614 insurers were able to resist a claim on a policy assigned to the plaintiffs on the ground of non-disclosure of a material fact known to the original assured but not the assignees.

Chapter 6

Payment by Documentary Credit

6.01 Introduction

Paying for goods in international sales presents special problems for both buyer and seller. Under the Sale of Goods Act 1979 it is the duty of the seller to deliver the goods and the duty of the buyer to pay for them. These obligations are mutually dependent: in other words, each side must be ready and willing to perform at the same time. The simple paradigm of the seller handing over the goods with one hand while receiving cash payment with the other breaks down, however, when the parties are dealing at a distance. How can a simultaneous exchange be effected when buyer and seller are in different locations? The parties can provide for some alternative timing of performance, but the seller is unlikely to be willing to part with his goods without some security for payment and, by the same token, the buyer is unlikely to be willing to part with his money without some assurance that the goods are in his control. The party who performs without this assurance runs the risk of the other's insolvency, dishonesty, or simple bloody-mindedness. The problem is, furthermore, exacerbated in those frequent instances in which one or both parties is in fact *unable* to perform without the necessary assurance. The seller may be handicapped because he cannot produce or acquire the goods until sure of payment; the buyer because he may be unable to raise the price (from resale or a creditor) until he has the goods or is sure to receive them.

A partial solution to this dilemma was achieved when bills of lading were recognised as documents of title, thus giving their holder symbolic control over the goods. In particular, the holder has the ability to sell or raise money on the goods before they come into his actual possession. The classic statements of the duties of parties to a cif or fob contract, as found for example in *Ireland* v. *Livingston* or *Biddell Bros* v. *Horst*, or *Stach* v. *Baker Bosley*, require the seller to tender documents to the buyer and the buyer to pay cash in exchange. Even if the buyer is willing to pay cash, this method requires the presence of one party, or his agent, at the other's place of business. Today the large majority of transactions substitute for this classic method of performance the use of a banker's commercial (or documentary) credit. Of these transactions, the major proportion are, by the express agreement of the parties, made subject to the Uniform Customs and Practice for Documentary Credits, a set of rules and principles of good practice first promulgated by the International Chamber of Commerce in 1933, and most recently revised in 1983. Through the intervention of the international banking system the problems outlined above are to a large extent obviated.

6.02   Nature of a documentary credit

Basically a commercial credit (also known as a letter of credit) is a written undertaking, given by a buyer's bank to the seller, that it will pay him the price of the goods in exchange for the shipping documents. This promise is usually communicated to the seller through a bank in his own locality, and the credit can be enjoyed at that, or another, local bank. All major banks either have branches, or associates, in all major trading centres throughout the world. In addition, all major banks have an established network of relationships with local banks in most other cities throughout the trading world. These are known as correspondents. The setting up of a documentary credit between any two banks in any two locations is in general a very straightforward matter, and the documentary credit system has been rightly described by one judge (Kerr J in *Harbottle* v. *National Westminster Bank* (1978) QB 146) as the life-blood of international commerce.

As such it is vital that it should flow freely. The law regarding commercial credits has largely developed with a view that the financing transaction should be autonomous, and proceed according to its own terms and provisions, independently of the underlying contract of sale and any difficulties or disputes that might arise from it. This underlying tenet can be found in Articles 3 and 4 of the UCP, and is the first response in the international banker's catechism. If the documents are apparently in order, and the terms of the credit satisfied, the bank will pay.

6.03 Types of credit

The buyer's bank is known, for the purposes of a documentary credit, as the issuing or opening bank. It will usually designate its customer, on whose instructions the credit has been opened, as the credit applicant, and the party in whose favour the credit is opened as the beneficiary. If the services of a bank in the beneficiary's locality are engaged, this bank will be known generally as the correspondent bank, and specifically as the advising or confirming bank, depending on whether or not the local bank has added its own confirmation of the credit. British banks tend to advise exporters not to accept a credit from a foreign bank unless it is at least advised locally. In a more complex transaction, other banks may be involved, whose functions are to handle, or reimburse a bank which has handled, the seller's drafts – that is, commercial paper which he has presented for payment.

Credits may be revocable or irrevocable. Under the UCP a credit is deemed to be revocable unless the opposite is clearly indicated. A revocable credit is one which may be amended or withdrawn without notice to the beneficiary. Since such a credit offers a seller very little security it is rarely used in practice, except in cases where there is absolute confidence in the buyer. Since it imposes the least liability on the issuing bank, it is, however, the cheapest form of documentary credit to obtain.

An irrevocable credit commits the issuing bank contractually to the seller, and cannot be unilaterally amended or withdrawn. The credit may, in addition, be unconfirmed, or confirmed to the benficiary by a local bank. (Typically, but not necessarily, confirmation is given by the bank which advises him of the credit.) Confirmation commits the confirming bank contractually to the beneficiary. A local bank would be foolhardy to confirm a revocable credit, and in practice only irrevocable credits are confirmed. A confirmed irrevocable credit offers a seller maximum protection, since he has contractual rights against the issuing and the confirming bank, one of which will be in his own country. It is, in consequence, the most expensive. Again, in practice, it is less usual for confirmation to be required where the issuing bank is of major international standing.

6.04   Contracts generated by a documentary credit

An international sale of goods to be paid for through a confirmed, irrevocable credit involves contracts between: (a) the buyer and seller; (b) the issuing bank and the buyer; (c) the issuing bank and the seller; (d)the confirming bank and the seller; and (e) the issuing bank and the confirming bank. Generally speaking, there is no contract between the confirming bank and the buyer. Problems relating to the credit can arise in each of these contracts.

Although a confirmed irrevocable credit generates this web of contracts, the courts have so far been happy to fudge over the question of quite how the seller's relationship with either the issuing or confirming bank can be contractual at all, since it is far from clear just what consideration he provides in return for their undertaking to pay. The banker's commercial credit is in fact included by Lord Wilberforce, in *The Eurymedon*, in a list of relationships generally regarded as contractual but which, in his words, 'fit uneasily into the marked slots of offer, acceptance, and consideration'.

6.05   When does the bank become contractually bound to the seller?

Though the courts have proceeded on the assumption that the bank's undertaking is contractually binding, the question of when it becomes so has been the subject of judicial comment. Unfortunately, these observations are not consistent. On one view the credit becomes binding when the beneficiary acts on it. On another it is binding when notified to him. The lack of consistency (indeed, some comments seem to combine both views) is explained by the fact that in no case so far has it been necessary to give a precise answer to his question.

Thus, in *Urquhart Lindsay & Co. v. Eastern Bank* (1922) 1 KB 318, Rowlatt J said that 'upon the [sellers] acting upon the undertaking contained in this letter of credit consideration moved from the [sellers], which bound the [bank]'. Similarly, in *Dexter v. Schenker & Co.* (1923) 14 LlLR. 586, Greer J, following Rowlatt J, took the view that the credit became binding upon the bank when the seller, having received notice of the credit, forwarded the goods to the buyer. In *Benjamin on Sale* (3rd Edn, pp 2169 and 2234) this case is cited for the alternative proposition that the credit becomes binding as soon as the seller has notice of it. Although, it is submitted, this involves a misreading of Greer J's judgment, (which at more than one point seems to regard the fact that the sellers dispatched the goods in reliance on the credit as crucial), nevertheless this alternative analysis has been adopted in other cases. (It is regarded by the learned Editor of *Benjamin* as both the prevailing, and the preferable approach, despite the theoretical difficulty of showing consideration moving from the seller to the bank at that point.) In *Hamzeh Malas & Sons v. British Imex Industries Ltd* (1958) 2 QB 127, for example, Jenkins LJ regarded it as plain that 'the opening of a confirmed letter of credit constitutes a bargain between the banker and the vendor'. Once more, however, it would seem that the learned Editor of *Benjamin* misreads a later comment by Jenkins LJ, taking it for an explanation of why the contract comes into being at this point. Jenkins LJ noticed that 'an elaborate commercial system has been built up on the footing that banker's commercial credits are of this character'. However, it seems clear from the context that this observation was directed to the fact that credits are regarded as autonomous, and not to the question of when precisely the contract between banker and beneficiary comes into being.

In *Bunge Corp. v. Vegetable Vitamin Foods* (1985) 1 LlR 613, Neill J stated that 'a letter of credit does not become irrevocable until it has been communicated to the beneficiary'. It is clear from the context in which this remark was offered, however, that the learned judge was not concerned to identify the precise moment the contract is formed, but to refute the suggestion that it was in fact formed at a point prior to notification of the credit to the seller. At a theoretical level, it is difficult to see what reciprocal promise a seller makes to a bank, upon receipt of its contractual offer in the letter of credit, sufficient to constitute consideration, still less what communication of acceptance is made at that time. If, on the other hand, the letter of credit is regarded as the offer of a unilateral contract (for which no notification of acceptance is generally necessary) acceptance of which is constituted by shipping the goods and tendering the documents, familiar theoretical difficulties arise should the bank purport to withdraw its offer after the seller has begun, but before he has completed, performance of the requested acts. Furthermore, in performing these acts the seller is simply doing what he is bound to do under his contract with the buyer. Despite the decision of the Privy Council in *The Eurymedon*, the question whether such performance can constitute good consideration has yet to receive a satisfactory response.

6.06   *Problems relating to the credit in the contract of sale*

It is a condition of the contract of sale that the buyer ensures the opening of a credit, should the parties have agreed that payment shall be made by this means. In *A.E. Lindsay & Co. Ltd* v. *Cook* (1953) 1 LIR 328 English buyers contracted to purchase goods from Australian sellers, who nominated a little known local bank at which the credit should be made available. Although the buyers did their best to comply with this instruction, they were in the event unable to establish the credit before the goods were due to be shipped. Pilcher J, after a thorough review of the authorities, concluded that the buyer's obligation to open a credit, available for the seller's use before he parted with his goods, was a condition precedent to the seller's obligation to ship. It was not enough that the buyer had done his best. This view is also borne out by the judgment of Denning LJ in *Trans Trust SPRL* v. *Danubian Trading Co. Ltd* (1952) 2 QB 297. Denning LJ also pointed out, however, that the opening of the credit may be a condition precedent to the formation of the contract of sale itself: in other words, something which must be done before any contract comes about. In such a case (which, it is submitted, will be exceptional) there would appear to be no obligation on the buyer to open the credit at all.

The authorities referred to by Pilcher J in *Lindsay.* v. *Cooke* do not make clear precisely when the credit must be opened, because, once more, no case seems to have turned on this particular question. Dicta in *Pavia & Co. SPA* v. *Thurmann-Neilson* (1952) 2 QB 84 suggest that, if the contract is cif and provides for a shipment period, the credit must be opened by the beginning of that period. A similar rule for fob contracts was accepted by Diplock J in *Ian Stach* v. *Baker Bosley.* If the contract fixes a single date for shipment then, according to Denning LJ in *Plasticmoda Societa per Azioni* v. *Davidsons (Manchester) Ltd* (1952) 1 LIR 527, the credit must be opened within a reasonable time before that date. In *Garcia* v. *Page & Co. Ltd* (1936) 55 LILR 391 the contract called for credit to be opened immediately. Porter J held that 'the buyer must have such time as is needed by a person of reasonable diligence to get that credit established'.

A failure by the buyer to open the credit in time entitles the seller to cancel the contract of sale. It does not automatically entitle him to an extension of the shipment period, however, although he may agree to continue with the contract provided an extension is allowed: see *Tamari & Sons* v. *Colprogeca* (1969) 2 LIR 18. In *Trans*

Trust SPRL v. *Danubian Trading Co. Ltd* (1957) 2 QB 297 buyers of steel on a rising market failed to open the credit in time, as a result of which the sellers cancelled the contract and sought damages. They were middlemen who had themselves agreed to buy the steel from a third party. The buyers knew that the sellers could not obtain the goods from the third party unless the credit was provided. The Court of Appeal held that the buyers were entitled to recover their lost profit. Denning LJ distinguished a failure to open a credit from a failure to pay money. A confirmed credit is a chose in action of immediate benefit to the seller, even before he draws on it, since it can provide the guarantee of eventual payment which may enable him to obtain goods, or the finance with which to buy goods, and so fulfil his own obligations.

6.07 Doctrine of strict compliance

In *Bunge Corp.* v. *Vegetable Vitamin Foods* the letter of credit contained a number of provisions which were inconsistent with the terms of the contract. Neill J decided that these discrepancies were *de minimis* and did not constitute a breach by the buyer of the contract of sale, even though the seller would be entitled to reject the letter of credit as a defective performance of the bank's obligation to him. This requires further explanation. In the contract between the seller and the bank there is no room for the *de minimis* principle. All documents – both the letter of credit and the shipping documents – must conform exactly with contractual requirements. As between buyer and seller, however, trivial discrepancies can be discounted. The result is that the seller cannot cancel his contract with the buyer because of such deviations, but he may nevertheless reject the credit. If time remains, the buyer can provide an exactly conforming credit. Only if he fails to do so will he be in breach. Implicit in this analysis is the assumption that the buyer has the right to cure a defective tender, and only by recognising such a right can the position of the seller *vis-à-vis* the buyer and *vis-à-vis* the bank be harmonised.

In *Soproma SpA* v. *Marine & Animal By-Products Corp.* (1966) 1 LlR 367 McNair J took the matter a stage further. He suggested that a credit which called for documents additional to those required by the contract of sale (rather than containing provisions directly at odds with the contract of sale) could not be rejected, provided the additional requirements were fair and reasonable.

6.08 Waiver and variation

Despite discrepancies in the letter of credit, the seller may choose to overlook them and proceed with performance. Generally speaking, the seller in such a case will be deemed to have waived the breach, and will not be allowed to cancel the contract of sale without at least affording the buyer a reasonable opportunity to correct the discrepancies. A waiver does not, however, constitute a variation of the contract terms and if the buyer cannot eventually provide a conforming credit, having been given reasonable notice to do so, the seller will then be entitled to cancel the contract of sale. Both these points emerge in *Panoutsos* v. *Raymond Hadley Corp. of New York* (1917) 2 KB 473. Here a contract for the sale of four thousand tons of flour called for payment by confirmed credit. The credit which the buyer opened was unconfirmed, but the seller nevertheless proceeded to ship some of the flour. He then refused to ship the balance, without giving any notice to the buyer. The Court of Appeal held that the seller could reinstate the condition precedent that the credit be confirmed, but only upon giving reasonable notice.

In certain circumstances, however, a failure to insist upon strict compliance with the terms of the contract of sale regarding the letter of credit may amount to a variation of that contract, in which case the seller will be unable to call for the original provisions to be observed. Such a situation arose in *W.J. Alan & Co. Ltd* v. *El Nasr Export and Import Co.* (1972) 2 QB 189. In this case a contract for the sale of coffee called for a credit to be opened in Kenyan currency. The buyers in fact provided a credit in sterling, which the sellers drew on as payment for the initial shipments. Before payment was claimed for the final shipment, however, sterling was devalued. The sellers claimed to be entitled to an additional payment, to bring the amount up to the equivalent sum in Kenyan currency. The Court of Appeal held that the original contract had been varied, and sterling become the new currency of account. Variation comes about in the same manner as a contract is formed: in other words, by a fusion of offer, acceptance and consideration. Here the buyers offered to pay in sterling, the sellers accepted that offer by operating the credit, and each side provided consideration by giving up a right under the original contract – the right to pay, on the one hand, and the right to be paid, on the other, in Kenyan currency. Since Kenyan currency and sterling stood at par at the time of the variation, there was mutual benefit and detriment in the alteration of the currency of account.

Lord Denning MR, however, explained the outcome of this case in somewhat different terms. In his opinion, it provided an example of the operation of the doctrine of promissory estoppel. This is not the place for a detailed examination of that still controversial doctrine. Suffice it to say that, by a typically Denningesque sleight, cases involving the waiver of provisions relating to time of performance (which, once foregone, can obviously not be recovered) were herded together with cases involving non-contractual agreements to accept less than full payment, in a disingenuous attempt to demonstrate that the latter form of promise is as irrevocable as the former. No case has decided that a promise to accept less than one is owed is binding in the absence of consideration, and it is submitted that it was only the presence of consideration in the *El Nasr* case which prevented the seller from recovering the additional payment.

6.09   Residual liability of buyer

The question has also arisen whether the provision of a letter of credit displaces the buyer's obligation to pay the price. In other words, should the bank (or, in the case of a confirmed credit, the banks) fail to make payment, can the seller look to the buyer directly? The question was considered by Denning MR in *Alan* v. *El Nasr*. In his opinion, unless the contract of sale clearly provides otherwise, a letter of credit constitutes a conditional method of payment only, and the seller has recourse to the buyer in the event that the method miscarries. This presumption can be displaced by sufficient evidence that the seller has accepted the risk of the bank's failure. The fact that, contrary to usual practice, the seller has nominated the bank will be important, although not conclusive. This approach was endorsed by Ackner J in *Man Ltd* v. *Nigerian Sweets* (1977) 2 LIR 50 and in *Maran Road* v. *Austin Taylor* (1975) 1 LIR 156.

6.10   The contract between the buyer and the issuing bank

The applicant for credit may or may not already be a customer of the issuing bank. In either event, the agreement relating to the credit will form a separate contract, usually made subject to the UCP. The UCP, however, has no independent force under English law, and must therefore be specifically incorporated by the parties into their agreement. The UCP lays out the liabilities and responsibilities of customer and bank in some detail. Its precise provisions are beyond the scope of this work, but two basic features can be noted. First, as Articles 4 and 17 emphasise, the bank's business is with documents, not goods. Its central obligation is to take reasonable care in the examination of documents. Secondly (in accordance with the general principles of the law of agency) a bank is entitled to interpret ambiguous or unclear instructions in a reasonable way. The customer will be bound by this interpretaiton even though, when freed from the pressure of time under which banks must act, it may be possible to demonstrate that some other interpretation is preferable: see *Commercial Banking Co.* v. *Jalsard* (1973) AC 279.

6.11   *Restraining payment in cases of fraud*

If a bank is satisfied on reasonable grounds that the documents it has received from the seller are such that he is entitled to be paid, the buyer cannot prevent the bank from making payment, even though the goods themselves are below contract standard, or the contract of sale has been breached by the seller in some other way. Exceptionally, however, the issuing bank can be restrained by its customer from making payment where there has been fraud on the part of the seller. Because the integrity of the international banking system, and the free flow of finance which, through the documentary credit format, it guarantees, are of paramount importance to world trade, the customer will be allowed to interfere only in the most extreme and clear-cut cases. Before 1975 there was no English authority on this matter. Since then a series of cases, starting with *Discount Records Ltd* v. *Barclays Bank Ltd* (1975) WLR 315, has established the relevant principles. In *Discount Records* the plaintiffs purchased a quantity of records and cassettes from French sellers, and arranged for the defendant bank to issue a letter of credit. The goods turned out to be substantially defective. The plaintiffs sought an injunction to restrain the defendants from making payment, alleging that the French sellers were guilty of fraud. Megarry J dismissed the plaintiffs' motion, stating that he 'would be slow to interfere with banker's irrevocable credit . . . unless a sufficiently grave cause is shown'. The plaintiffs' interests were adequately protected by the availability of an action for breach of contract against the defendants, who had given the plaintiffs certain misleading information. As Megarry J pointed out, there was no question that the bank was not good for the money at issue.

In *RD Harbottle* v. *National Westminster Bank* (1978) QB 146, Kerr J expressed even greater reluctance to intervene between bank and seller, being prepared to do so 'possibly in clear cases of fraud'. In his view, banks must be allowed to honour their commitments, free from interference by the courts. 'Otherwise, trust in international commerce could be irreparably damaged.' In *Edward Owen Engineering Ltd* v. *Barclays Bank International Ltd* (1978) 1 All ER 976, the Court of Appeal admitted an exception to the general rule that the bank must pay if the documents are apparently in order where, to the knowledge of the bank, fraud has been clearly established. It is not enough that fraud is suspected or alleged. Browne LJ added the further qualification that the documents must be presented by the beneficiary himself. If they are presented by a party who is not tainted by the fraud, there should be no scope for interference with payment.

The risk to a bank's reputation and standing which interference with irrevocable credits represents was once more stressed by Sir John Donaldson MR in *Boliventer Oil SA* v. *Chase Manhattan Bank* (1984) 1 All ER 351. He also emphasised that evidence both of fraud and the bank's knowledge of it must be clear. In the light of these authorities (in none of which was an injunction issued) it cannot be emphasised too strongly that banks are totally unconcerned with disputes between buyer and seller, and that their contract with the buyer is independent of the contract of sale.

Perhaps the most extreme illustration of the sacrosanctity of documentary credits is provided by the decision of the House of Lords in *United City Merchants (Investments) Ltd* v. *Royal Bank of Canada* (1982) 2 All ER 720. In this case the shipment date on the bill of lading was falsely and fraudulently misstated by a shipping agent. The defendant bank, having discovered this fact, refused to pay under the letter of credit. The House of Lords ruled that the exception of fraud only applied where the party presenting the documents had himself been fraudulent, or was privy to the fraud. Lord Diplock, delivering a speech with which the rest of their Lordships agreed, was not even prepared to accept that a bank is entitled to reject a document which it knows to be a complete forgery (or a buyer enjoin them from accepting it) unless the forger himself were presenting it to the bank. Lord

Diplock pointed out that the bank's duty to its customer is to examine the documents with reasonable care in order to ascertain that they appear *on their face* to conform. As Article 17 of the UCP stipulates, the bank accepts no responsibility to its customer for the accuracy of the documents. There would appear to be some difference, however, between paying out on a forged document which is apparently genuine, and paying out on one which the bank knows to be false. In the former case, as *Gian Singh* v. *Banque de L'Indochine* (1974) 1 WLR 1234 demonstrates, the bank is entitled to debit its customer's account with the amount paid. The bank's position in the latter case remains to be determined, and it may be that the approach of Lord Diplock is too extreme.

6.12   *The contract between the seller and the issuing bank; the seller and the confirming bank*

As we have already seen, there is some doubt as to when the contract actually comes about, and what consideration the seller supplies. Nonetheless, the existence of the contract is one of the foundation stones of international trade, and it is inconceivable that any court would find, on purely theoretical grounds, that no such contract had been formed. According to Lord Diplock in *United City Merchants*, the bank's duty to the seller mirrors its duty to the buyer. In other words, it is bound to accept and pay against apparently conforming documents. As Article 6 of the UCP affirms, however, the seller cannot take advantage of the contract between the buyer and the bank. Hence the seller can only draw on the credit by providing the documents which the bank requires. The fact that the buyer has not stipulated for these documents in his contract with the bank is of no concern to the seller. The issuing bank's duty to the beneficiary is set out in Article 10(a) of the UCP. The duty of a confirming bank is precisely the same, and is to be found in Article 10(b). In *Forestal Mimosa Ltd* v. *Oriental Credit* (1986) 1 WLR 631, confirming bankers argued that their contractual duty only arose as and when bills of exchange drawn on the buyers were actually accepted by the buyers. The contract incorporated the UCP, which (by Article 10(b)(iii)) makes the confirming bank responsible for obtaining the acceptance of bills of exchange. The Court of Appeal rejected the bank's contention that other terms of the contract were inconsistent with this provision and that it therefore should be excluded. As Sir John Megaw pointed out, although the parties could, if they wished, allow a buyer to negate a credit, simply by refusing to accept a bill of exchange, such an arrangement would not be regarded by the commercial community as a confirmed irrevocable credit, for which the contract in this case called.

The fundamental principle that banks deal in documents, not goods, applies with equal rigour to the contract between the seller and the issuing bank or confirming bank. In *Urquhart Lindsay* v. *Eastern Bank* (1922) 1 KB 318 a confirming bank, on instructions from the buyer, refused to pay against conforming documents which included an invoice covering sums for which the buyers disputed liability. Rowlatt J held the bank to be in breach of their contract with the seller.

Banks are bound, under their respective contracts, to take up only those documents which correspond exactly with the terms of the contract. As Lord Sumner pointed out in *Equitable Trust Co. of New York* v. *Dawson* (1927) 27 LILR 49: 'there is no room for documents which are almost the same, or which will do just as well'. In this case it was decided that a confirming bank should have rejected documents which included an expert's certificate, when the credit called for certification by *experts*. Similarly, in *J.H. Rayner & Co.* v. *Hambros Bank Ltd* (1943) 1 KB 37, the Court of Appeal held that a bill of lading for machine-shelled ground nut kernels should have been rejected, when the credit called for a bill covering Coromandel groundnuts, even though it was accepted that the two commodities were regarded in the trade as identical. As McNair J points out in *Moralice (London) Ltd* v. *Man* (1954) 2 LIR 526, there is no room for the maxim *'de minimis non curat lex'* to apply here, and otherwise insignificant discrepancies will nevertheless justify – indeed, dictate – rejection.

In *Banque de l'Indochine* v. *J.H. Rayner* (1983) 1 All ER 1137 Kerr LJ referred to expert evidence which established that two-thirds of documents presented against letters of credit in London are defective in some respect. It would appear that the same statistic is also true for the rest of the country, and is an alarming indication of a lack of professionalism in commerce. In practice, however, banks do not invariably reject defective documents, but have available a number of practical responses designed to keep matters moving as far as is possible. They may, for example, seek the authority of the buyer to pay, despite the discrepancies. They may send the documents to the buyer on a collection basis, in other words, leaving the decision to pay or not to the buyer's bank after it has seen them. For relatively minor errors the bank may take an indemnity from the seller, to cover any loss to the bank should the buyer refuse the documents. Finally, the bank may pay the seller 'under reserve'. The implication of such a payment was considered by the Court of Appeal in the *J.H. Rayner* case. It was decided that a bank paying under reserve could insist upon repayment from the seller if the issuing bank in the event rejected the documents for at least one of the reasons for which the confirming bank had first queried them. It was not necessary to establish that the grounds of rejection were in fact valid.

6.13   The contract between the issuing bank and the confirming bank

In return for paying in accordance with the terms of the credit, the issuing bank undertakes to reimburse the correspondent bank. They will also pay a commission, which will be higher if the correspondent bank has added its confirmation to the credit.

6.14   The mechanics of a documentary credit

The dilemma outlined at the beginning of this chapter, in which a seller will be unwilling to release his goods unless paid (or at least assured of payment) while a buyer will be unwilling to pay unless in possession (or at least assured of it) is exacerbated by the fact that a buyer, typically, will wish to postpone payment until as late as possible, while a seller will wish to be paid at the earliest possible moment. The banker's documentary credit provides a seller with what Rowlatt J termed 'a responsible paymaster in [his own] country'. The system allows for actual payment to be made in a variety of ways. These are designed to meet the particular desires or requirements of the two parties to the contract of sale and, to a large extent, resolve the exacerbated international trade dilemma. Article 10 of the UCP refers to four methods of payment: sight payment; deferred payment; acceptance and payment at maturity; and negotiation. These terms require explanation.

Sight payment obliges the issuing or confirming bank to pay the full price as soon as the relevant documentation is delivered to the bank. The seller may draw a bill of exchange, payable by the bank on demand or 'at sight'. The nature and significance of bills of exchange are explained below.

Deferred payment obliges the bank to pay at a stipulated date in the future. Again, a bill of exchange drawn on the bank and payable at that later date (variously known as a time or tenor bill) may be employed.

The latter two methods of payment actually require, rather than allow, the use of bills of exchange. In the one case the bank undertakes to pay, or ensure the payment of, the bill when it becomes due; in the other case the bank agrees to pay the bill before maturity and (usually) to take the risk of it not being paid by the person on whom it is drawn when it falls due. (This is known as negotiation without recourse.) Naturally the bank will only agree to do this for less than the face value of the bill, the amount of the discount reflecting the degree of risk of non-payment as well as the length of time the bank will be out of its money. It is the negotiability of bills of exchange which allows a seller to receive immediate payment, and the buyer at the same time to defer paying until the bill falls due. This, above all, represents the genius of the bill of exchange.

6.15   Bills of exchange: definition and terminology

The law relating to bills of exchange is to be found in the Bills of Exchange Act 1882. According to s.3(1), a bill of exchange is 'an unconditional order in writing, addressed by one person to another, signed by the person giving it, requiring the person to whom it is addressed to pay on demand or at a fixed or determinable future time a sum certain in money to or to the order of a specified person, or to bearer.' A bill which is payable at a future time will first be presented to the person on whom it is drawn (the 'drawee') for acceptance. This is signified by the drawee's signature on the bill, with or without words of acceptance and with or without the introduction of qualifications or conditions. The drawee upon acceptance becomes known as the acceptor. The bill, unless it signifies that it is not transferable, can be negotiated, either before or after acceptance, by written endorsement (if the bill is an 'order' bill) or by delivery (if it is a 'bearer' bill). The person to whom the bill is negotiated will, under the Act, be either a holder, a holder for value, or a holder in due course. The significance of these different categories should emerge later. Bills of exchange have a much wider use than in international trade, and a highly complex body of case law has grown up around the detailed and extensive provisions of the Bills of Exchange Act. What follows is a necessarily brief examination of the leading cases, drawn so far as possible from international trade, which may serve to illustrate the types of situation which might be encountered by buyers, sellers or banks.

The attachment of any condition to the order, or requiring anything to be done in addition to the payment of money, prevents the document in which the order is given from being a bill of exchange. If the drawee is ordered to pay out of a particular fund or account the order is conditional. However, an indication which merely advises the drawee of a particular fund or account from which he can pay does not.

Nor, too, does a reference on the bill to the transaction to which it relates. Bills of exchange drawn to pay for goods commonly refer to the documentary credit from which they are to be paid. It has yet to be considered whether such a reference would prevent the seller's draft from being a bill of exchange. In *Guaranty Trust Co. of New York* v. *Hannay & Co.* (1918) 2 KB 623 it was contended that an indication on the face of a bill of the transaction to which it related imposed a condition that the bill would not be accepted unless conforming documents were presented with it. In this case forged bills of lading were tendered with the bill of exchange, indicating a sale of cotton. Buyers sought to recover the amount paid on the bill by their unsuspecting bankers. The Court of Appeal ruled that the bill was unconditional and that the bank had been correct to pay it. Scrutton LJ noted the difference between a condition of the contract of sale, and a condition on the bill itself. The mere fact that, under the contract, the buyer's obligation to pay was conditional upon genuine documents being tendered did not render a bill which referred to that contract conditional.

The same point is made by Megaw LJ in *Korea Exchange Bank* v. *Debenhams (Central Buying) Ltd* (1979) 1 LIR 548, where a bill was drawn using the familiar abbreviation 'D/A'. This signifies 'documents against acceptance', and means that the buyer is only to accept the bill if proper documents accompany it. It was not suggested that the presence of this notation made the bill conditional. Not all the words and expressions appearing on the face of a bill (which, paradoxically, includes its reverse side) are a part of the bill. It is a matter of construction which go to make up the bill, and which relate to the underlying transaction or other matters. In *Roberts* v. *Marsh* (1915) 1 KB 42, for example, a document on which a bill was written contained the phrase: 'to be retained'. The Court of Appeal ruled that this was merely a part of the agreement between the parties, and that the actual order to pay was unconditional.

If a bill is not payable on demand (which can be indicated by appropriate words, or simply by omitting any time for payment) then it must indicate the time for payment with sufficient certainty. According to s.11 of the Bills of Exchange Act 1882, this can include payment at a fixed time after the date of the bill, or after sight of it by the drawee. It can also include payment upon, or at a fixed time after, the happening of a specified event. Such event must, however, be certain to occur, even though the exact date of its occurrence may not be known. In the *Korea Exchange* case, the bill was expressed to be payable ninety days after acceptance. The Court of Appeal held that the time of payment was not 'fixed or determinable', as required by the definition of a bill of exchange in s.3(1), since acceptance of the bill was not certain to occur. Section 11 further provides that the actual happening of the contingent event does not cure this particular defect. Hence the bill did not become valid upon Debenham's acceptance of it.

6.16 The holder in due course

The principal practical importance of bills of exchange as a method of payment is that, generally speaking, they can be immediately turned to cash, even though not due to be paid until some time in the future. (Indeed, bills of exchange are frequently said to be the virtual equivalent of cash.) This is achieved by selling, or 'negotiating' the bill to a discount buyer. A party to whom a bill is negotiated becomes a holder of the bill. He will be a holder 'in due course' provided the additional requirements of s.29 are satisfied. The importance of this status is set out in s.38(2). Quite simply, the holder in due course 'holds the bill free from any defect of title of prior parties, as well as mere personal defences available to prior parties among themselves, and may enforce payment against all parties liable on the bill.' The parties liable on the bill are the acceptor, the drawer, and all previous endorsers of it.

The first requirement of s.29 is that the bill be 'complete and regular on the face of it'. In *Arab Bank Ltd v. Ross* (1952) 2 QB 216, Denning LJ said that a bill is regular if there is nothing on it to give rise to suspicion, and that it is essentially a question for the banking profession to decide what matters do give rise to doubt. The requirement is, however, one of superficial or apparent conformity. The fact that parts of the bill may be invalid – for example, a forged endorsement – does not prevent the bill being regular on its face, unless the invalidity is obvious. In *Barclays Bank Ltd* v. *Aschaffenburger Zellstoffewerke AG* (1967) 1 LlR 387 a seller's bank advanced approximately three-quarters of the amount of time bills, and the balance when the bills were paid by the buyers on maturity. The Court of Appeal held that the bank was a holder in due course as to three-quarters of the amount of the bill, and therefore to that extent held it free of a personal claim which the buyers had against the sellers.

The second requirement of a holder in due course, to be found in s.29(1)(a), is that the holder became such before the bill was overdue, and without notice that it had previously been dishonoured (i.e. not knowing that the drawee had refused to accept it) if such be the case. Finally, s.29(1)(b) requires that the holder take the bill in good faith, for value, and with no notice of any defect in the title of the person negotiating the bill to him.

Neither the original payee (i.e. the party in whose favour the bill is first drawn) nor the drawer of the bill (assuming that they are not the same) are holders in due course, since the definition in s.29 requires that the bill be negotiated. However, an original party to a bill may become a holder in due course if the bill is negotiated back to him after he had previously parted with it. Even if a party fails to satisfy the definition of a holder in due course, he may attract equivalent protection from s.29(3). This provides that any holder of the bill who derives his title through a holder in due course, and is not a party to any fraud or illegality affecting the bill, has the same rights as that holder in due course in regard to the acceptor of the bill and all parties to it who precede the holder in due course from whom title was derived.

This provision was applied by the Court of Appeal in *Jade International* v. *Robert Nicholas Ltd* (1978) 3 WLR 39. Plaintiff sellers of steel sued for the amount of a bill of exchange drawn on and accepted by the defendant buyers but dishonoured by them on the ground that the steel was substandard. The plaintiffs had negotiated the bill to a German bank, who had in turn negotiated it to the Midland Bank, who had presented it for payment. When it was dishonoured the Midland Bank recovered their money from the Germans under s.47(2), which gives a holder an immediate right of recourse against the drawer and any indorsers if the bill is dishonoured by non-payment. The German bank similarly recovered from the plaintiffs, to whom the bill was duly returned. The Court of Appeal held that, although the plaintiffs were not holders in due course (since they took the bill with notice that it had been dishonoured) they nevertheless had all the rights of a holder in due course against the acceptor, under s.29(3). They were thus immune from any personal defence which might have been raised against themselves as original parties to the bill.

6.17 Defences

Because bills of exchange are treated as the virtual equivalent of cash, the circumstances in which a defence to liability on the bill can be raised, even between original parties, are closely circumscribed. This was well explained by Lord Wilberforce in *Nova (Jersey) Knit v. Kammgarn Spinnerei* (1977) 1 WLR 713, where he pointed out that, unless the seller can treat a bill of exchange as a virtually guaranteed payment, he might just as well give the buyer credit. Lord Wilberforce was therefore only prepared to recognise defences based on fraud, the invalidity of the bill, total failure of consideration, or a partial failure in which the amount claimed or sought to be set off by the defendant is precisely ascertained. Though the occasional judge has jibbed at the apparent or potential harshness or injustice of this approach (see, for example, the brief comments of Harman LJ in *Brown, Shipley & Co. Ltd v. Alicia Hosiery Ltd* (1966) 1 LlR 668 at 669) it is justified by the pre-emptive demands of international commerce. The defendant, in most instances, must bring separate proceedings.

In cases of partial failure of consideration the court has a discretion whether or not to grant the defendant leave to defend the action on the bill. Because of the importance attached by the commercial community to the inviolability of bills of exchange, however, this discretion is rarely exercised in a defendant's favour. In *Cebora SNC v. SIP Industrial Producers Ltd* (1976) 1 LlR 271, Sir Eric Sachs warned against the dangers of looking sympathetically upon the claims of buyers who were refusing to meet their bills. The mere fact that the seller was a foreigner, and that enforcement of a judgment obtained against him in separate proceedings in this country might be difficult to achieve, will in all probability not be sufficient to persuade a court to exercise its discretion.

The fact that the foreign party would be unable to satisfy any such judgment might be a stronger ground. (The foreign party might, however, be restrained by injunction from removing the proceeds of any judgment obtained by him in an action on the bill, pending any separate action which the buyer might bring against him.) In *Saga Ltd v. Avalon Promotions Ltd* (1972) 2 All ER

545 the Court of Appeal granted leave to defend an action on an unpaid bill of exchange. The defendants had offered to pay the whole amount of the bill into court, and there was, in Salmon LJ's opinion, 'a very real issue' to be tried between the parties. In the *Cebora* case, however, a differently constituted Court of Appeal deprecated such leniency. In their view, the combination of payment into court and the existence of a viable counterclaim was not sufficient to displace the rule that bills of exchange must be honoured in full. A defendant will be no more successful in seeking a stay of execution of the judgment on the bill, pending trial of his counterclaim.

Chapter 7

Conflict of Laws Problems in International Trade

7.01 Introduction

In an international sale the transaction will, by definition, have contacts with more than one so-called law district (i.e. country, or part of a country, with its own laws and law enforcement). The parties themselves may be based in different law districts, and performance of the various contracts which make up an international sale may involve yet others. As a result, a party who is contemplating litigation is faced with two preliminary questions. First, in the courts of which law district can the action be brought? Secondly, what law will be applied by the court hearing the case to resolve the dispute (for the court will not necessarily apply its own domestic law)? Once litigation is begun or concluded, further problems might arise. A litigant suing in one law district may, for example, wish to have proceedings initiated by another party elsewhere stopped. Problems may arise concerning the enforcement in one law district of a judgment obtained in another. All these matters belong to that part of the law known as the conflict of laws or, alternatively (and erroneously) private international law. The rules and principles of the conflict of laws (which title derives from the fact that the laws of different law districts may give different answers to the same problem and hence be in conflict) are as much a part of English domestic law as all the other rules and principles which have been examined thus far in this book. Though some of them may have had their origin in international conventions, or have first been promulgated by international organisations, they owe their authority as law either to their incorporation in English legislation, or through acceptance in case law.

Basically, a conflict of laws issue arises whenever the situation out of which a dispute has arisen has contacts with more than one law district, as a result of which more than one set of laws might appear to be of relevance. It is the function of the conflict of laws to choose between the competing sets.

7.02   *The jurisdiction of English courts*

The jurisdiction of English courts over personal actions involving a foreign element varies according to whether or not the defendant is domiciled in a member state of the European Community. If he is, the Civil Jurisdiction and Judgments Act 1982 will apply. If he is not, the jurisdictional rules of the common law (to be found in the Rules of The Supreme Court, popularly known as the White Book) will operate.

7.03   *Jurisdiction over EC defendants*

The 1982 Act incorporates the 1968 Brussels Convention on civil jurisdiction and judgments, described elsewhere as 'the Communities' greatest achievement in the sphere of private international law to date' (see Lasok and Stone: *Conflict of laws in the European Community*). The Act came into force on 1 January 1987. It is detailed and complex, and a full exposition goes beyond the scope of this work. However, its basic provisions can be identified. Article 2 of the Convention (which forms an appendix to the Act) establishes the fundamental principle: 'subject to the provisions of the Convention, persons domiciled in a Contracting State [i.e. a Community member state] shall, whatever their nationality, be sued in the courts of that state'. Different law districts have different definitions of a person's domicile, and Article 52 provides that the court which is hearing a matter shall apply its own internal law to the question. English law has a particularly complex concept of domicile. However, for the purposes of the Act, this has been replaced by the provisions of s.41. Basically, by virtue of this section, a person is deemed to be domiciled in the law district of England and Wales if he is both resident there and has a substantial connection with it. A person who has been resident for three months is rebuttably presumed to have the necessary connection. According to Article 53, a company or other association has its domicile wherever it has its seat. This is a novel idea to English law, and is defined in s.42. This provides that a company or association has its seat in England and Wales if it is incorporated or formed under English law and has its official address there, or if its central management and control is in that law district.

The following Articles create exceptions or additions to the basic rule which are relevant to international trade. Under Article 5(1) a domiciliary of a contracting state may be sued in the courts of another contracting state 'in matters relating to a contract, in the courts for the place of performance of the obligation in question'. Under Article 5(3) he may be sued 'in matters relating to tort . . . in the courts for the place where the harmful event occurred'. This has been interpreted by the European Court in *G.J. Bier BV & Reinwater Foundation* v. *Mines de Potasse D'Alsace SA* (1976) ECR 1735 as giving the plaintiff the option to sue either in the courts of law district in which the defendant's actions took place, or where harm was suffered in consequence of them. Under Article 6(1) an EC domiciliary who is one of a number of defendants may be sued in the courts of the law district in which any one of them is domiciled. By Article 6(3) he may be sued on a counterclaim arising from the same contract or set of facts on which the original claim is based, in the court in which the original claim is pending. The Article does not provide what shall happen should the original claim be abandoned. Article 8 stipulates that an insurer, domiciled in a contracting state, may be sued in the courts of the law district in which the insured party is domiciled. All the above identify courts which may have jurisdiction in addition to the courts of the defendant's domicile. Article 17, on the other hand, grants exclusive jurisdiction to any court of a contracting state which the parties have agreed shall have it.

The Act has been in force for a relatively short time, and as yet has generated no case law. In the light of European experience, however, it seems inevitable that difficult problems of interpretation will come before the English courts in due course.

7.04   *Jurisdiction over other defendants*

By contrast, the jurisdictional grounds which apply outside the Act have given rise to a considerable number of decisions. According to Lord Diplock in *The Siskina (Cargo Owners)* v. *Distos SA; The Siskina* (1979) AC 210, 'the general rule is that the jurisdiction of the English court over persons is territorial. It is restricted to those upon whom process can be served within the territorial limits of England and Wales'. Although this is expressed in terms which suggest that jurisdiction is constrained, the general rule has in fact been liberally applied. In *Maharanee of Baroda* v. *Wildenstein* (1972) 2 QB 283, for example, the defendant was present from abroad for a day's visit to Ascot races, and was served with a writ on the racecourse itself. His temporary presence was held sufficient to give the High Court jurisdiction over him.

7.05 *Jurisdiction under RSC Order 11(1)*

The jurisdiction of the High Court is even wider than this. Under Order 11 Rule 1 of the Rules of the Supreme Court, the High Court has jurisdiction over overseas defendants in no less than seventeen separate instances. This jurisdiction, however, is discretionary, and the leave of the Court must be obtained before process can be served upon an overseas defendant. This leave will in practice be granted only in the most exceptional circumstances.

The instances which are of particular relevance to international trade are to be found in Order 11, Rule 1(a), (b), (c), (d), (e), and (f). According to (a) service abroad is permissible with leave if relief is sought against a person domiciled within the jurisdiction. The common law concept of domicile will apply here. According to this, a person is domiciled in the law district in which he makes his home indefinitely. If there is no such place, he will, generally speaking, take the domicile of his father. (b) confers discretionary jurisdiction if an injunction is sought ordering the defendant to do or refrain from doing anything within the law district itself. Under (c) it is available where the claim is brought against a person duly served (whether or not he be a domestic or overseas defendant) and an overseas party is a necessary or proper party to that action. (d) applies where the claim is brought to enforce, rescind, dissolve, annul, or otherwise affect a contract, or to recover damages or obtain other relief in respect of the breach of a contract, being in either case a contract which (i) was made within England or Wales, or (ii) was made by or through an agent trading or residing within England or Wales on behalf of a principal trading or residing elsewhere, or (iii) is, by its terms, governed by English law, or (iv) contains a term to the effect that the High Court shall have jurisdiction to hear and determine any action in respect of the contract. Under (e) there is discretionary jurisdiction if the claim is brought in respect of a breach committed within England or Wales of a contract wherever made. It is immaterial that the breach was accompanied or preceded by a breach committed elsewhere which made it impossible to carry out that part of the contract which ought to have been performed in England or Wales. Finally, under (f) there is discretionary jurisdiction if the claim is founded on a tort and the damage was sustained or resulted from an act committed in England or Wales.

7.06   Exercising the discretion

In exercising its discretion under Order 11 the court must decide two questions. First, does the case fall within one of the listed exceptions to the general rule? Second, is the case an appropriate one in which to assume jurisdiction? These two requirements will now be briefly examined.

Order 11, Rule 1(a): This ground appears to overlap with the basic jurisdictional rule of the Civil Jurisdiction and Judgments Act 1982, where the plaintiff has a *right* to serve process on an English domiciliary. However, the discretionary rule, and not the mandatory one, will apply, by virtue of Order 11, Rule 1(2)(a), when proceedings arising out of the same cause of action are already pending in another Community law district.

Order 11, Rule 1(b): In *The Siskina*, cargo owners sought a *Mareva* injunction to prevent a foreign shipowner from removing insurance monies out of England and Wales. The House of Lords ruled that an injunction could issue under this sub-rule only where a violation of the plaintiff's rights within the law district was threatened. Here the plaintiffs had no proprietary claim to the insurance monies. They sought to restrain the defendant's removal of them only in order to ensure that a claim for breach of contract, over which the English court had no jurisdiction would, if successful, be satisfied. If the plaintiff's rights within the law district are threatened, however, an injunction can issue under this heading even though, paradoxically, the court would have no jurisdiction over an actual infringement. In *James North Ltd* v. *North Cape Ltd* (1984) 1 WLR 1428 the Court of Appeal held that an injunction could be issued against a Scottish defendant to restrain threatened breaches of contract in England, even though at that time the Order 11 sub-rule relating to breaches of contract within England and Wales did not extend to Scottish defendants.

In *Castanho* v. *Brown & Root* (1980) 3 WLR 991, Lord Wilberforce, in a speech with which the rest of the House of Lords expressed agreement, approved the judgment of Megaw J in *The Tropaioforos* (1962) 1 LlR 410 to the effect that the Court could issue an injunction restraining a foreign defendant who had been a party to English proceedings which had now ended, from taking proceedings abroad. In Megaw J's opinion, it is a question of fact whether sufficient connection exists between the foreign litigant and this country to justify the granting of an injunction. Lord Wilberforce's subsequent comments, in *Amin Rashid Corp.* v. *Kuwait Insurance* (1983) 3 WLR 241, that cases relating to Order 11 and those concerned with the enjoining of foreign proceedings proceed on different principles were not directed to the question of whether an injunction *can* be issued, but whether it *should*.

Order 11, Rule 1(c): A foreign defendant can be brought within the jurisdiction by being made a party to an action against a defendant who has already been properly served, provided the action against the first defendant has a reasonable prospect of success. In other words, a plaintiff cannot use the claim against the first defendant merely as a bridge to reach the second: see *The Brabo* (1949) AC 326.

Order 11, Rule 1(d) and (e): There is jurisdiction if the contract in issue was made in England or Wales. In determining where a contract is made for jurisdictional purposes the courts have invariably applied the principles of English domestic law, without considering that the contract might be subject to a foreign law of contract, whose rules regarding formation are different. Hence, in *Entores* v. *Miles Far Eastern Corporation* (1955) 2 QB 327 plaintiffs in London made an offer by telex to defendants in Holland. The offer was accepted by the same means. The Court of Appeal held that a contract formed using an instantaneous form of communication is made where the acceptance is received. The rule relating to contracts made by post – that the contract comes into being when and where the letter of acceptance is posted – was held inappropriate. No consideration was given to the possibility that the contract may have been subject to Dutch law (or the law of a third law district) under which telex contracts are made where acceptance is transmitted. Many foreign law districts do not follow our postal rule, but hold a contract formed by post when and where the letter of acceptance is received. Whether such an alternative approach would be regarded as relevant, should a jurisdictional issue arise in relation to a postal contract, remains to be seen.

The rule in *Entores* was approved by the House of Lords in *Brinkibon Ltd* v. *Stahag Stahl* (1983) 2 AC 34, where it was noted that exceptions might exist (and thus the postal rule would apply) if the parties are not in fact in instantaneous communication, although using machines such as telex or the telephone. This might occur where, for example, the parties are in different time zones, and a telex or a telephone message is received and recorded out of office hours, but not actually read or played back for some further period of time.

A contract is still regarded as having been made in a particular law district, despite the fact that amendments to it have been made elsewhere, unless the amendments in effect amount to a new contract: see *BP Exploration Co. (Libya) Ltd* v. *Hunt* (1976) 3 All ER 879. (The question whether a contract is governed by English law is considered below, [7.08]–[7.11].)

In *Cordova Land Co. Ltd* v. *Victor Bros Inc.* (1964) 1 WLR 793, buyers of animal skins cif Hull sought leave to serve the American sellers out of the jurisdiction on the ground that a breach had been committed within it when the skins arrived at Hull in a damaged condition. Winn J refused to hold that there was a warranty that the goods on arrival would be of the contract description and quality. If the implied condition of merchantability in a cif contract includes an undertaking that the goods are fit to withstand a normal voyage and, in addition, will remain merchantable for a reasonable time after arrival, this condition is nonetheless broken when and where sub-standard goods are loaded on board. Their arrival in a defective state is merely evidence of the earlier breach.

Sub-rule (e) was amended following the decision of the House of Lords in *Johnson* v. *Taylor* (1920) AC 144. Here English buyers purchased pig iron from Swedish sellers on cif terms. The sellers failed to ship the goods. This, it was eventually conceded, constituted a breach outside the jurisdiction, since the cif seller is not obliged to ensure ·. delivery at destination. The buyers, however, contended that a breach within the jurisdiction had been committed, by the failure of the sellers to tender contract documents in England. The House of Lords held that it must look to the substantial breach, and not breaches consequent upon it, in determining jurisdiction. Now any local breach, whether or not consequent upon an external breach, will suffice to found jurisdiction.

The latest form of Order 11(1)(f) avoids a problem of inter-pretation which had divided courts when faced with an earlier version. This extended jurisdiction to actions 'founded on a tort committed within the jurisdiction'. The difficulty was to deter-mine where a tort had been committed, when the defendant's behaviour had occurred in one place, but the harmful conse-quences of it were suffered in another. Jurisdiction now clearly exists if either event occurs within England or Wales.

Even if a litigant can bring himself within one of the sub-rules of Order 11(1), the courts have repeatedly made it clear that the discretion to grant leave must be exercised with great caution and circumspection. The reasons for this are two-fold. First, Order 11 jurisdiction goes beyond that which English law concedes to the courts of other law districts. In other words, a judgment of a foreign court based upon an equivalent jurisdictional ground to those in Order 11(1) would not necessarily be recognised in England and Wales. Second, the courts must be constantly alert to prevent so-called forum-shopping, in which a litigant brings an action in a particular law district simply because it will regard his cause of action more favourably.

In *Spiliada Maritime Corp.* v. *Cansulex; The Spiliada* (1986) 3 WLR 971, Lord Goff delivered a speech (regarded by his brother judge, Lord Templeman, as definitive) in which the relevant principles are analysed. The rest of the House of Lords agreed with it. Nevertheless, ironically, these principles are perhaps best summarised in the brief concurring speech of Lord Templeman himself. His Lordship noted three salient matters. First, the plaintiff must satisfy the court that it is the most appropriate forum in which to try the action. Second, the circumstances which may be taken into account in deciding to hear a case 'are legion'. Third, regardless of the above, the court will hear a case where the plaintiff could not obtain justice elsewhere. The self-same principles will be applied in determining whether or not an action begun in England and Wales as of right should be stayed in favour of foreign proceedings.

7.07   Admiralty jurisdiction

By virtue of s.20(2)(g) of the Supreme Court Act 1980, the Admiralty Court has jurisdiction over ships in territorial waters, in regard to 'any claim for loss or damage to goods carried in a ship'. In pursuance of this jurisdiction either the carrying ship or a sister vessel (i.e. one in the same ownership) can be arrested. In *The Hollandia* (1982) 3 All ER 1141, cargo owners sued in respect of damage caused to their goods while being carried from Scotland to the Dutch Antilles. The bill of lading provided that the contract of carriage should be subject to Dutch law, and that the Court of Amsterdam should have exclusive jurisdiction. The House of Lords nevertheless held that, since the Carriage of Goods by Sea Act 1971 had mandatory force and applied to the voyage, the forum selection clause was void under Article III(8) of the Hague–Visby Rules. This invalidates attempts to limit the carrier's liability below the level set by the Rules. Dutch law, at the time, applied the Hague, not Hague–Visby Rules. Under the Hague Rules the carriers' liability was lower than under Hague–Visby. Though an English court will normally stay an action brought in violation of an agreement that the courts of another law district shall have exclusive jurisdiction, it is not bound to do so. In *The Hollandia*, the very agreement itself was ineffective.

By contrast, the Court of Appeal in *The Benarty* (1984) 3 All ER 961 stayed an action in which the facts were superficially similar to those in *The Hollandia*. The limit to the defendant's liability here flowed from a provision of the Indonesian Commercial Code entitling carriers to quantify liability by reference to the tonnage of the carrying ship. Article VIII of the Hague–Visby Rules allows such limitations, by way of exception to Article III(8).

7.08 The law or laws which determine international contractual disputes

By reference to which law or laws are contractual disputes determined? Any discussion of this question must begin with the judgment of the Privy Council, delivered by Lord Wright, in *Vita Food Products Inc.* v. *Unus Shipping Co. Ltd* (1939) AC 277. Goods were carried from Newfoundland to New York on board the defendant's vessel. The contract of carriage contained a provision that it was to be governed by English law. Owing to the master's negligence, the goods were damaged in transit. Both the bill of lading, and the Hague Rules, which were in force in Newfoundland and in England, exempted the carrier from liability. Nevertheless, the goods owner claimed damages. He alleged that the contract of carriage was void for illegality, since the bill of lading did not contain an express statement that it was issued subject to the Rules, as required by Newfoundland law. Since the defendant had actually transported the goods, however, he must have done so as a common carrier, whose liability to care for the goods in his charge is strict.

The claim failed. The Privy Council ruled that the parties had, in effect, contracted out of Newfoundland law by choosing English law to regulate their contract. Since at that time the Hague Rules were applied by English law only to voyages from English ports, the parties, by their choice of law, had totally removed themselves from the reach of the Rules. As *The Hollandia* demonstrates, this can no longer happen, since the applicability of the Rules has widened and, being given the force of law, they have pre-emptive effect over any choice of law which the parties might make.

The abiding importance of the *Vita Foods* case, however, lies in the statement of principle by Lord Wright regarding the so-called proper law of a contract. This statement has three elements. First, parties to a contract are free to choose whatever law they wish to govern their contract. Second, it is not necessary that the chosen law have any connection with the contract, its performance, or the parties themselves. In *Vita Foods*, the parties were not English, the contract was not made in England, nor was it to be performed there. Nevertheless, the choice of English law was a valid one. Third, the only limits to this freedom of choice are that 'the intention expressed is *bona fide* and legal, and . . . there is no reason for avoiding the choice on the ground of public policy'.

This statement of principle has been consistently adopted and applied by English courts. (The comment by Lord Diplock, in *The Hollandia*, that an express choice of the proper law is 'one, but by no means the only matter to be taken into consideration', must be read in the particular context of that case, in which the choice of Dutch law was negated by an overriding provision of an English statute. Judgments by Lord Diplock in other cases, both before and after *The Hollandia*, would seem to establish that he did not demur from the *Vita Foods* principle.)

Nevertheless, *Vita Foods* leaves several important questions regarding the proper law of a contract unanswered. The first concerns the position when the parties fail to exercise the option to choose. As Lord Diplock pointed out in *Compagnie D'Armement Maritime SA* v. *Compagnie Tunisienne de Navigation* (1971) AC 572, the parties have a liberty to choose, not a compulsion. What law applies in default of choice? Secondly, does the proper law, however ascertained, regulate all possible issues under a contract, or are certain of them determined by a different system? Finally, what is the scope of the qualifications to the freedom of choice to which Lord Wright draws our attention?

7.09 *Where no express choice is made*

If the parties have failed to make an express choice of the proper law, it may nevertheless be the case that they have made an implied one. It would be unusual (not to say positively eccentric) for English parties dealing in English goods in an English location – for example, buying a pint of beer in a public house – to specify that the contract is subject to English law. It would be equally eccentric were the customer not English. An international contract might have such a preponderant connection with a particular law district that the proper law of the contract goes without saying.

In cases where the points of contact are spread more evenly among two or more law districts it may not be so straightforward. To suppose, as some authorities do, that we are still embarked upon a search for the parties' implied choice – their implicit agreement about the law to regulate their contract, even though it may be apparent that their individual interests are best served by different laws – is to indulge in a somewhat artificial exercise. The alternative approach is to apply criteria which have nothing to do with the supposed intentions of the parties. This approach, though it is an incursion into the conceit that a contract is a manifestation of the parties' intentions, is more realistic. Whether any practical difference flows from the adoption of one or other of these methods is itself a matter of controversy.

7.10 *Implied intention or weighing of circumstances?*

In *Miller* v. *Whitworth Street Estates Ltd* (1970) AC 583, a contract between an English and a Scottish firm, to be carried out in Scotland, was held by the House of Lords to be subject to English law. The contract was made on an English standard form, the use of which was regarded as an implied choice of English law. Had the court not been seeking the supposed common intention of the parties, it would seem that greater weight would have been given to the practical, rather than the legalistic aspects of the agreement. In that event Scottish law, as the law of the place of performance, might have been recognised as the proper law.

In the *Tunisienne* case, decided a short time later, the House of Lords again faced the question of how the proper law of a contract should be determined. Here a contract made in France between French carriers and Tunisian oil producers provided for the carriage of oil between Tunisian ports over a fixed period. A standard English contract was used, with additional clauses typed in French. One of these provided that the oil was to be carried in ships owned, chartered or controlled by the French firm. Clause thirteen of the standard form stipulated that the contract should be governed by the law of the flag of the carrying ship. In the event six vessels were employed, flying different flags. A bare majority of the House of Lords decided that clause thirteen constituted an express choice of French law as the proper law of the contract. In their opinion, clause thirteen, read in conjunction with the clause stipulating for French ownership, chartering or control, when generously construed, indicated an intention to nominate French law.

Lord Reid, dissenting, took the view that the search for the proper law should be divorced from the parties' intention, since they had failed successfully to express it. It therefore required the court to determine with what country or system of law the contract had the closest connection, by weighing out the various relevant contacts with the competing systems. Lord Wilberforce, also dissenting, accepted the formulation in Dicey and Morris, *Conflict of Laws*, 8th Edition, that the proper law is, in the absence of express choice, to be found from all the circumstances of the case. He seems, however, to have doubted whether, as Dicey and Morris suggest, such an inquiry is a matter of seeking an inferred intention.

The parties had included in their contract a clause referring disputes to arbitration in London. The Court of Appeal, applying the maxim *'qui elegit iudicem elegit ius'* ('a choice of judge is a choice of that judge's law) had decided that it gave rise to an irrebuttable presumption that the parties intended English law to govern their contract. The House of Lords ruled that an arbitration, or forum selection clause is simply one indication (albeit a strong one) of intention. Lord Diplock, however, went so far as to say that such clauses should be regarded as a choice of proper law unless there were compelling reasons to the contrary.

7.11   The Bonython approach

Perhaps the most well-known definition of the proper law of a contract is that given by Lord Simonds in *Bonython* v. *Commonwealth of Australia* (1951) AC 201. It is, he said, 'the system of law by reference to which the contract is made, or that with which the transaction has its closest and most real connection'. Perhaps the most useful exposition of this formula is given by Megaw LJ in *Coast Lines Ltd* v. *Hudig & Veder Chartering NV* (1972) 2 QB 34. In this case English shipowners chartered their vessel to Dutch charterers on terms which exempted the owners from liability for damage to goods carried in the ship. The master issued bills of lading to goods owners, on behalf of the shipowners, on terms which made the shipowners liable for want of due diligence. The cargo was damaged by want of due diligence during the voyage. The shipowners, having admitted liability under the bills of lading, sought an indemnity from the charterers.

Under Dutch law no such indemnity could be claimed. Under English law it could. The Court of Appeal held that the proper law of the contract was English law. Lord Denning MR, having stated that the parties themselves had given no thought to the matter, nevertheless placed great emphasis on the fact that the shipowner's exemption was valid under one system but not the other. The Dutch charterers, on an objective view, must, in his opinion, have intended to be bound by all the terms of their agreement and so to have intended English law – the system under which all terms were valid – to apply.

Megaw LJ indicated that the *Bonython* formulation involves a three-stage inquiry. If, first of all, the parties have made an express choice, effect will, generally speaking, be given to it. So too, secondly, will effect be given to an implied choice. In both these instances the contract will have been made with reference to a particular system of law, within the first part of the *Bonython* definition. If no choice has been made, however, the third stage is reached, and a court must examine all the circumstances and decide on balance with which system the *transaction* is most closely connected. At this stage emphasis falls upon what is actually to be done under the contract. Matters relating to performance assume importance over matters of form or legal interpretation. In Megaw LJ's opinion, once the third stage is reached, no especial weight should be given to the fact that a provision is valid under one system but not the other.

204

Although no particular factor (apart, perhaps, from an arbitration or forum selection clause) will assume preponderant importance, the nature and circumstances of the individual contract will generally indicate which elements of it deserve emphasis. In shipping cases, the flag of the carrying ship will often be decisive, if only by default. Indeed, in the *Hudig & Veder* case, the Court of Appeal, having been seduced by its own balancing-of-factors metaphor into deciding that the various relevant factors weighed out evenly between English and Dutch law, gave double weight to the flag. Its importance was also stressed by an earlier Court of Appeal in *The Assunzione* (1954) P 150. Here the form and place of payment, and the fact that a government was a party to the contract, were also singled out as circumstances of particular importance.

It can be seen from this brief glance at the leading cases that the determination of the proper law of a contract is a matter fraught with both conceptual and practical difficulty. In view of this, perhaps the best general assistance can be found in the words of Bowen LJ in *Jacobs* v. *Credit Lyonnais* (1884) 12 QBD 589, which were quoted with approval by Lord Wilberforce in the *Tunisienne* case. 'The only certain guidance', said Bowen LJ, 'is to be found in applying sound ideas of business, convenience, and sense to the language of the contract'; and, it might be added, to the surrounding circumstances in which the contract was made. As Bowen LJ also observed in the same case: 'there can be no hard and fast rule by which to construe the multiform commercial agreements with which in modern times we have to deal'.

7.12 Contractual issues not determined by the proper law

The next question to consider is whether the proper law regulates all issues which might arise out of an international contract. The answer is almost certainly no, although the question has never actually arisen for direct decision. In the *Tunisienne* case, Lord Diplock confined the proper law to 'the interpretation and validity of the contract and the mode of performance and the consequences of breaches of the contract'. While the *continued* validity of an initially valid contract might well be an appropriate subject for the proper law as chosen by the parties, it is less easy to concede that its original status should be determined by the law which the parties have, or are deemed to have, selected. That choice is effective only on the assumption that the contract itself is effective: deciding the one by reference to the other smacks of proving a matter by reference to itself.

Just what law should determine questions relating to the initial validity of a contract is not clear. One possibility is that it should be the law which has the closest connection with the particular issue, choice of law provisions apart. Hence, if the issue is, for example, whether one party has capacity to contract, it may be resolved by reference to the law of that party's domicile, place of business, or of the place where he is called upon to perform, depending on the precise nature of the contract in question. But in any event, it is difficult to imagine that a party can confer capacity upon himself simply by choosing as the proper law a system under which he has capacity.

7.13 Illegality

One of the most difficult and controversial subjects in this area of the conflict of laws relates to illegality and its effects. A transaction may be illegal under English law, under the proper law of the contract, or under the law of the place where the transaction is carried out. The illegality may, furthermore, relate to the contract itself, or to something or someone associated with the contract but not directly involved in it. Though some leading cases contain wide dicta concerning the nature and effects of illegality, there are relatively few decisions in which the question has been directly raised.

A useful starting point for a consideration of this subject is the judgment of the Court of Appeal in *Ralli Bros* v. *Compania Naviera Sota* (1920) 2 KB 287. Here an English firm chartered a Spanish vessel to carry a cargo of jute from Calcutta to Barcelona at an agreed rate of freight. Half the freight was to be paid upon arrival of the ship in Spain. Before this occurred, a Spanish decree fixed the rate of freights payable in Spain at a ceiling lower than the sum specified in the contract. The Spanish owners sought to recover the full amount. It was decided that they could not do so. A contract which has become illegal by the law of the place of performance is no longer binding. Scrutton LJ ascribed this rule to an implied term in the contract itself.

Although the rule is stated as one of general application, it should be noted that the proper law of the contract in *Ralli*

Bros, and in later decisions applying the rule, was English. Commentators have questioned whether the rule should apply when the proper law is that of another law district. Dicta in subsequent cases, notably the decision of the House of Lords in *Reggazoni* v. *Sethia* (1958) AC 301, suggest that the rule will still operate. Its basis is properly put, not on an implied term (since the implication of terms is a matter for the proper law) but on grounds of public policy. English courts will not enforce a contract if to do so would involve the violation of laws of a friendly foreign state. As a comcomitant to this, neither will they grant a remedy for failure to perform a contract, if performance would involve such violation.

It is quite a different matter to decide whether or not performance would involve this, however. The proper law of the contract may, for example, provide that payment must be made elsewhere, if it can no longer legally be made in the first named law district. Recourse to the proper law in order to determine whether or not enforcement of an illegal act is being sought is entirely appropriate.

A rather different, and more difficult, question arises when performance of the contract itself is not illegal, but some related transaction or event is. Suppose, for example, that goods are sold which, to the seller's knowledge, the buyer intends to smuggle into a friendly state. Would an English court enforce the contract of sale or give a remedy for its non-performance? In *Foster* v. *Driscoll* (1929) 1 KB 470, whisky was sold in England with the object that it should be smuggled into the United States during prohibition. The Court of Appeal held that a contract of sale is illegal when the seller participates in the illegal use of the goods, but not when he merely knows that the buyer intends an illegal use. This decision ignores the judgment of the Court of Exchequer in *Pearce* v. *Brooks* (1866) LR 1 Ex 213, where it was decided that knowledge of illegal intent rendered a contract of hire-purchase itself illegal.

7.14 The doctrine of 'taint'

Foster v. *Driscoll* was in turn overlooked by Staughton J in his extensive and profound review of the conflicts principles of illegality in *Euro-Diam Ltd* v. *Bathurst* (1987) 2 WLR 1368. An English contract of insurance was taken out on jewels, which were subsequently the subject of illegal dealings in West Germany. The insurers refused to meet a claim when some of these jewels were stolen. The learned judge drew upon the judgment of Diplock LJ in *Mackender* v. *Feldia* (1967) 2 QB 590. There the law of illegality was summarised under three heads. According to Diplock LJ, English courts will not enforce a contract (a) if it is contrary to English law; (b) if it is illegal under its proper law; and (c) to the extent that performance is illegal in the place of performance. Staughton J offered a modest criticism of the first category: a foreign contract which is valid by its proper law and by the law of the place of performance will sometimes be enforceable in England, even though in some respect contrary to English law. This will be the case where, for example, there is no consideration given for the defendant's promise, but the proper law imposes no such requirement (see, for example, *Re Bonacina* (1912) 2 Ch 394). However, although Diplock LJ's dictum, taken out of context, is clearly too wide, it would seem that he was in fact referring to contracts which were not merely void under English law, but were actually illegal, or, if it is preferred, contrary to English public policy.

The contract in *Euro-Diam Ltd* v. *Bathurst* was fully valid under all three heads. However, a related transaction – the disposition of jewels in West Germany – was illegal by the law of the place where it occurred. Staughton J held that the principal contract – here, the contract of insurance – will be tainted by this illegality, and consequently unenforceable in an English court, in two instances. The first derives from the case of *Bowmakers Ltd* v. *Barnet Instruments Ltd* (1945) KB 65. A plaintiff will fail if he needs to plead or prove illegal conduct in order to establish his claim. For example, a buyer may purchase goods in order to sell them abroad. If the resale is illegal, and the buyer needs to refer to it in order to quantify his damages in an action against the seller, his claim will fail (cf *Marles* v. *Philip Trant & Sons Ltd* (1954) 1 QB 29).

The second instance of taint derives from the case of *Beresford* v. *Royal Insurance Co. Ltd* (1938) AC 586. This arises when a claim is so closely associated with the proceeds of crime as to offend the conscience of the court. If, for example, a seller understood that he was to be paid with money that was obtained criminally, or a buyer purchased goods which he knew to have been illegally exported from a friendly foreign state, no action would lie on the contract.

7.15   Lord Wright's limitations in Vita Foods

The qualifications to the *Vita Foods* principle which Lord Wright himself acknowledged – that the choice of proper law must be *bona fide*, legal, and not contrary to public policy – though frequently repeated, have never been the subject of detailed judicial scrutiny. It should therefore first be said that there is nothing necessarily improper in the parties choosing a governing law specifically in order to avoid legal provisions which might otherwise apply to their contract, unless such a choice is specifically prohibited, as in the Unfair Contract Terms Act 1977, s.27(2) (and see also *The Hollandia*, above [7.08]). A choice made in order to obtain an unconscionable advantage over the other party would presumably be invalid, however. It is somewhat surprising, though, that in the half-century since Lord Wright's limitations were first enunciated no challenge to a choice of proper law has ever been based upon them.

7.16   Each contract carries its own proper law

Finally, it should be noted that it is theoretically possible for each individual contract in the web of transactions which make up an international sale to be subject to a different proper law. The only exception arises when a charterparty is incorporated into a bill of lading. Here, as the result of a doctrine known as infection, the bill of lading contract acquires the same proper law as the charterparty: see *The Njegos* (1936) 53 LlLR 286. In all other instances, the contract of sale, of carriage, of insurance, stevedoring and storage contracts, financing arrangements, and contracts arising under the *Brandt* principle, will have their proper law separately determined. However, the fact that each is made as part of the greater whole may be a relevant factor if it becomes necessary to balance competing circumstances. In *The Elli 2* (1985) 1 LlR 107, a *Brandt* contract was made in Saudi Arabia in circumstances which had no transactional connection with England. However, the bill of lading, by virtue of incorporating charterparty terms, included an English arbitration clause. The Court of Appeal regarded this as a decisive factor when deciding that, on balance, English law was the proper law of the *Brandt* agreement.

7.17 International torts

A party to an international sale, typically the buyer, may often wish to bring proceedings against more than one defendant, suing one in contract and another in tort, or to bring alternative actions against a sole defendant. Where, for example, goods are damaged by the carrier's negligence, the buyer may found his action both in contract and tort.

The question of which law district's tort law an English court will apply, when the tort has connections with more than one, has received a peculiarly complex response. The seminal case is *Phillips* v. *Eyre* (1870) LR 6 QB 1. English law has struggled to make sense of Willes J's judgment in this case ever since it was handed down. The Rule in *Phillips* v. *Eyre* is easy enough to state. Willes J said that 'in order to found a suit in England for a wrong alleged to have been committed abroad, two conditions must be satisfied. First, the wrong must be of such a character that it would have been actionable if committed in England . . . Secondly, the act must not have been justifiable by the law of the place where it was done.' Controversy over this principle has centred on the legal implications of the contrast between the requirement of 'actionability' in the first leg of the rule, and of 'justifiability' in the second.

To the present writer it seems almost certain that Willes J intended by the first leg to lay down a jurisdictional rule and by the second a choice of law. In other words, he was saying that English courts should refuse to hear cases involving acts which were not regarded as litigable under English domestic law. Given that they had jurisdiction, they should decide the issue by reference to the law of the place where the tortious act was committed. The word 'justifiable' was appropriate to the particular facts in *Phillips* v. *Eyre*, in which the defendant had caused to be passed a law retrospectively exonerating his previously tortious behaviour.

7.18 Interpretations of the rule in Phillips v. Eyre

Whether or not this interpretation is historically correct, it is not one which has been adopted by later courts. The two-part rule in *Phillips* v. *Eyre* is universally regarded as a composite choice of law provision in which the defendant's conduct must be shown to be in some sense wrongful by, not one, but two, legal systems.

The only problem is to determine the extent of that wrongfulness which the rule requires each system to identify.

There are two possibilities. The first derives from the much-maligned, and possibly defunct, decision of the Court of Appeal in *Machado* v. *Fontes* (1897) 2 QB 231. (It is symptomatic of the general confusion surrounding the present state of English law in this area that it is not even clear whether or not this decision has been overruled.) Briefly, the Court of Appeal decided here that foreign torts should be adjudicated according to English domestic law – in other words, as if they had no foreign connection at all – subject only to the rider that the defendant's behaviour was in any sense wrongful according to the law of the place where it occurred. Once that is established, foreign law has no more to say in the matter. In *Machado* v. *Fontes* itself, the defendant's actions attracted criminal, but not civil, liability abroad. This was held to be sufficient to found an action in tort in England.

This is not so much a principle of the law of conflicts as the virtual negation of any such principle. Nevertheless, it is one which has been frequently applied, both in England and the Commonwealth. The *Machado* interpretation of the rule in *Phillips* v. *Eyre* was praised by Lord Pearson in *Chaplin* v. *Boys* (1971) AC 356. In his view it possesses the double merit of certainty and of allowing an English court to give judgment according to its own ideas of justice. In this writer's opinion, it possesses the double demerit of being both jingoistic and mechanical.

The second interpretation of *Phillips* v. *Eyre* is in the ascendant, and indeed may be the sole survivor, following the decision of the House of Lords in *Chaplin* v. *Boys*. It is known as 'double actionability'. Under it, a plaintiff will recover to the extent that English law and the relevant foreign law overlap. Thus if, for example, there is a duty of care under one system but not the other, or there is a valid defence under one but not the other, there is no overlap and no liability. If there is a partial defence under one system and no defence under the other, there will be recovery to the extent of the partial defence. If a head of damage is recognised only by one system, the plaintiff's claim under that head will fail. In *Chaplin* v. *Boys*, two of their Lordships favoured the double actionability approach, and specifically rejected *Machado* v. *Fontes*. Two others did the opposite, favouring *Machado* v. *Fontes* and specifically rejecting double actionability. The fifth judge was noncommittal.

Subsequent decisions, not involving Lord Denning, have utilised double actionability. This has been done, however, not in preference to the alternative, but because a plaintiff who can establish his case under double actionability will necessarily succeed under the far more favourable *Machado* v. *Fontes* approach. Lord Denning, however, has strongly advocated a totally different criterion of liability. This is based upon developments in the United States where, by analogy with the proper law of the contract, the proper law of the tort is applied. This is the law which has the closest connection to the specific issue before the court. In *Chaplin* v. *Boys* the two judges who favoured double actionability also favoured the introduction of a proper law rider in exceptional cases.

7.19   Torts on board ship

The torts of which a party to an international sale is likely to complain might well be committed on board ship. If the vessel is in territorial waters at the relevant time, the law of that law district will be applied in combination with English law, whether or not the tort has consequences outside the ship and regardless of the ship's flag. If the ship is on the high seas, the law of the flag will be used, provided no other vessel, or property external to the ship, is involved. If it is, English maritime law will apply. It is arguable, however, that if a carrying vessel collides with another as a result of actionable negligence and the cargo is damaged, the consequences of the negligence are confined within the carrying ship as far as the cargo is concerned, and the rule in *Phillips* v. *Eyre* will continue to operate.

7.20   Proof of foreign law

In all conflicts actions, foreign law must be proved as a fact. To the extent that it is not established in this way, it will be assumed to be the same as English law. In practice, litigants are often content to allow actions involving overseas torts to be decided solely according to English domestic law.

Index